This book is dedicated to all those who care for animals.
Below are some of the groups that are helping save gorillas.

Wildlife Conservation Society – www.wcs.org

Gorilla Doctors – www.gorilladoctors.org

The Dian Fossey Gorilla Fund International – gorillafund.org

World Wildlife Fund – www.worldwildlife.org

Virunga National Park – virunga.org

International Gorilla Conservation Programme – igcp.org

Goualougo Triangle Ape Project – www.congo-apes.org

Mbeli Bai Study – www.mbelibaistudy.org

African Wildlife Foundation – www.awf.org

Gorilla Rehabilitation and Conservation Education Center (GRACE)
gracegorillas.org

Ape Action Africa – www.apeactionafrica.org/index

Limbe Wildlife Center
limbewildlifecentre.wildlifedirect.org/category/gorilla/

www.mascotbooks.com

Raising America's Zoo: How Two Wild Gorillas Helped
Transform the National Zoo

For more information, please contact:
Mascot Books
560 Herndon Parkway #120
Herndon, VA 20170
info@mascotbooks.com

Library of Congress Control Number: 2017901699

CPSIA Code: PBANG0617A
ISBN: 978-1-68401-170-4

Printed in the United States

RAISING AMERICA'S
ZOO

How Two Wild Gorillas Helped Transform the National Zoo

Dear Kathleen,

I am so grateful for all you do for the animals and the

Kara Arundel

National Zoo!

Kara Arundel

Author's Note

This is a work of nonfiction based on four years of researching thousands of documents at the Smithsonian Institution Archives, where the National Zoo's records—starting from its founding in 1889—are preserved. SIA, located in Washington, D.C., is free and open to the public. Additionally, I interviewed more than two dozen people for various aspects of this book. All the people and animals named in this book are real. Although most of this book focuses on situations in which I was not present, I have not created anything, including dialogue, that I had not read or heard in my research. Please refer to the endnotes section for details on my sources.

"In the end we will conserve only what we love, we will love only what we understand, and we will understand only what we are taught."

– Baba Dioum, 1968 at General Assembly meeting
of the International Union for the Conservation
of Nature and Natural Resources

ACKNOWLEDGMENTS

I began research for this book in 2013 simply because I was curious about the story of my father-in-law Arthur "Nick" Arundel capturing a pair of gorillas in Africa and bringing them to the National Zoo in Washington, D.C. What evolved over the next four years was a larger story about the gorillas' legacy in relation to the current captive gorilla population in North America and the contributions of the many people at the National Zoo who worked tirelessly to make "America's Zoo" a model in the zoo community.

My utmost gratitude goes to the people most familiar with the National Zoo and its gorillas in the 1950s, 60s, 70s, and 80s when the science, understanding, and compassion about animal care finally intersected to make real differences. These people helped me understand the reasoning behind many decisions in these crucial years. William Xanten, who rose from a landscaper to animal curator over his six decades at the zoo, was a treasured resource. I am also thankful to Lisa Stevens, Melanie Bond, Robert Shumaker, Benjamin Beck, Michael Davenport, Mitchell Bush, Judith Block, Katherine Ralls, Miles Roberts, and Chris Wemmer. Mark Reed's memories of his father, National Zoo Director Theodore Reed, and the elder Reed's tenure at the zoo was invaluable. Smithsonian Conservation Biology Institute Director Steven Monfort, a friend and someone I greatly admire, patiently explained to me the zoo's trajectory and commitment to saving animals.

The complex and comprehensive story of the zoo would have been impossible to tell without the thousands of documents preserved by the zoo through the Smithsonian Institution Archives. SIA Historian Pamela Henson had the foresight to record more than 40 hours of interviews with Theodore Reed and other zoo insiders. Tad Bennicoff was essential in helping me pull the personal letters, reports, photos, and animal records from SIA storage areas in Washington, D.C., and Maryland. I am also so grateful for the assistance of SIA's Miguel Argueta, Ellen Alers, Heidi Stover, Mary Markey, and Marguerite Roby.

Many others helped in my goal of recovering this important period of time. Stephen Hosmer and Robert Lamb shared the history of Friends of the National Zoo's (FONZ) support to the zoo. Rufus Phillips provided clarity about Nick Arundel's involvement in Vietnam. Jim Bugg, who sadly passed away as I was writing this book, helped me understand how a group of exotic animal hunters could transform into animal conservationists. Lee Talbot, an extraordinary man who gave so many contributions to national and international environment and animal conservation practices, offered critical information about Africa in the 1950s and of the world mindset toward animal preservation in the 1960s and 70s. Former Rep. Pete McCloskey recalled the country's political cooperation in creating the Endangered Species Act.

I am indebted to my friends and talented journalists Pat Harden and David Johnston who offered valuable feedback on early versions of this book. Friends Connor Herman, Paige Kevill, Virginia DeWees, Maria Acebal, and Christine Malcomson Young read sections of the manuscript. John Warren at George Mason University Press believed in this project and helped guide the conservation focus of the book in its early stages. I am extremely grateful to Mimi Dornack at National Geographic Creative for her assistance in recovering several photos used in this book, including the cover photo.

Special appreciation goes to the entire team at Mascot Books. I am extremely grateful for Publisher Naren Aryal's enthusiasm for this project. To Jenna Tea, Kate McDaniel, Jasmine White, Kristin

Perry, and my loyal editor Wendy Strain—my deepest gratitude.

This effort would have been impossible without the support of my parents Richard and Mary Urbanski, my sister Beth White, and the Arundel family, especially my mother-in-law Peggy Arundel, and Nick Arundel's sister Jocelyn Sladen. My love and heartfelt appreciation go to my sons Nathan and Jack, who enjoyed countless trips to the zoo with me. And finally, to my husband Tom, who offered valuable feedback on every step of this project and a never-ending supply of his love and support in my quest to tell this story.

CHAPTER 1
LEAVING AFRICA

Standing with straight posture and looking directly at the camera, Arthur "Nick" Arundel posed with his arms tightly and protectively holding a small gorilla to his chest. The little ape also stared intently at the camera. Both seemed at ease with each other among the surrounding grass and trees in the Belgian Congo.

Nick and the young gorilla had met only a few days earlier. Before this pleasure trip in February of 1955, Nick Arundel had never held a gorilla or even been to Africa before.

The female western lowland gorilla who seemed so comfortable in Nick's arms was born almost two years earlier in the humid, forested area of the Likouala-Mossaka region near the Congo River in French Equatorial Africa. A French mining company reportedly captured her as a six-month-old baby, killing her parents in pursuit of the infant.[1] Nick named her Moka to honor the place of her birth.

At Nick's feet and out of the photo's image, a baby male gorilla played in the grass, waiting for Nick to return his playmate, Moka, to the ground. He was smaller and slightly younger—a year and a half old—and was born in the same region along the Congo River. When he was about 10 months old, native hunters trapped him. He was the only member of his family taken alive.[2]

Nick named him Nikumba for a village in the region where he was captured.[3]

Soon after their captures, both gorillas were turned over to French colonial government authorities who housed the young apes together. The two formed a close bond by sleeping and playing together and giving each other the attention and touch they were missing from their mothers.

Nick held Moka as the camera took several more pictures. She was timid, affectionate, and content to be in Nick's arms. Nikumba, on the other hand, did not like being separated from Moka. He was curious and needy and would violently resist, even bite, anyone who handled him independently from Moka.

Nick scooped both orphaned apes into his arms and held them against his khaki safari shirt. Together, the apes felt heavy; their development helped by four daily feedings of infant formula and their natural vegetarian diets of fruits and vines. Moka weighed 22 pounds, and Nikumba carried 17 pounds. The camera captured another picture just as the toddler apes were losing their patience.

The gorillas lived most of their short lives in captivity in the French Equatorial African capital of Brazzaville. Now it would be Nick who would comfort, snuggle, and hand feed the babies while escorting them out of the Congo and to their permanent home at the National Zoo in Washington, D.C.

It took Nick several days to find an airline willing to fly the gorillas across the Atlantic Ocean. Pan American Airlines refused to fly the trio, spooked at the thought of transporting "King Kong" in an airplane across the Atlantic, an airline official told Nick. Other airlines that flew from Leopoldville in the Belgian Congo also rejected Nick and the gorillas.[4]

Not helping matters was that a veterinarian in the Belgian Congo who examined both animals before their cross-Atlantic flight discovered Nikumba had a slight cold and a more serious parasitic disease that causes diarrhea and weight loss. The *balantidium coli* also can be a serious threat to humans. But neither gorilla was showing signs of being lethargic and Nikumba was put on medication right away.[5] Nick did not explain Nikumba's illness to the airlines he called.

Nick finally called Sabena, a small Belgian airline with a reliable history of flights in the Congo. He made a promise to the airline that if it took him and the two baby gorillas out of Africa, he would have reporters and photographers on the tarmac in New York City taking pictures of its plane.[6] That was the incentive the airline needed, and it agreed to fly Nick and the apes.

On February 23, 1955, Nick dressed Nikumba and Moka in diapers, packed a bag full of infant formula and baby bottles, and, with a gorilla in each arm, boarded the Sabena Airlines DC-6. The apes' closeness with each other and their tameness from being in captivity at such young ages made them excellent airline passengers as they flew away from their homeland.

Brussels was the first stop after leaving Leopoldville. "You may expect twins on Tuesday," Nick telegrammed his sister Jocelyn, who was working in Belgium for the International Union for the Protection of Nature. She, along with the Antwerp Zoo director, were waiting on the tarmac. As soon as the plane's propellers stopped rotating and Nick emerged with the apes, they wrapped the baby gorillas in blankets to protect them from the European winter. A heated truck drove the gorillas through a cold sleet to the Antwerp Zoo where they rested for the night.[7]

From Brussels, the gorillas and Nick flew directly to Idlewild Airport in New York City. The flight over the Atlantic was the dangerous part because, had the gorillas flown in cages in the cargo hold, the near freezing temperatures could have killed the young animals. Instead, Moka and Nikumba sat with Nick in the passenger cabin, with entranced passengers taking turns feeding the babies bottles of formula.[8]

As Nick promised, a waiting press corps was ready to greet the gorillas in New York. The next day, the *New York Herald Tribune* ran a front-page picture of a weary looking Nick holding a gorilla in each arm as Moka played with Nick's necktie. The accompanying brief article mentions Nick and the gorillas' journey from Africa on Sabena airline.[9]

After only a few hours in New York City, a chartered plane took the gorillas on the last leg of their journey to Washington, D.C.

Despite the transition, the two baby gorillas were in good spirits and eating well. Nikumba was "extremely aggressive, playful, and physically strong for his age," Nick wrote in a memo on the day he brought the young gorillas to the National Zoo.

"It is my feeling that this younger and smaller member of the pair needs the more careful handling and development in the months and years to come. Continuation of his present dependence on her company and lack of trust in humans, appears both a developing (with size and strength) danger to his own self-sufficiency (should we lose her) and to his human keeper."

"But he is young, probably a perfectly normal little male and these judgments may be premature. He certainly balances her affectionate feminine personality, and I am not sure we would want him any other way," wrote Nick.

Moka, it seemed to Nick, displayed the opposite personality. She clung to whoever was feeding her and was indifferent to Nikumba's presence. She never bit and never sulked.

Her easy-going temperament compared to the higher-maintenance Nikumba might make her the favored child, Nick worried.

"All in all, an ideally well-balanced female personality. She needs, perhaps, only to have her affection better divided over the years ahead in favor of our hoped mate-to-be," Nick wrote. "Difficult though it may be at present, I suggest strongly that she be shown no preference to him in human attention and that this be held over the years of their development."[10]

When they arrived at the National Zoo, Moka and Nikumba were placed in the same small barred cage in the Small Mammal

House, one of the zoo's more comfortable, elegant looking and structurally strong animal buildings. As newspaper photographers captured the long-anticipated moment, Nick climbed inside the cage to play with the apes. Nikumba clung tightly to Nick's neck and wrapped his toes around his finger, as if anticipating that Nick would soon leave the cage without him. In his other arm, Moka also gripped tightly to her surrogate parent.[11]

Nick felt accomplished. His mission was to bring gorillas to the National Zoo and with militaristic determination, he met his goal. The journey to bring the baby gorillas from Africa to the National Zoo, however, was only the beginning of dramatic changes for the young gorillas, for the zoo that would be their home for the rest of their lives, and for Nick, who at first bragged about capturing the gorillas himself, but then spent the rest of his life dedicating his time, money, and energy to improving the National Zoo and protecting future generations of wild African animals.

Nick's devotion to Moka and Nikumba would continue. The intertwined lives of Nick, Moka and Nikumba, and the National Zoo brought national and global improvements to the compassion and conservation of captive animals and their wild relatives.

But before evolving into an internationally respected center, the zoo—and its gorillas—first had a lot of growing to do.

The zoo in the nation's capital had waited decades to exhibit gorillas. Gorillas were and still are some of the star animals at zoos. Their size and strength can both impress and frighten people. Their emotional and physical resemblance to humans draws crowds that linger to watch how gorillas move, where they cast their eyes, and how they interact with the other gorillas and the people watching them. They are one of the few types of animals at a zoo that seem to observe people as much as people watch them. Not only are gorillas genetically similar to people, their behavior is human-like, too.[12]

They get sad and mad. They laugh and scream. They can develop memories of people and places.

The gorilla that preceded Moka and Nikumba, N'Gi, died 23 years earlier in 1932. Ever since then, the National Zoo's director, Dr. William Mann, wanted to bring other gorillas to the park. He was in competition with other American and international zoos. By 1955, many big city zoos, such as those in New York City, Chicago, Milwaukee, and Cleveland, had gorillas. In fact, several zoos, including San Diego, San Antonio, and Cincinnati, had at least two gorillas.[13]

There was no rhyme or reason for which zoo got their desired gorillas. Those decisions were left to lucky timing and knowing the right connections in colonial Africa. But as well-connected internationally as "Doc" Mann was, every angle he pursued for the last two decades to get gorillas met with failure. It was one of his biggest frustrations as leader of the zoo.

In the end, it was his long-time friend Russell Arundel and Arundel's son Nick, a 27-year-old former Marine and CIA operative, who promised to bring gorillas from Africa—even if they had to capture them—and followed through.

Outside the Small Mammal House, where Nikumba and Moka could not see, was the rest of the National Zoo that sat on nearly 200 acres in the Rock Creek Valley. While the quiet, hilly, and naturally wooded site in the center of the growing city was an oasis for visitors who wanted the convenience of a city zoo, the organization had major problems.

Animals were dying unnecessarily. Most of the buildings were poorly constructed and falling apart. And zoo leaders begged for every dime they could get to run the place.

The zoo was a victim of budget fights between the U.S. Congress and the District of Columbia city government. While Congress financed zoo projects on a whim and with no plans for its continued fiscal needs, city leaders grew resentful of pulling money away from schools, hospitals, and other pressing needs for what many viewed as simply a place of entertainment.[14]

This dysfunctional partnership between the city and federal officials started more than 60 years earlier when the free-to-the-public zoo opened in the city's Rock Creek Valley under an agreement that both the city and federal governments would split the costs.[15]

This unique city-federal relationship was rooted in the U.S. Constitution, which put the nation's capital under the authority of Congress. It was a defense move on the part of the young federal government—one that would prohibit a rogue state from having the influence of proximity on national interests. The District of Columbia was not a state and therefore could not make any financial decisions without the collective approval of Congress.[16]

Congress created the National Zoo in 1889 with a basic mission—to save American species threatened by extinction. In the nation's capital, large and exotic animals at that time were only seen as lifeless, stuffed exhibits. Animal skins were stretched over rags shaped into the animal's body and positioned in display cases in the National Museum. Within the display cases, scenes were designed to mimic the animals' natural habitats.

The National Museum sat to the side of a stretch of tree-covered land crisscrossed with winding paths known as the National Mall.[17] Located between the Capitol Building and the newly completed Washington Monument, the museum was an ambitious project of the Smithsonian Institution, which possessed a growing collection of artifacts, art, and research under the responsibility of Congress.

The Smithsonian Institution's head taxidermist, William T. Hornaday, became alarmed by the dwindling number of American bison and traveled west to collect the hides of these animals to display in the museum. In 1865, the American bison, also called buffalo at the time, numbered in the millions across much of Northern America.

Bison were so plentiful, Hornaday had later commented, "Of all the quadrupeds that have lived upon the earth, probably no other species have ever marshaled such innumerable hosts as those of the American bison. It would have been as easy to count or to estimate the number of leaves in a forest as to calculate the number of buffaloes living at any given time during the history of the species previous to 1870."[18]

But by 1872, an average of 5,000 bison were killed each day. By 1880, the great animal was slaughtered to near extinction—their demise caused by the popularity of their meat, hides, and tongues.[19]

When Hornaday set out in 1886 to collect buffalo skins and skeletons for the Smithsonian, he was conflicted about killing the animals just to publicize their plight.[20] Years earlier, as a young man, Hornaday dreamed about traveling to western Africa to capture another mystical animal: the gorilla. He never went, being talked out of the deadly adventure by a concerned uncle.[21]

Hornaday's four-sided, glass-enclosed display of the buffalo was popular with visitors and the envy of other museums, but what Hornaday really wanted was to feature the actual animal and breed the species to sustain its population. Before Congress created the National Zoo, the Smithsonian Institution had a Department of Living Animals, which opened in 1887 on the National Mall. Four donated bison grazed outside and a dozen other animals of American importance were soon collected.[22]

People delighted in seeing the bison grazing in the shadows of important American monuments, and soon an eager public started giving a variety of creatures to the Smithsonian. Many of these donated quadrupeds, birds, and reptiles were crowded into a small

Smithsonian-owned building on the Mall that had little ventilation and a hard-to-control steam heating system. Larger animals were squeezed into yards so small that museum curators worried that they might injure or kill each other. Within two years—by 1889—the Smithsonian had 341 animals to care for and feed, yet Congress refused to approve the requested sum of $5,000 for their upkeep.[23] In desperation, the Smithsonian sent many of the animals to zoos in Philadelphia, New York, and London. Some were given to the United States Insane Asylum, located in the District of Columbia, to entertain patients.[24]

Hornaday and Smithsonian Secretary Samuel P. Langley, an animal lover, urged Congress to support the building of a zoo at the larger Rock Creek location a few miles north of the Mall. The men envisioned a simple zoo that focused on scientific efforts of preserving, protecting, and observing certain species while allowing the animals large areas to roam as they would naturally. The secondary mission of the new zoo was for the "instruction and recreation" of visitors.[25]

Passage of the law gave Hornaday and Langley the funding and encouragement to move the zoo to the Rock Creek location.[26]

The spot featured acres of sunny slopes, wooded hillsides, steep cliffs, and open meadows. Its waters flowed directly into the Potomac River. The tract of land was much larger than most zoos of the day; New York City's Central Zoo was 10 acres at the time and held about 900 animals.[27]

Washington, D.C.'s mid-Atlantic locale seemed to beckon a variety of captive animals. Hot, humid summer days felt tropical, and frigid winter nights were glacial. A temperature swing of 100 degrees between the two seasons was possible.[28] Blizzards, hurricanes, derechos, and droughts could potentially come through town, even within the same year. But the District of Columbia also enjoyed a true four-season calendar year. The bursts of color and comfort the fall and spring seasons bring remind creatures and humans to enjoy it while it lasts because the next season is right around the corner.

Although geographically located in the middle of Washington, D.C., the large swath of land was largely undeveloped and so remote from the busyness of Capitol Hill that some early Smithsonian papers described the site as being outside the city.[29] Langley later described it as "probably the most beautiful in its diversified natural features of any similar park in any capital of the world." He also said that in developing the zoo, he used as a guiding principle, "to leave nature largely to herself, and to not attempt to beautify what is already beautiful."[30]

For the grand opening of the National Zoological Park's Rock Creek Valley home on April 30, 1891, two former circus Asian elephants Dunk and Gold Dust—known troublemakers— walked more than 10 city blocks, with horse carriages awkwardly hurrying out of the way, to their new home. Thousands came to greet the new animals. James Cooper, owner of the Adam Forepaugh Circus, donated the elephants to the federal government most likely because he couldn't handle them. Dunk, who weighed more than 6,000 pounds, often charged at other circus elephants. Gold Dust, who carried more than 5,000 pounds, was "a man killer" with a "mean and treacherous disposition,"[31] wrote the zoo's first head keeper William H. Blackburne.

It was Blackburne who took responsibility for escorting the rebellious pair through the streets of D.C., from the circus grounds to the new zoo. He had previously worked as an animal keeper for the Barnum and Bailey Circus, and large beasts didn't intimidate him. He was particularly gifted at performing with big cats and was the first to enter a lion cage during circus shows.[32]

With the parade of these two huge animals into the zoo grounds, the National Zoo at the Rock Creek location was officially born. Dunk and Gold Dust's feet were immediately chained to trees where they stayed for several months because there was no shelter for them. There was no running water at the park, so workers dipped buckets into Rock Creek, poured the water into two barrels, and carried the barrels on horse-drawn carriages up the hill to the elephants. Keepers repeated this process twice a day, estimating that the elephants drank 80 gallons daily.[33]

A few months later, Blackburne borrowed a wagon from the Humane Society to transport the rest of the animals from the Living Museum on the Mall to the new zoo grounds.

It was a shaky first year. The zoo requested $35,000 from Congress to care for the animals—the same sum New York's Central Park Zoo spent to run its program.[34] But Congress approved only $17,500 to be paid equally by the federal and city governments—an amount too little to keep up with the needs of nearly 450 animals.[35]

Officials tried to force the zoo's survival by getting emergency funding of $1,000 from the Smithsonian Institution and the city. They refused any gifts of animals, cut the workforce, and had only one watchman on duty at a time.

In one of the most dangerous incidents of this chaotic first year, a grizzly bear escaped its enclosure by climbing over a nearby 50-foot wall; it was shot dead when it made its way outside park boundaries. No one could fault the bear for trying to flee—the park manager acknowledged the bear's den was too cold in the winter, too hot in the summer, and damp year-round.[36] A few years later, a valuable sea lioness died from fright after engineers set off explosions when building a sewer system through the park.[37]

Other animals died from being overfed by visitors. More unnecessary deaths occurred because animals of varying origins and needs were kept in the same "Animal House." Lions and tigers, which can tolerate colder climates, were living under the same roof as tropical birds and monkeys.[38] Some smaller, timid animals reportedly died of fright after hearing the calls of larger beasts that are their natural predators.[39]

The zoo had eight enclosures, all but one were described as temporary sheds; Congress wanted to see if this experimental zoo would succeed before dedicating money to build permanent animal buildings.

But despite the ramshackle buildings, the zoo's limited labor force, and many unfinished and unsafe roads, visitors arrived in surprising numbers. An average of 7,500 guests a day enjoyed the park that first year, putting strain on the developing and ill-prepared zoo. The Smithsonian Board of Regents, which oversaw zoo operations, feared for the safety of the visitors because of rickety animal enclosures and dangerous roads. Board members gently told Congress that if guests or animals were injured, Congress' elected members would shoulder the responsibility. And with such limited funding, the Regents doubted the park could stay open.[40]

Not helping matters, city leaders were pressured to cut off zoo funding.[41] The city didn't have a say in Congress about what it could or could not afford to give to the zoo; it was just told what to do. And the rapidly growing city did not have much to give.

While Congress and the District of Columbia continued to provide minimum funding for park improvements, salaries, and food for the animals, Congress prohibited zoo staff from purchasing any new animals or expanding any current programs for six years in the mid-1890s.[42] The zoo survived one winter by leasing space to the circus that previously owned the elephants Dunk and Gold Dust. The zoo got to keep any babies born to these visiting animals, and while no elephants were born, the zoo did get to keep a kangaroo and a monkey.[43]

Bickering escalated between officials in Congress and in the District of Columbia over who should fund the zoo's upkeep[44] with both barely committing to a trickle from their spending spigots.

Fed up with the budget stalemate, Smithsonian officials started using the clout of their federal status to get what they wanted. Secretary Langley sent letters to State Department officials and military officers stationed in foreign lands asking them to be on the lookout for interesting animals in exotic locales. "Almost any foreign animals would be gladly received," he wrote in 1899.

Langley listed particularly desirable animals by region. From Cuba, the Smithsonian wanted manatees and flamingos; from Central America, it sought tapirs and sloths; from Australia, it desired kangaroos and wombats; and from Asia, it wanted cheetahs.

But the most extensive list was for animals in Africa. "No other region is so rich in animal life as this continent," Langley wrote. Giraffes, zebras, and gorillas were among the most wanted African animals sought by the zoo.

"The gorilla has never yet been brought to America," Langley's letter challenged.[45]

CHAPTER 2
NOAH'S ARK

After Smithsonian Secretary Samuel Langley's plea for animals, many curious and unusual animals made their way to the National Zoo thanks to the servicemen abroad. Gorillas from Africa were not among the new arrivals.

When the zoo hired Dr. William Mann as superintendent in 1925, he also made it a priority to fill the zoo with a variety of animal species, which he knew would increase the zoo's coffers and clout. He did not shy from making waves or have any interest in pretending there was harmony between the federal and District of Columbia governments. When he began working at the zoo, he was appalled at its status and was vocal about it.

In his first report to the Smithsonian Board of Regents, he criticized the quality of the buildings and declared that the zoo lacked certain important and interesting species. He even chastised the U.S. Treasury for keeping profits from the zoo's restaurant rather than reinvesting the money into projects for the animals.[46]

Mann's outspokenness made a difference. Over the next three years, the zoo budget grew by 18 percent.[47]

William Mann was 39 when he became head of the National Zoo. Every significant event in his life until then prepared him for the top job at the zoo. Once he got to the pinnacle position at the National Zoo, nothing would hold him back from doing whatever it took to succeed in his lifelong pursuit, even the federal government's sluggish pace of action.

As a quirky kid, Mann occupied himself with dreams of joining a circus or living in a jungle among animals. He ran away from his Montana home when he was 12 so he could travel to South Africa.

He got as far as a ranch 40 miles away. When he was 14, he wrote to explorer Robert Peary to see if he could join Peary's next expedition to find the North Pole.[48]

After his failed attempts at international exploration and the numerous snakes and lizards Mann brought home, his mother tried to contain his wild side by sending him to a military school in Virginia. Still, he kept trying to get closer to animals and adventure. He applied for a job as an animal keeper with the Ringling Brothers circus, but was rejected with these words from Charles Ringling: "Advise a boy of your age to choose some other line of occupation as more desirable in every respect."[49]

While on break from the Staunton Military Academy in Virginia as a teen, Mann took a part-time job at the National Zoo cleaning animal cages for $1 a day.[50] His supervisor, William Blackburne, the same man who led the unruly elephants Dunk and Gold Dust on the first day of the zoo's opening at the Rock Creek Valley location, was not impressed with the teenager's awkwardness with the routines and schedules of the zoo. One day when Mann was cleaning the spittoons of chewing tobacco, Blackburn said to him, "Billy, you don't like to clean spittoons, do you?"

"No, sir," Mann replied. Blackburn took the spittoon away from him, rubbed a handful of sand into the bowl, handed it back, and said, "You ought to learn, no matter what job you have, as long as you live. There's always going to be some spittoon connected with it."[51]

Mann failed to get hired there or at any other zoo and was packed off to Washington State College to find a sensible career.[52]

But his studies at Washington State College, then Stanford University, only strengthened his vim and vigor to work with animals, taking advantage of every course, contact, and opportunity to get him the knowledge and experience he needed. He eventually became proficient in the study of insects and earned a doctorate in entomology from Harvard University.

His profession took him around the world studying and collecting various bugs. Of the thousands of insects discovered or waiting to be discovered, Mann was fascinated with ants. He was amazed at the armies of ants working together to protect one another and accomplish a mission. He dug under logs and slept in forests all over Central and South America to find new species of ants.[53] He soon gained the reputation as a world-wide ant expert. More than 100 species of insects are named in honor of Mann. Before he retired as the director of the National Zoo in 1956, Mann gave the Smithsonian his personal collection of 117,000 ants, described at the time as among the world's finest.[54]

As an adult, Mann was quite a prankster and loved to make people, especially children, laugh. Although he didn't have children of his own, he never outgrew his fascination with the circus. When the circus came to Washington, Mann would go to the show every day, even if the show was in town for three weeks.[55] And even as an older adult, he often leveraged his humor to make a point. While working in the zoo's decaying administrative headquarters built on zoo grounds in the early 1800s, he let loose an anteater in his office to control the building's termite population and underscore the blighted state of the building.[56]

When he got requests for zoo animal manure to be used as fertilizer, Mann responded that the solicitor needed permission from the U.S. Surplus Property Division of the Treasury since he, as a federal employee, was forbidden to sell government "property."

And when he first became zoo superintendent, days before President Calvin Coolidge's cabinet was to visit the zoo, Mann worked with a Southeast Asian bird called a myna, which can reproduce human voices, especially when in captivity. When Coolidge's budget director passed by the bird's cage, the bird jumped up and down screeching, "How about the appropriation? How about the appropriation?"[57]

An unexpected ray of hope came on January 16, 1935, when the zoo received $680,000 from the Public Works Administration. The influx of money was the result of New Deal legislation and the effort to boost the American economy after the Great Depression. When Secretary of the Interior Harold Ickes, who also ran the Administration of Public Works, called Mann at his desk to tell him the news, the zoo director nearly dropped the phone.

Mann later said this moment was the most exciting in his 30 years as zoo director. It wasn't being chased by charging buffaloes in Africa, keeping a fragile, newborn tiger cub at his house, or discovering a new species of ant; it was the great relief that money brings when the organization you lead is constantly on the edge of collapse. "Any zoo director will understand," he stated proudly, even while disappointing those who hoped a wild animal exploit would be at the top of Mann's professional memories.[58]

The PWA money was enough to build a brick exhibition house for small mammals and great apes, an addition to the Bird House, two maintenance buildings, a central heating plant, and finally, a stone exhibition house for large mammals, such as elephants and giraffes.[59]

This new exhibition house was a long-time dream for zoo leaders. The zoo's first elephant house, or more accurately a shed, was built in 1891 to house the circus elephants Dunk and Gold Dust. It was a small wooden building that started rotting ten years later[60] and had no chance of keeping out the winter chill. A new barn-like elephant house with an outside yard and pool opened in 1903,[61] but after 30 years, that facility also became practically unusable.

By 1937 many of the building projects paid for by the PWA

grant were finished or nearing completion. The small mammal house opened to the public in May 1937. The large mammal house was nearly completed in June 1937, but needed more work before animals could move in. It measured 227 by 90 feet and was designed to hold elephants, rhinos, hippos, tapirs and giraffes within its 13 cages. The smallest cages measured about 12 by 19 feet, or about the size of a one-car garage. The largest cage measured 22 by 58 feet, or about the perimeter of a large, above-ground swimming pool. Some of the inside cages had pools, and each cage connected with an outside yard blocked off by dry moats instead of fences.[62]

It was to be the best fiscal year in the zoo's history to date.

Now all these new zoo buildings needed were some animals. To build up support and excitement for the project, Mann didn't rely on Congress or the city government. He turned to the well-known and respected National Geographic Society and a bright and mischievous eight-year-old boy he knew—his friend Russell Arundel's son, Nicky.

In 1936, Nicky launched a neighborhood newspaper he named *Nicky's News*. On a November night, in his parents' Washington, D.C., living room, Nicky and his friend Lawrence Battey couldn't contain their restlessness. Nicky's father Russell Arundel, a former newspaperman, suggested the boys start their own newspaper. The boys ran into the next room to start writing.[63]

The inaugural edition of *Nicky's News* featured an ambitious mix of national news and local gossip from their neighborhood of Wesley Heights—a planned community of modest homes set a few miles away from the bustle of Capitol Hill and the growing business district of downtown D.C. and within blocks of the National Cathedral, whose limestone towers were still being erected over the city skyline.

The two third graders, using Nicky's Royal portable typewriter, wrote disparate articles with such headlines as "Madrid is Bombed," "The President has Gone to Buenos Aires for Peace," "Lady Loses Keys to Her Clothes Closets. Is Lucky," and "Millers Visiting New York and Coming Home Soon."[64]

To make the paper more authentic, if not particularly ethical, Nicky wrote and drew advertisements for a local pharmacy and for a large downtown department store. "Beds to sleep and bicycles cheap," reads one early, unpaid, unapproved ad written by the editor.[65]

The newspaper also needed a purpose, Nicky decided. He added two editorials to round out that first newspaper. One argued that children should have longer recesses at school: "Don't you see that if we don't have to go back in the room so soon we can breathe more nice fresh air and then won't have tuberculosis…"[66]

The other editorial urged the nearby National Zoo to add giraffes to its animal collection. Nicky visited the zoo occasionally, and his parents were close friends with Mann and his wife, Lucile. Nicky likely overheard Mann talk about his need for more animals for the buildings under construction and decided to help with the effort.

Nicky incorporated the biggest health scare of the day into his persuasive essays, writing that visits to the zoo to see giraffes would prevent children from getting tuberculosis. He often misspelled the respiratory disease.

One passionate early editorial pushed the giraffe agenda with the determination, creativity, and randomness of thought characteristic of eight-year-olds:

"Children get lots of fresh air at the zoo, and they would like to go there if the giraffes were there. Not so many children would die of tooberkulowsis if there were giraffes to look at. Giraffes eat leaves and leaves don't cost much. Chickens cost lots to raise and children don't want to look at chickens."[67]

"You should work hard for your little boy and girl and get them some giraffes and make the teachers give them more recess," read another editorial.[68]

Nicky recruited his six-year-old sister, Jocelyn, and more friends to fill his news staff. They kept pressing for the long-necked mammals in subsequent weekly editions of *Nicky's News*. The giraffe campaign was always listed on the editorial pages.

Week after week, except during school breaks, *Nicky's News* was distributed to a growing number of subscribers. The paper was typewritten and multigraphed on both sides of an 8½ by 14 inch paper, folded in half for a four-page leaflet with two columns of news and ads or hand-drawn illustrations on each page. In just eight weeks of its launch, *Nicky's News* had 60 subscribers, four of whom paid $1 each for a commitment of a year's subscription. Others paid 10 cents a month.[69]

The children took their subscription base seriously. In one of the first editions, this was written in the paper: "This is the week when all who want *Nicky's News* for another month should pay their dimes. It costs something to publish a newspaper. We will keep going for one year because one subscriber paid up for that long."[70]

The paper continued to cover all levels of news, from critical international developments down to the nitty gritty of importance to children. Headlines included; "Adolph Hitler of Germany is Dumb," "The Editor was In Bed for Two Days with Asthma," and "Managing Editor Loses a Tooth."[71]

The kid-run newspaper started getting noticed by important people in Washington. Eight U.S. senators bought subscriptions, with Nicky charging them an increased rate of 15 cents a month.[72]

Russell Arundel's connections as a former secretary to Senator Jesse Metcalf of Rhode Island, his public relations business, and his position as a member of the Mount Rushmore Memorial Commission[73] likely helped develop this prestigious readership. But general knowledge of this start-up paper took off when Nicky attended a contentious and historical Senate Judiciary Committee hearing in March of 1937.

Senators gathered to debate President Franklin D. Roosevelt's proposal to expand the number of Supreme Court justices from nine to 15 to win favorable rulings on New Deal legislation. Of course, Roosevelt's proposal never did formalize, but court scholars suspect it led to more acceptance of measures aimed to boost the economy.[74]

Looking adorable in serge knee breeches, an Eton collar, tie, and a homemade Editor-In-Chief badge pinned to his jacket, but acting very much like a veteran Capitol Hill beat reporter by vigorously taking notes on the proceedings, Nicky's presence at the hearing lightened the mood, with at least one paper writing a feature story on the towheaded boy's attendance[75] and another running a front-page picture of Nicky sitting on Senator Pat McCarran's lap, notebook in hand.[76] After the hearing, Nicky sold copies of that week's *Nicky's News* with the headline "Supreme Court Hasn't Been Made Bigger Yet. Still Try."[77]

How a grammar school student could steal the show from U.S. senators arguing over a president's overreach of the Supreme Court was likely due to Nicky's supreme confidence and unusual tenacity. This self-determination and methodical behavior was Nicky's alone, but was slightly influenced by his parents' attentive, yet hands-off upbringing of their son. They expected a lot from their only son, yet they were mostly absent in providing direct oversight.[78]

Russell and Marjorie taught young Nicky that anything was possible if he worked hard for it. The exact steps, however, were left for him to discover, stumble over, and get right.

At the same time young Nicky was getting his newspaper off

the ground, Russell was finishing his own writing project. His access to Capitol Hill players led to an interest in collecting doodles made by political celebrities, the quiet lawmakers, agency leaders, Capitol Hill journalists, and artists. Over 10 years, he obtained nearly 100 mindless sketches from past and present–day Washington, D.C., elite, sometimes after House or Senate committee meetings adjourned and sketched–on agenda sheets were left behind in chairs and on tables. Psychologists analyzed the sketches and Russell turned the drawings, descriptions, and interpretations into the book, "Everybody's Pixillated."[79]

The book labeled Theodore Roosevelt a "dreamer" for his doodles of ships. George Washington's sketches of checkered designs with alternate squares filled in was interpreted as coming from someone who was, "Meticulous, generous, studious, well-balanced; and neat to the point of fastidiousness." President Franklin D. Roosevelt's drawing of a small stick person with a large sailfish at the end of a fishing line must have meant that Roosevelt's recent Caribbean fishing trip was on his mind. Seeing this drawing, the psychologist said its doodler is "Enthusiastic and a lover of sports. Fond of the outdoors. Has a mind which 'races' and works continuously! Fine sense of humor."[80]

Nicky, the Editor–in–Chief, started becoming the news. As *Nicky's News* became more widely known, the "other" city newspapers started following the young journalists' coverage and picked up on the newspaper's giraffe agenda.

Six months after *Nicky's News* began its campaign, the *Washington Post* featured Nicky's push for giraffes on its front-page Sunday edition. Under the headline "D.C. Editor, 9, Begins Crusade To Get Two Giraffes for Zoo," was a picture of Nicky and Jocelyn intensely reviewing news copy still rolled into the typewriter.[81]

Nicky and his staff held press conferences at his Wesley Heights home as interest in their movement grew. At one press conference, Nicky admitted he didn't know how many giraffes the zoo had in the past. He also used the opportunity to advance his push for longer recesses at Horace Mann Elementary School.

"All zoos ought to have at least two giraffes," he told those gathered. "And recesses of less than 15 minutes aren't worth a hoot."[82]

The *Nicky's News* staff started ramping up their persuasion efforts, offering to collect donations to pay for the giraffes. "Nobody has sent $5,000 for these giraffes to *Nicky's News*. Somebody send the money quick. Call the president up and ask him to send some money to Doctor Mann for these animals or your little boy might die of tuberkuloshus (sic)," Nicky wrote.[83]

Pressure grew both on the zoo and on Congress. Behind the scenes, Mann was making plans to bring many new animals to the zoo, including giraffes.

The National Geographic Society was financing an expedition to Asia, the East Indies, and Africa. Mann headed the expedition that would take nine months, traverse 3,000 miles, and gather the largest and most unusual assortment of live animals that had ever before traveled to this country in one shipment.[84] Mann and Lucile left Washington, D.C., on January 12, 1937—Nicky's ninth birthday—with a group of 26 wild animals from America, such as raccoons, black bears, and salamanders, to offer as exchanges.

With Mann on leave from the zoo, Ernest Walker filled in as acting director. Walker supported Nicky's push for giraffes: "Nicky's not the only one who wants giraffes. Visitors out here are always asking us, 'Now where are giraffes?' And the only thing we can do is point to the big, new mammal house and explain that's where the giraffes would be if we had some, but we don't," Walker told the *Washington Post*.[85]

Walker said that zoos and circuses that already had giraffes didn't want to give any away and that to transport giraffes from Africa would cost $2,000 to $3,000 each—a cost the zoo couldn't afford. Blackburne, the head keeper, also debunked the possibility of seeing giraffes anytime soon at the zoo.

"Why in rough weather they are almost sure to suffer—maybe with broken necks," Blackburne told the *Post*.[86]

Blackburne's prognostication was eerily close to the truth. Included in the nearly 900 animals Mann and his group gathered from their expedition were four Sudanese giraffes. For the return sea voyage back to the United States, each young giraffe was secured in its own wooden and padded crate, constructed on the spot. One window in each crate allowed the giraffe to poke its long neck out of the 11-foot tall cage to drink water and eat from pails raised by the ship's crew.[87]

"Oh, they just looked beautiful," Lucile Mann recalled years later. "There were two males, two females, and very tame. We could pat their noses. The captain, up to that point, had not cared very much about having animals all over his ship. After the giraffes came aboard, he weakened. He wouldn't go to bed at night unless he'd been down and said good night to the giraffes."[88]

The captain guided this modern Noah's Ark—a motor vessel named *Silverash*—first north toward the Suez Canal and through the stifling heat of the Red Sea where William Mann splashed water on the monkeys and bears to keep them from collapsing in the 117-degree heat.[89] The journey continued through the choppy waters in the Mediterranean, and then out into the calm of the Atlantic Ocean.

"The Atlantic was kind to us almost until the end," William Mann wrote in an essay for *National Geographic Magazine*. "Two days out of Halifax, however, we ran into a gale that made animal-keeping a nightmare."[90]

The midnight storm kicked up the sea. The giraffes' crates broke free from the railings and slid on the heaving deck. The captain worked to correct course and yelled for all hands on deck to secure the cages, which were once again lashed to the railings. When the ship left the Gulf Stream, the temperature dropped and the ship's engineer and electrician spent hours installing heat lamps in the giraffes' cages so the animals wouldn't get sick.[91]

After a 50-day sea journey, the ship finally reached New York on September 27, where the animals were unloaded. The hoofed animals, including the giraffes, stayed in New Jersey for quarantine; the rest were immediately shipped via express train to the zoo in Washington.[92]

On October 13, 1937, Nicky and his family were invited to welcome the giraffes to their new home at the zoo, along with the public. Seven railway express trucks carried the giraffes and other animals down the street to the zoo. In what must have seemed like forever to the children, but was about 15 minutes, the giraffes were guided into the pachyderm house. The first giraffe entered tentatively, but then began to explore its new home. An artist had painted a large mural of a jungle landscape on a wall of the cage, and the confused giraffe began licking the painted leaves, and then, appearing to quench its thirst, began licking the painted water. The crowd laughed. The second giraffe to enter the cage also licked the mural, to the delight of all the observers.[93]

After the giraffes were unloaded, Mann asked Nicky which giraffe he wanted to be named after him. Nicky picked the smallest one that had light colored hair, but when Mann said that giraffe was a girl, Nicky picked another small giraffe to carry his name. The littlest giraffe would be named Spring Song, Mann's nickname for Jocelyn.[94] (The name later changed to Kitty.) The other two giraffes were named Nageoma for *National Geographic* and Bob.[95]

Nicky was thrilled at the success of his campaign to bring giraffes to the zoo.[96]

"I expected to get only two giraffes, but I am going to get four giraffes so I'm twice as happy. Children cannot get run over by automobiles while they are looking at giraffes," he wrote in a column for the *Washington Herald*.[97]

Bringing giraffes to the National Zoo was a goal he worked hard to achieve. He boasted of his victory in his newspaper and through interviews in city newspapers.

With growing knowledge and success of the giraffe campaign, demand for *Nicky's News* skyrocketed. In a move that is rare in the print news business, the young editor refused to increase the number of subscriptions. The paper ran scratched-out subscription requests on the editorial pages.

It's unknown whether Horace Mann Elementary expanded recess time, but with at least one of his objectives achieved, Nicky could have folded his newspaper and focused on pursuits more typical of his age. Instead, the attention and success drove him, and he sought to fix another problem.

Now he aimed to replace the zoo's restaurant, built only 14 years earlier.

"This awful building should be rebuilt and a brand new one put up. Because every time it rains, the water leaks through the top and then all the popcorn is ruined and the keepers can't tell very well without opening the box and eating some of it and then of course it is no good after it is opened," reads Nicky's typed notes on the first anniversary of the launch of *Nicky's News*.

"The resturant (sic) needs to be much bigger because on Sundays the store is so jammed that you can hardly breathe. The editor almost got crushed trying to get some peanuts for Highknee the Elephant. If you don't want your little boy to get crushed or have tuberculoshus you had better get a new restaurant quick."[98]

Again, adults took Nicky seriously. He was invited to talk on the radio about his restaurant platform, and a U.S. congresswoman arranged to meet with Nicky and Mann.[99]

A new restaurant opened three years later.[100]

CHAPTER 3
ELUSIVE ANIMAL

Visitors gathered around the indoor and outdoor giraffe cages, excited to see the long-necked animals move gracefully in their enclosures. The giraffes' neighbors in the new large-mammal house included massive animals that previously lived in other buildings at the zoo. Zoo staff closed the park's gates and spent days carefully crating the elephants, hippopotamuses, and a rhinoceros to move them into the new building.[101]

Once all the animals were settled, Mann could finally appreciate the enormous effort, time, and money it took to open the building and to find places for all the other animals that were collected from the National Geographic Society-Smithsonian Institution East Indies Expedition. And he also had time to ponder how to bring other creatures from faraway lands to the Washington, D.C., park. Ten years earlier—in 1928—the zoo's first gorilla arrived. Now, Mann was unsure the zoo would ever again want to be a home for a gorilla.

N'Gi was the first gorilla at the National Zoo. He arrived quite by accident in December 1928, as a baby weighing less than 30 pounds.[102]

N'Gi's dramatic capture in west Africa was made by an American man known more for collecting snakes than great apes. Julian L. Buck made several trips to Africa to collect animals for his family-run zoo in Camden, New Jersey. Although he told people gorillas were plentiful in Equatorial Africa, he only captured three gorillas over the course of eight trips there.

During the trip through Spanish Guinea when he caught N'Gi, Buck traveled with 23 Batwa natives. The group followed the gorillas—four adult females, one male, and baby N'Gi—for 17 days through the tropical rainforest of what is now Equatorial Guinea on the western coast of Africa. Over the weeks, the gorillas became less edgy about their followers but still kept a brisk pace of walking, sometimes up to 20 miles a day, according to Buck. For most of the time, N'Gi's mother, with her baby on her back, kept well ahead of the troop. But she started slowing down and, on the 17th day of the trek, the Batwas saw the opportunity to take aim. They shot her with a poisoned arrow. She tried to fight off the poison's effects, but grew weak and died an hour after being shot.

Taking off his shirt, Buck caught the baby and put his shirt in the young gorilla's mouth so it wouldn't bite him or call out to his family. The Batwas gathered wood for a fire and roasted N'Gi's mother's body, then ate the meat.[103]

For nearly a year, N'Gi was in Buck's care before Buck decided to take the growing gorilla to Cuba to sell him. Before leaving New Jersey on the train to Florida, Buck called Mann to see if the zoo director wanted to look at N'Gi while the train stopped in Washington, D.C. Mann and Lucile met Buck and his gorilla at Union Station, but the busy station was too chaotic and the threesome plus the gorilla got in a taxi. As the taxi passed the Capitol Building and other significant sites near the National Mall, N'Gi sat on Buck's lap looking intently out the window[104] before the taxi reached the zoo where N'Gi would have a chance to stretch and play.[105]

Buck and Mann placed N'Gi in the largest ape cage the zoo had, which happened to be the home of Jiggs, the orangutan. After some initial hesitation and darting back and forth in the cage, Jiggs grabbed N'Gi for an embrace and planted kisses all over the gorilla's face.

"The longing in Bill's eyes as he watched the little ape was unmistakable," Lucile remembered.

Buck was just as emotional. "N'Gi's just like one of the family," he told the Manns. "My wife cried like a baby when I brought him away. I'd a heap rather see him here in Washington, where we could visit him occasionally, than down in Cuba, I would."

"How much rather, in dollars?" Mann asked Buck. After the men settled on a price of $3,500, the gorilla became the newest resident of the National Zoo.[106]

"No one could have resisted him," Doc Mann wrote in his book.[107]

Jiggs' cage also held two white-handed gibbons who were less enthusiastic about the newcomer. Bob, one of the gibbons, teased N'Gi by using his long arms to swing down on him, whacking him on the head and then quickly gliding back across the cage. N'Gi was soon moved to his own newly-built cage under two skylights that allowed 10 percent of ultraviolet rays inside. But he cried out in protest and seemed lonely.[108]

Toys made N'Gi happier, and he attracted a lot of visitors. So many visitors came that, for the first time in the zoo's history, guests lined up to wait their turn to glimpse a zoo animal.[109] Pediatricians suggested a diet that was compatible to a three-year-old child, and N'Gi was fed orange juice, apples, eggs, milk, cod-liver oil, and cooked and raw vegetables. Curious psychologists who wanted to compare gorilla and human characteristics also came to see N'Gi, and one even determined that the young gorilla had the mental capability of an 18-month old child.[110]

"For the first week, whenever I wanted to look at my own gorilla it was necessary to elbow aside some distinguished scientist," Mann said.

Mann wrote to Buck frequently to let the hunter know how the ape was fairing. "He is comfortable in his new cage, and shows a great deal of ingenuity in playing with his physical culture apparatus and his toys," Mann wrote Buck. "Yesterday he stood on his head for us, and played pat-a-cake with his front feet at the same time. We get fonder of him personally, while professionally and scientifically there is no limit to our pride in having him here."[111]

N'Gi grew to enjoy the audiences in front of his bars and would get more playful as more people gathered. Certain children would visit N'Gi on their way home from school each day. Mothers called the zoo at night saying their children wouldn't go to bed without knowing how N'Gi was doing.[112] The ape recognized his little admirers and would get extra active when they stood in front of his cage.[113] Visitors were also content to watch the ape when he was placid. N'Gi seemed to enjoy watching his visitors too.

Lucile Mann also stood in front of N'Gi's cage for long periods of time, "never tiring of his tranquil busyness—for he did not romp impulsively like the chimpanzees or sit and mope like the orang-outangs (sic), but had every appearance of giving dignified consideration to each detail of his play, whether it was balancing dumbbells on his shoulders or a drinking pan on his head," she wrote in her published memoirs.[114]

The human fascination for gorillas could be explained by the genetic and anatomical similarities between the two. Ten million years ago, gorillas and humans likely shared a common ancestor and still have several biological commonalities. Relatively speaking, in the animal kingdom, gorillas and humans are both slow breeders whose females have gestation periods for about nine months, with subsequent births being years apart. Humans and gorillas also move through childhood and adulthood at similar pacing. The hairless hands of gorillas resemble ours, and they have unique individual fingerprints.[115]

But it's really gorillas' behaviors that hold a connection for humans who see them in person. Gorillas can show anger, fear, and desire. They laugh and they recognize familiar faces.[116] They can get fiercely jealous, resentful, and can hold grudges. They can show bravado or they can be insecure. Their majestic and exotic presence can intimidate with a scowl, yet their gentle mannerisms and tenderness unveil their emotional sophistication.

They are smart and can manipulate objects by using problem-solving skills to turn some objects into tools to accomplish a task. Some gorillas have even been taught to communicate using hand gestures.[117]

Most of the visitors who came to see N'Gi were entranced with his human-like stare, his rapidly-developing show of strength, and his curiosity. But at least one guest protested that it was "degrading to keep an animal so much like a man in captivity." The woman demanded to know why the young gorilla was taken from its family, according to Mann.

The ape is not a man, Mann reasoned. Measurements of skull cavities compared to humans prove gorillas are not as smart as man, the zoo director argued. Additionally, the gorillas held in captivity, with their easy access to food and shelter and toys, may seem human-like, but wild gorillas, for which there was limited research, may have different characteristics as they struggle moment-to-moment for survival, Mann said.

And although Mann defended the divide between humans and gorillas, he was concerned about the capture of wild gorillas and the closeness humans and apes were sharing at zoos. "It is doubtful if many live gorillas will be exhibited in the future, as a serious attempt is being made to have them protected throughout their range—a wise move, indeed, and badly needed right now. No animal is more interesting, and the very few thousand that still remain in Africa should be preserved," he wrote in his 1930 book. "It is to be fervently hoped that sportsmen will no longer feel that they must shoot a gorilla."[118]

But without Buck's dramatic capture, N'Gi wouldn't be at the zoo. And N'Gi was, as Mann called him, "easily the most important animal the zoo ever had."[119]

"A gorilla is an event in the lifetime of a zoo," Mann wrote in his book. "This animal is, without doubt, the most spectacular that can be secured, and because of its rarity, the difficulty of transportation, and the great risk of illness and death, the price is generally so high that few zoos can afford to buy one."[120]

In fact, in 1930, very few zoos had gorillas. They were difficult to capture and keep alive, both during the transport and once they were living at a zoo. Several gorillas that did make it from Africa to the U.S. died after only a few years.[121]

N'Gi's run as the zoo's star resident came to a halt in September of 1931, when another gorilla joined the ape exhibit. Okero, who keeper William Blackburn nicknamed "Snowball" despite the black hair covering the young gorilla's body, was donated to the zoo by husband and wife filmmakers and photographers Martin and Osa Johnson.

In December 1930, the adventurous duo was in Tanganyika near the Ruanda-Urundi border trying to film gorillas for their movie *Congorilla*, which was to be the first movie with sound produced entirely in Africa.[122] They already captured two juvenile gorillas—one more than they were allowed by colonial Belgium authorities—when natives approached them with a very young, thin and sick gorilla. They bought him anyway for $60 and while getting the necessary permits for the two extra gorillas, nursed him back to health.[123] The Johnsons donated him and a chimpanzee named Teddy to the National Zoo.[124]

Okero, which the zoo and Johnsons believed to be a mountain gorilla, but was likely an eastern lowland gorilla,[125] was just as popular with zoogoers as N'Gi and maybe more so because of Okero and Teddy's playfulness and tight friendship. Soon after Okero arrived, N'Gi became ill. Constipation was the first sign the ape was sick, but then he got a bad cold. Quickly the illness progressed to pneumonia and emphysema, and he struggled to breathe.

Veterinarians stayed with N'Gi day and night, trying to make him comfortable and helping the animal fight the infection. Eleanor "Cissy" Patterson, a Washington, D.C., journalist and later owner of the *Washington Times-Herald*, paid for several X-rays to be taken of the ailing gorilla and even arranged for an oxygen chamber, including equipment and technicians, to be flown from New York to D.C. Doctors put N'Gi's 105-pound body into the oxygen chamber and were hopeful as his condition progressed enough to be cleared for surgery.

The phones at the zoo and at the Manns' home rang constantly with people wanting to know N'Gi's status. Lucile Mann cooked him special meals and even tried to lift his spirits by giving him eggnogs laced with brandy.[126] Word got out that the National Zoo's sick gorilla was sipping brandy,[127] and several people offered to donate high-grade brandy.[127] N'Gi, however, kept getting weak and his weight dropped to 62 pounds. He died on March 10, 1932. Jojo, a chimpanzee in a nearby cage, also died. Okero and Teddy developed pneumonia, but soon got better.[128]

The D.C. community mourned N'Gi's death, which was reported in newspapers locally as well as nationally and internationally.[129] The loss of N'Gi was heartbreaking to Mann and was compounded later that year at the sudden death of Okero from an intestinal tumor. Within seven months, his two beloved gorillas were gone.

Gorillas were one of the most popular animals at a zoo, but also one of the hardest to care for. Mann began to think it was pointless to have gorillas in a zoo and told people that N'Gi's and Okero's fatal illnesses were like "standing helplessly by and watching a baby die."[130]

For the next 10 years, Mann kept busy improving buildings for the animals already at the zoo and acquiring other animals of interest, such as the giraffes and hundreds of other animals, gathered from the National Geographic–Smithsonian Expedition to the East Indies in 1937.[131]

Then, just as the National Zoo was entering a period of stability and increasing credibility, the onset of World War II put a stop to any hopes for growth. Much of the zoo's male staff was called for military duty, making it hard to keep a stable roster of employees. Zoo attendance increased, however, forcing it to accommodate the crowds despite fewer employees and resources. Many visitors were soldiers recovering in nearby hospitals who yearned to be outdoors and take their minds off their injuries.[132]

The zoo, like other quasi-federal agencies, made very few improvements during this time, as any extra money went to war efforts. Shipments of animals to the zoo nearly stopped, and gas restrictions limited all but essential travel for zoo business. To save money, the zoo accepted discarded vegetables from several nearby grocery stores. The U.S. Marshals Office sent condemned food to the zoo that was unfit for human consumption but apparently okay for the animals. Paralyzed with fears of air raid strikes, the zoo removed every poisonous snake to avoid accidental escapes during an attack on D.C.[133]

After the war, Mann renewed his intrigue with gorillas. He was once again ready to have gorillas at the National Zoo, and his suppressed desire for the apes could no longer be contained. The gap in time, however, was filled with an array of protections put on African wildlife. In 1933, the London Convention pushed colonial African governments to establish wildlife parks where human activity was limited. The agreement also aimed to prevent the hunting and killing of certain animals unless for scientific or critical purposes. Gorillas fell into Class A of the protected animals—the highest level.[134] Gorilla purchasers could no longer use the animals for entertainment purposes, and natives were dissuaded from eating gorilla meat.

It was now nearly impossible for zoos to directly contract with hunters to find gorillas for them without securing permits from government authorities in Africa. The number of gorillas allowed to be captured from western Africa was also limited. Sure enough, very few gorillas were sent to American zoos between 1930 and 1947.[135]

Smithsonian leaders were careful and strategic in their quest for gorillas when contacting the ministers of the colonial African nations where gorillas lived, mostly in territories ruled by the French and Belgians. They wanted to be aggressive in their pursuit without being annoying. They strove for diplomacy, with an edge of urgency. They acknowledged the growing efforts to protect African wildlife, but unabashedly asked to display the animals to further the zoo's conservation efforts.

"We are very desirous of cooperating with the French government in their efforts to protect vanishing species of flora and fauna in Africa," Smithsonian Secretary and former National Zoo superintendent Alexander Wetmore wrote to the French minister in 1947. "In view of the numbers of gorillas in various parts of French-controlled areas of Central Africa we feel justified in making this request for two young live gorillas at the present time."[136]

Wetmore, soon after, was asked to head a commission for the Belgian African colony that would be the exclusive authority of all requests by American institutions for protected animals. While it's unclear if Wetmore took on this responsibility, just the fact that he was offered the position shows the mutual respect the Belgians and Smithsonian leaders had for each other.[137]

The Belgian government also appeared eager to get the National Zoo its long-awaited gorillas. "A first priority has been granted to the National Zoo of Washington for one okapi and a couple of young gorillas. The three animals I heard would be free of all charge except the transportation from the Congo to Washington," Louis van den Berghe, head of the Belgian agency in charge of research and science projects in the Congo, wrote to Mann. But, van den Berghe wrote, the capture of gorillas hadn't started yet.[138]

A year later, van den Berghe wrote Mann again: "There is no doubt that, in an exceptional way, at least one gorilla will be secured for the zoo." In fact, eight recently caught gorillas were being examined by scientists in the Congo, van den Berghe added.[139]

Another year passed without gorillas at the National Zoo, despite the French finally granting a permit for the capture of four gorillas, including two for the National Zoo. Even with all the protocols and paperwork in order for the zoo to claim two young gorillas, it appeared the animals were difficult to find. But as more time passed, the restrictions on capturing gorillas tightened further.

"Many thanks for the efforts you are making to secure us the gorillas," Mann wrote to an administrator at Paris' National Museum of Natural History who was helping French Equatorial African leaders determine whether requests for animals were truly for scientific purposes.

"On account of the many abuses in the past concerned with the capture of gorillas, I do not want anybody to violate any of the rules and regulations, but would like to obtain them strictly legally and with the consent of the French authorities,"[140] Mann wrote.

The back and forth between French officials and Mann and others helping the zoo was cordial, but tensions rose when it became obvious the National Zoo did not have several thousands of dollars to purchase gorillas and was hoping the French would donate the animals to the zoo if they had them. The typical price of a young gorilla was between $2,000 and $5,000. Mann's government-funded zoo only had $600 to buy one gorilla.

Harold Jefferson Coolidge Jr., a long-time friend of Mann's who was a founding member and U.S. representative of the Brussels-based International Union for Protection of Nature, even tried to help. "I feel sure that the National Zoological Park would consider this action on your part as a most generous gesture of international good will even if you are reimbursed for expenses up to the amount of $600 per animal you could still consider that these animals were being presented as a gift and were not being sold," Coolidge wrote to the chief inspector of hunts in French Equatorial Africa.[141]

A zoologist by training, Coolidge wanted to help his friend Bill Mann and his zoo, but his motive was also personal. In the late 1920s, when Coolidge was just starting his career, he traveled to Equatorial Africa to collect a variety of animals for study. He was particularly focused on the elusive mountain gorilla in eastern Africa. While in eastern Congo, Coolidge followed a number of mountain gorillas for two months, barely getting more than a quick glance of the apes. Finally, he caught up to one large gorilla and fatally shot him in the chest.[142] He later had the animal mounted for display at the Museum of Contemporary Zoology at Harvard College where he was a curator.[143]

Coolidge wanted to know more about this obscure animal and set the record straight about its taxonomy. In the early 20th Century, hundreds of skulls—partial and full—were saved and kept at a scattering of museums and universities throughout the world, leading to a mishmash of scientific knowledge about the animal.

He wondered: were the coast gorillas, found more in countries of western Africa, and the mountain gorillas to the east, one-in-the-same? Or were there more than a dozen subspecies of gorillas found throughout Africa's equatorial belt, as some scientists had concluded?[144] The tropical forests of Equatorial Africa are the only place on Earth where gorillas live in the wild.

By measuring skulls, viewing X-rays, studying photographs of carcasses, reviewing the animal's history of classification, and reading papers by fellow researchers, Coolidge concluded in a report that there is only one genus and species—Gorilla, gorilla. He also determined the gorilla had two slightly distinct subspecies, which he titled the coast gorilla and the mountain gorilla.[145]

The gorilla's classification continued to be debated. Not until this century were gorillas divided into two species, the eastern gorilla (Gorilla beringei) and the western gorilla (Gorilla gorilla) and each having two subspecies.[146] Western lowland gorillas are the most plentiful subspecies of gorillas in the wild and the only gorillas in American zoos.[147]

Even Coolidge's professional clout and international prominence couldn't help Mann's efforts to bring gorillas to the National Zoo. Gorillas were in high demand and the authorities in the F.E.A. didn't want to start giving them away.

Tired of the delays and setbacks, Mann started writing to hunters directly. He reached out to John Biname, the protégé of well-known gorilla hunter William "Gorilla Bill" Said, an American from Ohio. Said gained notoriety for the number of young gorillas he captured and brought back to the United States. He was unapologetic for his brutal tactics of capturing young gorillas by killing their adult protectors, and his strategy, with the help of natives, was detailed in a six-page article and photo spread in *Life* magazine in 1951. The article said that in one hunt led by Said, six gorillas were killed so that two could be captured.[148]

After Said died, Biname attempted to continue the difficult, yet prosperous, work of hunting gorillas in the Belgian Congo for American zoos and museums. For several years, he successfully captured several different types of small monkeys and a few other small animals, such as snakes for the National Zoo. At one point he told Mann he had a two-year-old male gorilla for sale at a price of $3,000 as long as the zoo had the export permits.[149] Although the offer was tempting, Mann wanted a pair of gorillas, and he didn't have $3,000 for the purchase.

By 1953, the Belgian Congo Game Service was refusing any request for gorillas from zoos or scientific institutions. F.E.A and Cameroon were limiting or prohibiting hunts. But Spanish Guinea, the tiny nation between F.E.A and Cameroon, was still granting authority for hunts, Biname wrote to Mann.[150]

In a letter, Biname told Mann he would hunt there in the following year, but would need Mann to get the proper permits for hunting and exporting the gorillas. "The permits are very difficult to obtain," Biname warned Mann. "But considering the Spanish government has nothing to refuse the USA and that you are the National Zoological Park, I think that if you pass through the Department of State and that you get his full help and assistance for your request, it will be possible for you to obtain the permits."[151]

Mann immediately wrote to the Spanish ambassador, who sent the request to officials in Madrid. Once again, Mann's hopes rose. "We shall be very glad to see you when you come to the States, and terribly glad if you will bring a gorilla in each arm," Mann wrote Biname, adding that the zoo finally raised the $6,000 for a pair of gorillas.[152]

The State Department did write a letter to the American Embassy in Madrid supporting the zoo's attempt to get gorillas from Spanish

Guinea through Biname, but only for the export of gorillas, not for hunting them. Biname, the letter added, was seeking U.S. assistance because he was having difficulty getting permits from Spanish authorities to ship gorillas.[153]

Perhaps it was miscommunication between Biname and Mann or an intentional effort from both to try to side step protocols so the zoo could finally have gorillas but Spanish authorities were livid at the assumption its government was being difficult to deal with. The Embassy in Madrid wrote back in a terse letter: "What is actually being solicited by Mr. Biname is a permit to hunt gorillas in Spanish Guinea. He does not have the gorillas or a permit to hunt them.

"It appears that [Biname] has, in an effort to obtain permission to hunt in Spanish Guinea, offered to supply various American institutions gorillas which he would catch if these U.S. Institutions could bring enough pressure to bear to get him the hunting permit. While the interest of the American institutions in obtaining these scarce animals may be perfectly genuine and meritorious, it is also believed that the viewpoint of the Spanish authorities in wishing to preserve the remaining specimens in their colony, also in the interest of science, cannot be ignored," the Embassy's commercial attaché wrote the State Department.[154]

A month later, the Spanish government officially prohibited the hunting of gorillas in Spanish Guinea "in order to conserve this species." A copy of the order was sent to the U.S. State Department, referencing the "Smithsonian Institution's Request for Assistance."[155]

Chapter 4
Congo Safari

Each failed attempt for gorillas from Africa disappointed Mann. Russell Arundel heard about his zoo director friend's discouragement. He sympathized with Mann and, like his son Nick, wished for their hometown zoo to be filled with many exotic creatures. They wanted large crowds to visit the zoo and for the zoo to become a safe haven for animals—big and small—threatened in the wild.

Thousands of animals lived at the zoo, some of which were the lone representative of its species. This uncoordinated collection of animals occurred in part because Mann accepted nearly every creature given to the zoo from generous contributors. Mann's policy of NRA—"Never Refuse Anything"—filled zoo displays with significant and not-so-significant animals.[156]

Leaders of countries around the world gifted animals to the President of the United States, which were in turn sent to the zoo. Children could walk right into Mann's office to give or exchange small animals they caught in their backyards, but weren't allowed to keep at home. He promised these young visitors he'd care for their pets, but often, keepers fed these donated bunnies or mice to larger zoo animals.[157]

Over the years, Russell gave horses and a snake to the zoo, but he wanted to make a more meaningful contribution. After hearing of Mann's inability to get gorillas, Russell began planning a trip to Africa. He wanted to see and learn more about elephants and cheetahs in the savannah and monkeys and hippopotamuses in the rainforest.[158]

Mann connected Russell with his friend Coolidge, whose involvement and influence in world conservation activities was increasing as he became one of the eminent Americans protecting vulnerable plants and animals.[159]

When Coolidge, a descendent of Thomas Jefferson's, helped form the International Union for Protection of Nature in 1948, the group became the first ever to use both government and non-government organizations to coordinate international attempts to protect a wide variety of wildlife in Africa. It was a difficult undertaking and, from the start, had ambitious goals of saving species, educating national and regional governments on conservation priorities, gathering research, and negotiating international agreements to preserve species.

Years later, the group's name changed to the International Union for the Conservation of Nature, and it formed a sister organization—the World Wildlife Fund—to help focus its fundraising and public awareness work.[160]

In the 1920s, when Coolidge shot the mountain gorilla in order to understand the animal's biological classification, he had plenty of company among those who chose to hunt and kill the animals they wanted to study and save. There simply was no method at that time to understand large, exotic animals in hard-to-reach locales without killing them and shipping the animals' bodies or body parts to a research lab.

Early conservationists justified these sacrificed slaughterings as a way to better understand how to save animals. Like the Smithsonian's William T. Hornaday, whose conservation work was still admired decades later, these academics who hunted animals were conflicted, but saw no other way. The sacrifices these dead animals made would lead to better understanding and protections, they told themselves and each other. And after they took apart the carcasses, examined the skins, measured the skulls, and inspected the stomachs, they would stitch the animal's pelts back together.

The stuffed body would stand on display at museums, such as the National Museum in Washington, D.C., continuing to educate and invigorate the public. Although the exhibited animal was just an inanimate shell, it was the closest most humans would ever get to this wild beast.

Many who hunted in the name of research would show signs of remorse for their kills many decades—or even sooner—after they fired the guns or shot the arrows into animals. Toward the end of his life, Hornaday wrote of his 1886 buffalo hunt, "If the reader now should feel doubtful about the ethical propriety of our last buffalo hunt, and the killing that we had to do in order that our National Museum might secure a few good wild skins out of the wreck of the millions, let him feel assured that our task was by no means a pleasant one."[161]

Coolidge helped form the American Committee for International Wild Life Protection in 1930, and although the group was headed by men in charge of museums, zoological parks, and conservation organizations, it made a priority for saving the over-hunted gorilla.[162] In its first five years, the group collected information about threatened species, pushed for prohibitions on smuggling animal parts across African borders and into the United States, and built relationships with colonial African countries in order to spread the message about animal conservation.[163]

By the mid-1950s, there was no doubt where Coolidge stood on the moral question of killing animals for the benefit of research. Expeditions for mysterious animals should take place, but no animals should be harmed, he concluded.[164] Coolidge set out to find benefactors who could understand this distinction and support expensive safaris that produced only memories, reports, and photographs, not trophy skins or hunter's bragging rights.

When Russell Arundel met Harold Coolidge, the two men

needed something from each other. Coolidge needed Russell's financial support. By now, Russell had the wealth to help. He grew his lobbying firm and acquired Pepsi-Cola as a client. Russell worked on Pepsi's behalf during World War II when sugar was in low supply due to wartime rations. Pepsi wanted Russell to convince Congress that developing part of the Everglades, a vast tropical wetland in southern Florida, for sugarcane crops would help the economy. Russell was soon so enamored by the company that he bought a Pepsi franchise and set up a bottling operation. His annual sales were nearly $250,000 in 1945, the first full year of his business.[165]

Intrigued by Coolidge's mission to prevent the extinction of certain animals, Russell gave him $8,000 to survey threatened animals.[166] Coolidge, in turn, offered Russell his knowledge and the connections Russell needed to carry out his African safari.

The Arundel trip to Africa was set for January and February 1955. The plan was to hunt non-threatened animals and explore central and western Africa. Russell would take his wife Marjorie, several friends, a guide, a photographer, and natives. His son, who was now 27 and referred to himself as Nick, would also join the safari. Getting gorillas for the zoo would be the highlight of the trip.

The day before Nick left for Africa, he met with Dr. Mann.
The zoo director was excited for Nick, who, nearly 20 years earlier, had been his young admirer helping the zoo get giraffes. Nick was now an experienced solider ready for a new assignment. Mann talked about his past difficulty getting gorillas for the National Zoo and his hopes that Nick and Russell could succeed in finally bringing the apes to Washington.[167]

When N'Gi lived at the zoo in the early 1930s, few other American zoos had gorillas. But by 1955, plenty of other American zoos featured western lowland gorillas. A few North American zoos had two or more gorillas. In all, there were around 25 gorillas in more than a dozen American zoos, including one young male gorilla caught in Cameroon and living at the zoo in Baltimore, Maryland, an hour's drive from Washington, D.C.[168] And many of these zoo gorillas, all of whom had been caught in the wild in Equatorial Africa, were living long lives—sometimes decades—in captivity.

Mann already secured permission from the French government to export gorillas from Africa, although, when granting the request, the Inspector-General of Game and of the Protection of the Fauna of the Ministry of France Overseas sternly warned the National Zoo director, "We no longer authorize, for any reason, the intervention of agents who are not specialists in the capture of these animals."[169]

More importantly, Mann had the promise of two young gorillas from the French Equatorial African authorities. He also had contact information for John Biname, who was by now director of the Leopoldville Zoo in the capital of the Belgium Congo. Although Biname disappointed Mann in his quest for gorillas before, the two zoo directors kept in constant contact over other animals for trade. It was hoped that Biname could help the Arundels while they were in the region.[170]

Days after meeting with Nick, Mann learned of a kink to his plans for getting the gorillas. Russell Arundel, who spent several days in Europe ahead of his trip to Africa, wrote to Mann that F.E.A. officials made the same promise of the two baby gorillas to Sweden, Germany, Denmark, and Japan.

"Somehow the French got their wires crossed and told six or eight persons, including you, that they could buy the pair in Brazzaville. ... So you can see much of the red tape and black market is caused by crossed wires in the government itself," Russell Arundel wrote to Mann while en route to Africa.

"Because of the multiple promises, a hunt by the Forester of Brazzaville may be necessary," wrote Russell Arundel, who offered to cut short his safari to go on the drive for gorillas, apparently disregarding Coolidge's and Mann's opposition to hunting gorillas.

"I don't know what will come of this, but I will try damned hard. My instructions from France are to deal only with the F.E.A. Forester so you see the problems. We have to capture them before we get them," he wrote to Mann.[171]

The Arundels' trip began in the prosperous city of Stanleyville in the Belgium Congo, located at the northernmost tip of the Congo River. With luxury hotels, modern transportation, and a plethora of comforts, Stanleyville mimicked glamorous European cities, rather than the wilds of the ancient continent the group probably expected.

They were visiting during a pivotal time in African history. Large swaths of the continent were under British, French, Belgian, or Italian power, but that was about to change. Central Africa in the mid-1950s was on the eve of decolonization after more than 50 years of European rule. Pro-independence movements throughout the great continent were starting to resist European control over African profitable resources and forced labor. A few regions had peaceful transitions, while others, including the Congo, repeatedly struggled to create autonomy.[172]

Before these tumultuous times, however, any foreigner who spent time pre-arranging their travel with the governors and district commissioners of the colonial countries could find hospitable and safe conditions and reliable natives to transport all the needed equipment for time in the field.[173] The Great Depression ended the days of the champagne safaris, but wealthy visitors could still enjoy the comforts of camping with a staff to cook and pitch tents, a fleet of cars to cover more distance, and a guide to lead the way and steer travelers away from danger.

The Arundel expedition was mixed with the comforts of local drivers, catered meals, and luxury hotel stays, along with the long days in the blazing sun, nights sleeping in simple tents, meals of antelope brains, unreliable vehicles that broke down often, and scary moments of close encounters with charging animals.[174]

Both Russell and Nick were primed for an international adventure.

Nick spent the previous two years as a Marine and CIA operative working covert missions in Korea and Vietnam. At the end of the Korean War, while Nick was working on an offshore island training South Korean soldiers in paramilitary exercises and rescues, he was asked to "volunteer" to join a mission into Vietnam. Not even knowing where Vietnam was, he agreed to go.[175] He would be one of 12 military officers chosen for the Saigon Military Mission under the direction of U.S. Air Force Col. Edward S. Lansdale.

A legendary leader who helped defeat a Communist campaign to take over the Philippines after World War II, Lansdale's main mission was to save South Vietnam from Communist influence by using political-psychological warfare. A secondary mission was to make the takeover of the North more difficult for the Communists. [176]

Lansdale focused on Nick's journalism interests. The tow-headed boy who once started a neighborhood newspaper to rally support to bring giraffes to his local zoo, now a military officer with CIA credentials, would use his writing skills to persuade the Vietnamese to resist socialist control. Nick met regularly with one Vietnamese pro-independence journalist to begin boosting the morale of the South Vietnamese people.[177] Late at night, Nick and the Vietnamese journalist would write propaganda articles, using Thomas Payne's "Common Sense"—the 18th century anti-British, pro-American independence tome—as a guide.[178]

On September 4, 1954, Lansdale ordered Nick to be part of a mission headed by Major Lucien Conein to Hanoi in North Vietnam. "Our mission is to mess up the North Vietnamese capitol city and make life hard for Ho Chi Minh when he arrives a week later after his rag-tag army's huge recent victory over the French Army at the big Battle of Dienbienphu (sic) northwest of Hanoi. Lansdale quietly tells me it could be a one-way trip," wrote Nick in a journal decades later.[179]

On a marked Civil Air Transport prop plane used to fly refugees from Hanoi to Saigon, the group landed at the Hanoi airport.[180] Operating from a safe house that U.S. diplomats and French officials had left a few days earlier, they moved largely at night around the city. Helped by a few friendly locals, the group contaminated the POL dump, a storage place for fuel for military vehicles, with lead chips. They also wrote and printed hundreds of leaflets that appeared to be written by the Communist Vietminh about Ho Chi Minh's intention to change the entire North Vietnamese currency.[181] The leaflets caused financial panic around Hanoi, according to Lansdale.

"The day following the distribution of these leaflets, refugee registration tripled. Two days later, Vietminh currency was worth half the value prior to the leaflets. The Vietminh took to the radio to denounce the leaflets; the leaflets were so authentic in appearance that even most of the rank and file Vietminh were sure that the radio denunciations were a French trick," Lansdale wrote in a 1961 classified report to Defense Secretary Robert McNamara.[182]

On the seventh morning of the mission in Hanoi, the CIA team rendezvoused with the CAT plane to fly back to Saigon. As the plane took off, Nick wondered what would happen next and if he would ever return to Hanoi.[183]

While Nick was helping end the war in Korea and assessing the need for American involvement in Vietnam, his father's boldness and zeal for fun sparked another not-so-well-known international conflict.

Several years earlier, in 1948, Russell and his close friend G. Prew Savoy Sr., were fishing in an area off Nova Scotia, Canada, known as the Tuna Capital of the World. Tidal rips helped to push the large, fast-moving Atlantic bluefins into the waters south of Nova Scotia and around a string of small, scarcely populated islands known as Tusket Islands. On one trip, a sudden squall forced the men onto one of the small islands and, while sitting in the pouring rain waiting for the storm to pass, Russell spoke of the outlandish idea of building a shelter on the tiny, treeless island populated with nothing but a flock of sheep. Once he got back to the comfort of Nova Scotia, he asked about the status of the family-owned island and immediately paid $750 for the title.[184]

He built a one-room house on the three-acre island using stones from the island, and there, he, Savoy, and other friends sat and drank rum while breaking from fishing competitions. The rum led to bodacious plans to formally rename Outer Bald Island the "Principality of Outer Baldonia." More rum was drunk and the group had a Declaration of Independence: "That fishermen are a race alone. The fishermen are endowed with the following inalienable rights: The right to lie and be believed. The right to freedom from question, nagging, shaving, interruption, women, taxes, politics, war monologues, care, and inhibitions." Russell crowned himself "Prince of Princes" and wore royal attire decorated with sashes of beer bottle tops and sardine cans.[185]

The friends, who were also titled princes, designed a flag, a great seal, and reset the Gregorian calendar so that the annual calendar started with the incorporation of Outer Baldonia. Motor vehicle registration cards were issued even though there were no cars or roads. If someone wanted to buy anything on the island—there were no stores—they would have to use the currency of "tuner." Fishing was proclaimed the constitutionally-mandated activity along with the production and exportation of empty beer bottles.

Back in Washington, D.C., the "Prince of Princes" listed his micronation in the city phone book, gaining enough clout that embassies in the city started inviting him to their most exclusive parties. The young United Nations even sent the nascent nation an invitation to the opening of its world headquarters in New York City.[186]

The Provincial Government of Nova Scotia didn't know what to make of this foreign entity, but a Canadian newspaper understood the joke and published a satirical piece about Outer Baldonia's government and culture. That article somehow traveled to Germany where a trade publication printed it under the guise of serious news, which got noticed by powers in the Soviet Union.[187]

This being the onset of the Cold War, the Soviets apparently saw the island as a threat. The *Literaturnaya Gazeta*, a state-controlled newspaper in Moscow, ran a column in 1952 denouncing the island nation and calling Russell Arundel the "fuehrer of Baldonia" and an "imperialist."

"It would not be worthwhile to consider the device of Mr. Arundel with his Outer Baldonia, if this would-be businessman were not attempting to introduce into the territory of one hectare the same set-up which many of his comrades of the U.S. government are trying to establish over the territories of the whole world," the column states.[188]

Delighted with being called a savage by the Soviets, Russell issued a formal protest, sent it to governments around the world and invited the column's writer—rumored to be a woman—to the principality's national holiday celebration, the Outer Baldonia Tuna Tournament. "Getting out of Russia will be her own problem," Savoy said.[189]

L. Chernaya never came, but Russell kept up defenses by appointing all local fisherman Outer Baldonia's eight and nine star admirals just in case the Soviets came calling or other threats were made.[190]

Perhaps the young nation peaked too soon. By the late 1960s, the Outer Baldonia press releases stopped flowing. The tuna wasn't as plentiful, so the island's princes stopped visiting. Nearly 25 years after its founding, the principality dissolved in 1973 without ceremony or international attention. Russell donated the island to the Nature Conservancy, which then turned the property over to the Nova Scotia Bird Society.[191] The society continues to this day to keep the island, still referred to as Outer Baldonia, as a preserve for nesting birds, who no doubt are enjoying the same freedoms as the tuna-loving princes once did.

Nick, the Marine, and Russell, the "Prince," brought all the bravado and machoism they could muster while they crisscrossed Equatorial Africa. They also carried with them the seemingly conflicting directives from Coolidge and Mann—to be respectful representatives of America while appreciating the wildlife of Africa and to end the 23-year absence of gorillas at the National Zoo.

The Arundel safari moved east from Stanleyville toward Uganda and Rwanda where they watched hippos, waterbucks, elephants, buffalo, and warthogs in Albert National Park, now Virunga National Park. They spent the next two weeks traveling in and near Albert Park, starting at the jagged Rwenzori Mountains through the calm of Lake Edward on boat toward Queen Elizabeth Park.

They moved into and out of Uganda and Rwanda, traversing vast low-lying lakes to grassy plains to towering volcanic mountains. Along the way, they viewed leopards, cheetahs, and zebras. At one point, two lions crossed right in front of their jeep.

They recorded the animals and scenery with their cameras and diaries and shot non-threatened animals, including leopards, which were considered nuisances then. Although the distance they covered in these two weeks was small compared to the vastness and diversity of the entire continent, the number of animals they came across surprised them. They were near the habitats of eastern lowland and mountain gorillas, but they never recorded seeing the apes.

They also took every opportunity to spend time interacting with the Batwa people, whose dancing and singing led Nick to call them "the happiest of all" people. A member of the safari had M-80s and threw the small explosives in the air to the amazement of the Batwa natives who oohed and aahed at the fireworks show. The group finalized their central and eastern African trip in Rwanda's capital of Kigali before driving back to Stanleyville and then flying to western Africa's Leopoldville, the capital of the Belgian Congo.[192]

On their first full day in Leopoldville along the Congo River, Nick and Russell went to the Leopoldville Zoo to meet with John Biname. The hunter-turned-zoo-director finally had a solid lead on gorillas for the National Zoo, he told Nick and Russell. There were two young gorillas—a male and female—being held by the French Equatorial African government at the Brazzaville Zoo, directly across the river from Leopoldville.[193]

It's unknown whether these two young gorillas were the same pair offered to the National Zoo and to the four other countries Russell Arundel mentioned in his letter to Mann. But when Nick and Russell saw the baby gorillas for the first time on February 15, 1955, there was "no doubt in Dad's mind at first sight we took them," Nick wrote in his journal. Russell likely paid around $10,000 for the pair, promising the F.E.A. authorities Nick would be back to visit the gorillas the next day.[194]

As Russell and Marjorie flew back to the U.S., Nick spent the next few days loyally traveling back and forth by ferry between Leopoldville and Brazzaville to visit with his gorillas. On the visits, Nick attempted to learn more about their histories and personalities. He called them both "baby" and carried them around so they would get used to his feel, his smell, and his voice.[195]

After several days, Nick went back to Brazzaville with John Biname's wife Madeline. The two hired a private boat to carry them and the gorillas across the Congo River back to Leopoldville as to not draw attention or questions. Instead of taking the pair to John Biname's Leopoldville Zoo, Madeline and Nick went to the Biname house and set up a play yard for the gorillas. Understanding his incredible responsibility, Nick carefully chose the pair's play toys and developed a firm feeding schedule for the gorillas. He bought baby bottles and learned how to mix infant formula, relying on advice from John Biname.[196] With Sabena Airline's promise to fly the gorillas, Nick was ready to bring them home to the National Zoo.

"Bill Mann all but in tears as we took two healthy babes into their new home in Washington, D.C.," Nick wrote in his journal after arriving back in the U.S. holding the gorillas.[197]

The press coverage of the gorillas' arrival at the zoo on a cloudy and cold February 24, 1955, was extensive, yet conflicting. Some articles described the gorillas as being taken from their mothers a week earlier by Nick.[198] A *Washington Post* article said Nick trapped the animals. "Strictly amateurs at the animal-trapping business, they did it 'just for the fun of it,'" the paper quoted Nick as saying.[199] The *Washington Star* also referred to Nick's capture of the gorilla pair.[200]

An article later that week called the acquisition of the gorillas a "modern-day, mechanized safari" saying Nick and his family caught the small apes.[201] Even the Smithsonian Institution's Board of Regents' 1955 Annual Report, in announcing the donation of the gorillas as the zoo's outstanding gift of the year, referred to the gorillas' captures by the Arundel Expedition.[202]

A few months later, The *Washington Post* and *Times-Herald* ran a story saying Nick purchased the gorillas from natives. Nick's own notes from this time in Africa did not mention spending time in the jungle or his capturing gorillas in the rainforest.[203]

But Nick kept perpetuating the story that he got Nikumba and Moka by hunting them on his own. He told friends and family a foreboding story of how he traveled up the Congo River from Brazzaville and with the help of natives, chopped down a giant tree where a gorilla family hid. Once the tree crashed to the jungle floor, the natives shot the mother gorillas and threw nets over the babies, he said.[204] No one seemed to publicly doubt his story.

He didn't tell the story often, and when he did, he had shame in his voice and embarrassment on his face. After a few years, he stopped sharing the story of his hunt for gorillas, saying he didn't want to be known as a "gorilla killer." When people asked about how he got the gorillas, he would tell them, "It's a sad story."[205]

It is unknown but unlikely that Nick actually captured the gorillas. Many of the reports from Nikumba and Moka's life in Africa say the gorillas were captured separately, nine months apart; that they were not brother and sister; and that the Arundels paid the F.E.A. for the gorillas in order to donate them to the National Zoo.[206]

But in 1955, the tale of a former Marine hunting gorillas in the African wilderness was a better tale to tell. It also was not as villainous then as it sounds now. Exploits of capturing big game on the mysterious and largely unexplored continent by non-natives could buoy a man's social status and reputation. There were bragging rights and trophies of animal parts to show off. And although efforts to educate the world on the declining population of certain animals and the need for conservation were expanding, it was still believable that a tourist, particularly a Marine, could capture a gorilla from the African jungle.

CHAPTER 5

NATIONAL DISGRACE

Gleefully, Doc Mann watched the toddler gorillas wrestle each other and the huge crowds that came to watch. He frequently checked in on the gorillas, monitored their growth and bragged in letters to friends about how the gorillas were thriving. By the end of their first year at the zoo, the younger Nikumba was covered with a heavy black coat of hair. He outweighed Moka, who wore lighter, thinner black hair, at 38 pounds to her 31 pounds.[207]

Nick also kept close watch of the apes' development. Nikumba, to Nick's surprise, quickly grew from a shy introvert to a hard playing, moody extrovert. In one of the last times Nick Arundel could climb into the gorillas' cage to play with the apes, Nikumba ripped apart Nick's necktie. Moka remained an "affectionate, tolerate little lady," Nick wrote in a memo to Mann.

Moka and Nikumba always stayed in the same cage together, and no one ever saw either show aggression toward the other. Nick's only advice was that the pair be provided with more toys so the two wouldn't depend solely on each other for entertainment.

"We plan to provide the pair with more diversions from each other (in the line of safe playthings) such as they would have in the struggle and exchange of life in more native surroundings," Nick wrote.[208]

While a lot of the zoo's attention and resources were focused on the gorillas and other high-profile zoo animals, the rest of the park seemed stuck in a pre–World War II time warp.

The National Zoo's mission when it was founded was for the "advancement of science and the instruction and recreation of the people."[209] But even by 1955, there were still a lot of animal management problems and very little education was taking place. Public outreach consisted mainly of attaching labels to animal exhibits, conducting tours to special groups, and speaking at community meetings about the zoo's animals.

The zoo's first notable educational campaign came in the shape of a fuzzy black bear cub named Smokey. The cub was rescued from a forest fire in New Mexico in 1950 and given to the National Zoo by the U.S. Forest Service. For years, the National Advertising Council ran a campaign about preventing forest fires featuring a fictional Smokey Bear as its mascot. The live cub would help boost the fire safety message. Smokey was a big draw for visitors, and he lived at the zoo for 26 years until his death.[210]

The significant scientific contributions that Congress expected of the zoo were only just beginning. The biggest discovery of this time was a much-improved technique to give medicine to difficult-to-control animals. The Cap-Chur gun, a CO_2 powered rifle or pistol, could shoot a hypodermic syringe surrounded by an aluminum shell that delivered medication on impact, replacing the dangerous work of roping, tying, or squeezing large and resistant animals. By the late 1950s, zoo staff were the first to demonstrate the Cap-Chur technique to the larger zoo community.[211]

Before there were medications such as anesthetics or penicillin, zoo staff improvised. William Blackburn, the zoo's first head keeper, once stood on top of a tiger's cage and tickled the cat's nose with a carriage whip. When the tiger roared, Blackburn poured a quart of castor oil into the tiger's mouth in an attempt to cure the cat's indigestion.[212]

Preventative medication and a comprehensive plan for animal preservation at the National Zoo were still undiscovered in the mid-1950s.[213] Reproductive plans were also undeveloped. Instead, the approach, like other zoos, was to gather as many species and specimens as allowable and leave them to reproduce. If breeding created a surplus, the zoo sold excess animals to other zoos or institutions.

If animals weren't breeding, zoo staff were encouraged to find out why. Animal keepers recorded animals' behaviors, illnesses, food preferences, housing conditions, sleep habits, exercise needs, and socialization habits.

If an animal wasn't eating, its temperament was not normal, or other uncharacteristic signs developed, keepers made changes and recorded those reactions, always searching for the ideal balance for healthy, happy animals.[214] Except in those days of trial and error, nothing could be perfectly balanced. An animal could appear to have the ideal diet and perfect companions but eat a toxic plant growing in its habitat. And animal care mistakes made by well-meaning zoo staff became part of the learning process.

Care of the animals improved when the Smithsonian hired Theodore Reed as the zoo's veterinarian in 1955. The bespectacled, crimson-haired doctor was born in Washington, but spent his youth living in cities all over the world as he followed his father's Army assignments. Reed had, in fact, wished for a career of military combat, just like his father and brother. His color blindness, however, led him into the Army's veterinary program at Kansas State University. During World War II, both his father and brother were killed in action and news of their deaths were delivered to Reed's mother just two hours apart.[215]

Reed earned his veterinary doctorate in 1945 and worked at the local zoo in Portland, Oregon. He wanted to help run a bigger zoo and applied for the head veterinary job at the National Zoo.[216] Before Reed, 15 years went by without a full-time vet at the zoo.

Reed's role at the zoo consisted of three parts: to establish a disease-preventative program through nutrition, sanitation, and parasite control; to nurse back to health diseased and injured animals; and to oversee research for better health for the animals in captivity.[217] He was responsible for nearly 3,000 different animals at the time of his hire.[218]

Reed inherited several projects started by Doc Mann that studied the habits and diets of a few zoo animals. Partnering with students and scientists from local universities and institutions, zoo staff tried to uncover mysterious animal problems. The staffs at the zoo and at nearby Walter Reed Medical Center cooperated on research into animal immune systems. The zoo sheltered and cared for the center's research animals. In turn, the hospital would often perform autopsies for the zoo's deceased animals to help the zoo understand why the animals died.

Other collaborations led to the understanding of parasitic worms and the damage they can do to reptiles. And less than a year after Moka and Nikumba arrived at the zoo, the city's George Washington University students studied the psychological behavior of the young gorillas.[219]

Before and after Reed came on board, trusted pediatricians or other specialists in town donated their time to analyze tricky animal illnesses. These doctors were eager to help. Their altruism may have come out of curiosity or even ego, but most likely they wanted to help the animals in their local zoo thrive.

Reed returned to Washington excited about working for the National Zoo. "I thought I had died and gone to heaven, because it was really great," he remembered years later.[220] But he soon learned of the obstacles the zoo faced. He sometimes walked to a drugstore across the street so he could purchase medication for the animals. He'd buy enough drugs for one day, and if the animal survived the night, he'd go back the next morning and buy enough drugs for one more day.[221]

When Doc Mann retired in 1956 after 30 years as head of the zoo, Reed was named acting director, and he inherited a host of problems. "I have to admit that we were a zoological slum," he said decades later.[222] As the new director, he wanted to learn everything about the zoo. As the zoo vet, he was already familiar with the animals, so he investigated the finances, the management, and the buildings. He climbed through steam tunnels and examined rooftops.[223] He met with nearly every zoo employee to learn about their duties.

What he discovered disappointed him. Buildings were falling apart, animal death rates were high, birth rates were low, and there wasn't enough money for all the staff that was needed.[224] Although these fragile conditions were decades in the making, they were embarrassing to the new director.

And like Doc Mann, he didn't shy away from venting about the zoo's shortcomings. When a group of residents living near the zoo asked Reed to speak at a meeting in the fall of 1957, he was upfront and honest. He abandoned his "aren't animals cute and don't zoo directors have fun" speech and told the truth; the zoo was in a desperate place.[225]

There was a list of embarrassing truths he may have mentioned; the zoo had 3,000 animals, but only 50 keepers.[226] The elephant pool water and waste flowed directly into Rock Creek. There were 40 cages that didn't have any animals. About 700 cages didn't even have labels. Because of wartime needs in the previous decade, the newest building at the zoo was 23 years old. Several simple stone or log buildings, constructed at the turn of the century or before, were falling apart. Reed's office, in fact, was in the same historic home on zoo grounds built in the early 1800s that Mann had worked out of and was still being "held together by termites," Reed said.[227]

The zoo blamed its embarrassing status on the lack of money

from the city and federal government. Federal funding for the zoo fell from the agreed-upon 50 percent in 1891 to just eight percent by 1958.[228] City leaders continued to complain of having to pay for the upkeep of a zoo that they had no control over. Other city pressures such as schools, hospitals, and infrastructure for utilities continued to leave only minimal funding leftover.

The citizens who heard Reed speak became motivated to act. They wrote to the District Commissioners asking that the city pay the full amount in the zoo's budget request for the following year. But the group had more long-term ambitions. Even if they won that year's budget battle, all the zoo's problems couldn't be fixed in one fiscal cycle. And these citizens were skeptical of the governments' passive interest in the zoo.

They decided to form a separate group committed to permanently boosting the finances of the zoo. Members of this new group could raise awareness and money by lobbying Congress and soliciting private donations. The group's involvement meant the zoo could potentially save a small amount of money for favorite projects without Congressional meddling.

Two of the early organizers, Barbara Robinson and Dr. Malcolm Henderson, met with Reed and Lear Grimmer, the assistant director of the zoo, to talk about ways the citizens' group could help. But instead of embracing the involvement, Reed was dubious. Did this group want control over the zoo? Would it make demands with the money it could possibly raise? Would he now have to justify the zoo's performance to this citizen group in addition to the Smithsonian's Board of Regents?

Reed approached his boss, Leonard Carmichael, Secretary of the Smithsonian. This idea of a citizen-organized support group for a Smithsonian museum or center was unprecedented, but Carmichael saw the group as non-threatening and persuaded Reed to welcome the aid. "Never discourage the active interest of citizens," Carmichael told Reed.[229]

The citizens' group moved quickly to establish a slate of officers and increase membership. Doc Mann gave the group one of its first donations. "His eyes shining with excitement, his grey hair half combed, he was one of the first to write a $50 check and become a charter member," a Washington newspaper reported.

"I never could get such a needed group started while I was at the zoo," he told the paper.[230]

The citizens' constituency called themselves Friends of the National Zoo (FONZ for short). The group chose Max Kampelman, a prominent D.C. attorney and later diplomat who negotiated war treaties with the Soviet Union, as its first president. Kampelman met with a dozen other supporters, including Nick Arundel, to plan their strategy.

Kampelman, at that time a Senate aide on Capitol Hill, suggested a slow and methodical approach concentrating on that year's budget request to the city and Congress. The group testified publicly in budget hearings and talked privately with politicians to educate them on the zoo's needs.

"In terms of federal funding priorities—A to Z—the zoo was definitely at the bottom of the appropriations list," Nick later said.[231]

And just as Kampelman, Nick, and the others were plotting out ways to get support from Congress and city officials, national and international attention beamed onto the zoo for the most tragic of circumstances—the mauling death of a young child by a lion.

Julie Ann Vogt was two and a half and from British Columbia when she visited the National Zoo on May 16, 1958, with her sister, grandparents, and mother. With a bag of peanuts in one hand and an independent streak running through her small body, she slid either between or over the bars of a perimeter fence outside the Lion House. That perimeter fence kept visitors about six feet away from the barred fence housing the lion's outdoor pen. Julie Ann's grandfather, Harry Jackson, had, moments before, asked his granddaughter to hold his hand. "I hold my own hands," the toddler told him. Now, he was screaming at her to get back over the fence.

Instead, she walked close to the lions' outdoor pen and glanced back at her grandfather. A lion quickly grabbed her leg and pulled her through the bars. Harry Jackson, who was 67, by now had climbed over the perimeter fence and was beating the lion with his cane while trying to rescue his granddaughter.

He couldn't save the child. The lion yanked her legs and lower body through the spacing in the vertical bars, reported to be only 3½ inches wide.[232] She was decapitated quickly as her lower body went through the bars. Another lion dragged her body around the enclosure. Zoo keepers rushed into the outdoor enclosure and fought the lions away from the toddler's body with a fire extinguisher and water hose.

Reed was eating lunch at another area in the park when the police captain found him and told him about the horrific event. Reed rushed to the Lion House and saw a big crowd standing around the perimeter fence. Harry Jackson was among the crowd. In his hands, he held his granddaughter's head in a paper bag.[233] Soon after, Harry Jackson started having heart pains.

In all the chaos, witnesses could not confirm which lion pulled little Julie Ann into the cage: either Pasha, a male African lion, or his mate, Queenie, who was also known as Princess.[234] Days after the tragedy, maintenance staff wrapped heavy wire mesh around the perimeter fence of the lion's outdoor pen.

News coverage of the child's death was everywhere. Newspaper articles followed for days and weeks about the dangers of the National Zoo, especially for its youngest visitors. One newspaper pointed out that the parking lot sat on the edge of a cliff with only logs separating the cars and people from taking a 100-foot plunge down into Rock Creek. Low fences, illegal paths, and dangerously decaying buildings were highlighted throughout the park.[235] The zoo closed several exhibits as a precaution. The main road that ran down the spine of the park and feet away from animal cages and buildings on both sides, was originally built for horse carriages, but was now used by cars. That road was cited as one of the worst safety hazards at the zoo, and the speed limit was lowered from 25 miles per hour to 15.[236]

Investigators ruled the tragedy an accident, and the zoo decided it would not euthanize the lions.[237]

"So there was some hue and cry that I should kill the cat, and I said I wasn't going to do it. They hadn't done anything wrong. They were cats," Reed recalled years later.[238]

Of the 115 million people who visited the park since 1908 when the zoo first started keeping guest counts, Julie Ann's death was its first fatality.[239] Her family sued, and the case was settled out of court for $11,500, a sum Ted Reed vaguely remembered decades later.[240]

"I remember going down to the district attorney's office and talking about the case. I did not want to settle because the lions had done nothing wrong. He pulled out of his drawer a picture of this little girl, of her poor little naked body with her head pulled off. Her head had been pulled off when he pulled her body through the wires. And this is why the grandfather was carrying it around in the paper sack. I agreed there could be no justice in this. There could not be any justice in this to me," Reed said years later.[241]

If there was any good to have come from this tragic accident, it was that the zoo was finally getting the attention it needed to make overdue improvements. By 1959, it received $120,000 more than the previous year, although less than requested. The additional funding paid for 14 more staff members, including four police officers. Another $50,000 was set aside to make structural improvements such as new fencing and repairs to run-down buildings.[242]

FONZ membership grew to 400, and the citizen support group gathered a relentless energy to push for long-term improvements. Its motto was "Protection, Education, Recreation." The group worked with Reed to create a plan to modernize the zoo's design and animal care. The ambitious proposal called for strengthening and improving the zoo's research, breeding, and educational efforts. To that end, the proposal advocated for a separate breeding center outside the city with space for animals to roam in herds. It also called for modernization of the animal exhibits and visitor experience.

The wish list included bigger and more natural exhibits. The new construction would reduce visual barriers between the animals and guests by using dry and wet moats, overlooks, and windows to view underwater animals.[243] Julie Ann's death was still on everyone's minds, and the renovation plans also prioritized visitor and keeper safety.

"Our National Zoological Park seems to be the only zoo in the world which has been decaying rather than progressing over the recent past," read a 1960 FONZ report. It continued: "One would expect our National Zoo to take a leading role in the preservation of species, at the very least in the preservation of North American species. But the aims of Secretary Langley have never been fulfilled. The National Zoo has never been able to perform this increasingly important mission adequately."[244]

While architects created a plan for modernizing, Congressional, city, and zoo leaders finally began serious talks about the parenting of the zoo. Reed, for one, was eager to have this issue settled. "It divided its control—District, financial; Smithsonian, administrative. The Bible says you cannot serve two masters for you'll love the one and hate the other. The Bible's wrong. You'll hate them both. You can do a little whipsawing, though, occasionally," he later said.[245]

The shared city-federal relationship was dysfunctional, but what would be better? Who really should be responsible for the National Zoo? Elected officials on Capitol Hill and at city commission meetings debated the issue, with some talk focusing on raising money for the zoo by charging an admission fee. The suggestion of 10 cents was made and Reed felt insulted.

"If an admittance charge is to be made, it should be worthy of the zoo," Reed wrote to a Smithsonian executive. "The National Zoological Park is not a 10-cent zoo. We have the best show in Washington. If we must collect an admittance fee, the amount charged should reflect the international importance and prestige of the Smithsonian, the National Zoological Park and the animals in the collection." If there were to be any admission fee, he suggested a minimum of 50 cents for entry.[246]

Officials also discussed putting the zoo under the bailiwick of the Interior Department because of its park-like status. The city ordered a study of the zoo's architectural and engineering assets and liabilities that showed many of the park buildings were still in dire need of upgrades. The Smithsonian commissioned a visitor study that showed a higher-than-expected count of guests who lived in all parts of the country, not just the Washington area.[247]

Back and forth it went until a compromise was reached in 1961; Congress, through the Smithsonian Institution, would shoulder the costs for construction and repairs at the zoo, and the District of Columbia would pay the operating costs. It would remain a free zoo.

In a show of good faith, Congress appropriated nearly $1 million to the zoo in 1962 toward the 10-year Master Plan.[248] Zoo administrators used some of the money to accomplish the goal of shutting down the public road cutting through the center of the park and building another road to carry car traffic along the perimeter. The former road became the main pedestrian walkway through the park.[249] By 1970, Congress assumed all fiscal responsibility.[250]

The zoo was finally finding financial footing, but now FONZ started suffering. By September of 1961, the group only had $22.14 in its checking account and $7.41 in petty cash. Its phone bill was two months late, and there were conflicts among officers about the future purpose of FONZ. Some wanted to concentrate on establishing the off–site breeding center and others wanted to focus efforts on the urban zoo. A few others wondered whether the group should exist at all given that they accomplished the original goal of boosting the zoo's budget.

Board members Nick Arundel, Russell Train, and then FONZ President John Perry urged the group to support both the breeding center and efforts at animal conservation at the city zoo. The growing awareness of endangered animals and the difficulty of obtaining animals from the wild was an issue that FONZ could not ignore. "For it is the life blood of this zoo," said FONZ board member C.R. Gutermuth.[251]

The group began its conservation mission on a very small scale by creating a simple guide to the park for school groups. One FONZ member paid for the printing of the maps herself. The outreach to the public was slow, and the group needed to find a money–making endeavor. It made a request to operate audio tours with all the proceeds going to the zoo. The proposal was rejected by the Smithsonian Board of Regents.

The FONZ board tried again in 1965 to get permission to run a souvenir stand. After a year of negotiations and legislative hurdles, the basic act of operating a simple gift stand at the National Zoo during the summer months became Public Law 89–772 once it was approved by President of the United States Lyndon B. Johnson.[252]

The first kiosk sold coloring books and animal food, including biscuits for the bears and monkeys, and fish for the sea lions. The disparate merchandise hardly helped promote a message about animal welfare and preservation, but at least it brought in some cash. The net profits totaled a few hundred dollars that first year, which covered FONZ's administrative costs.

A few years later, Reed approached FONZ with a request to fund the zoo's newly hired resident scientist's field study of elephants in Sri Lanka. The commitment of sending zoo staff to different parts of the world to study—not to acquire—animals in their natural habitat was a critical step toward the zoo's dedication to researching and protecting wildlife. Yet, FONZ could not be a part of it because it didn't have the $5,000 to give.[253]

FONZ leadership kept trying different ventures with varying degrees of success. A program to teach volunteer guides to lead school children through the zoo began in 1968 and kept growing in popularity and credibility. A trackless train to take visitors up and down the steep walkway was a steady source of income, as was FONZ's control of paid parking at the zoo. But an early move to take over food concessions was rejected.[254] And no one was buying the coloring books, leaving FONZ with expenses for storage and printing that was consuming the profits from other ventures.[255]

The group kept persevering, building on their successes and discarding failed initiatives. By 1972, the outlook for the zoo and for FONZ seemed even more optimistic. More unique and important animals were on display, which attracted a healthy number of visitors. FONZ was growing in membership and qualified for a bank loan to help their operation expand. Yet, when Nick Arundel became FONZ president in 1973, he declared, "This National Zoo is a national disgrace."[256]

To outsiders, the zoo made significant financial and managerial changes in the last 10 years, but Nick remained frustrated that the zoo hadn't made greater strides. Funding from Congress was unreliable year-to-year. The Master Plan was scaled back dramatically in order to pay for Vietnam War efforts, meaning big renovation projects at the zoo were put on hold.[257] Also, the zoo was still not receiving, nor was it worthy of, the national admiration it should command as the zoo in the nation's capital, Nick said.

Nick's sensational remark was forgotten a few months later when China gave an adorable pair of pandas to the children of the U.S. There was no doubt in Reed's mind that the National Zoo should become the pandas' American home, but other zoos were competing for the honor. After intense quiet lobbying, the decision was finally made that the pandas should go to the zoo in D.C.[258]

The male, Hsing-Hsing, and female, Ling-Ling, were around two years old at the time of their arrival. They became instant celebrities and brought the zoo the positive national and international attention it sought. Not only did the young pandas captivate the crush of visitors through their play and mild manners, the pair's arrival was seen as a historic moment in U.S. relations with Communist China. After two decades of adversarial Cold War relations between them and years of being worn down by national strife inside both countries, people seemed eager to let two cuddly and docile-appearing animals ease the tumultuous Chinese-U.S. relationship.

About 20,000 people came to see the pandas on their first day at the zoo on April 20, 1972. That following Sunday, 75,000 people waited in a quarter-mile-long line to welcome the furry diplomats.[259] Zoo and FONZ leaders rushed to accommodate the press and visitors by planning expansions to the restaurant and parking lot. The pandas appeared on magazine covers, and their likenesses were duplicated on T-shirts, notepads, and other merchandise.[260]

"It appeared that Washington, and indeed most of the country, spurred on by the media, might never recover from the excitement," according to a 25-year history booklet of FONZ.[261]

As a FONZ board member and zoo enthusiast, Nick was especially exuberant to have the pandas. Nearly a decade earlier, Nick started writing letters to various sources to build support to get a panda, and even offered to pay all expenses, but had no luck.[262] In 1967, he even obtained a license from the U.S. Secretary of the Treasury, under the authority of the Trading with the Enemy Act, to import two giant pandas from China through the exchange of another animal of equal value. But he never found the right contacts to negotiate with Chinese authorities.[263] At the announcement of Nixon's historic visit to China, Nick proposed that the elusive, yet captivating, black and white panda would be the ideal offering to improve international relations between the two countries.[264]

It's unknown how influential Nick's quiet campaign to acquire pandas for the zoo was in the end, but one of Nick's suggested animals for the goodwill exchange with China—the musk ox—was the eventual creature that America gave to China as a thank-you for the pandas.[265]

The large shaggy animals live in the Arctic, including the northernmost tips of Alaska. During mating season, the males give off a pungent odor, hence their name. Reed personally escorted a pair of musk oxen to China. The male, Milton, had a runny nose, a cough, and a skin disease that caused hair loss. The female, Mathilda, was a nervous wreck and also had skin issues that caused hair loss. It is unlikely Chinese zoo-goers lined up to view these unhappy, unattractive animals as Americans did for the pandas.

"Frankly, I just don't think musk oxen have the same sex appeal pandas do," Reed told the press.[266]

The positive impact of the pandas' arrival at the National Zoo led to an immediate financial windfall driven by zoo visitors' mad love affair with the black and white cubs. Ling-Ling and Hsing-Hsing were admired and doted on until their deaths in the 1990s. For the decades they lived there, they were the stars of the zoo and a source of pride for the city. They helped the zoo and FONZ mature and build clout among the zoo world. By 1976, FONZ had 11,000 members.[267] Between 1974 and 1980, FONZ raised $1.3 million for education, research, and conservation efforts at the National Zoo.[268]

The force of FONZ grew, and Reed, once again, became concerned with its potential play for power at the zoo. In 1976, FONZ leadership, including Nick Arundel who was still the group's president, put the issue to rest by clarifying that FONZ, a private, nonprofit, volunteer organization, existed solely to support the zoo and that zoo and Smithsonian directors had the final authority for all public programs. FONZ's role was clearly delineated from the zoo's—FONZ was to serve the interests of the visitors while the zoo would care for the animals.

"After 15 years, we are taking here a major step in the maturity of FONZ, and creating a perhaps unprecedented example of what can be achieved together between a major private citizen's effort and professional zoo management to build what we jointly shall see become the world's foremost zoological park and educational experience for its visitors," Nick Arundel wrote to the FONZ Board of Directors.[269]

CHAPTER 6

A BIRTH

Old zoo buildings were leveled and replaced with better-functioning facilities for both the animals contained inside and the increasing numbers of visitors coming to see the new pandas and other interesting creatures. Like the zoo around it, the gorilla section of the Small Mammal House in the 1960s and 70s was also expanding.

Around the fifth anniversary of the gorillas' arrival at the National Zoo, when Moka was six years old, she first showed an interest in sex. Keepers became aware of her maturity when she "got an evil look on her face and sucked her lips over her teeth," although she showed no other physical signs. During oestrus, Moka would be the aggressor. Otherwise, Nikumba was the initiator.

By late 1960, the pair's practice paid off. Moka showed no more cycles of heightened sexual desire, although she continued to submit to Nikumba's advances. When Moka stopped consuming her vomit as was often her habit, keepers suspected she may be pregnant. They collected her urine and sent it to a lab where doctors injected it into a female rabbit. This rabbit test is how pregnancies of some zoo animals were confirmed at the time. If the rabbit's ovaries became enlarged, it was a positive result. Rabbits used for these types of tests typically died after being surgically cut open to inspect their ovaries.

Moka's test came back positive.

Her breasts became enlarged by April, and in May, the normally happy and affectionate Moka became snappy and irritable. Supervisor Keeper of Great Apes Bernard Gallagher, a large, robust man, watched in amazement as Moka's sunny and gentle disposition changed toward him, Nikumba, and the other keepers. At the end of May, during a brief time when Moka allowed him to be close to her, Gallagher put his hand on her stomach, and he felt the baby inside move. Soon after, the fetal movements in Moka's belly were seen visually.[270]

Earlier that spring, in anticipation of a baby gorilla, zoo leaders built a bigger cage for the gorillas. The zoo renovated Moka and Nikumba's original cage three times in the first year and a half of their arrival as the gorillas grew bigger.[271] This most recent renovation was the largest yet. The new 40-foot-long cage was still in the same side wing of the Small Mammal House, but developers added a small outdoor pavilion for the animals to get fresh air and look down on Rock Creek Park. Corrugated fiberglass protected the concrete space from sun and rain. With more than three times the space of their old cage, a new tire swing and separate drinking faucets, zoo administrators thought the animals would be pleased. But instead they threw oranges at anyone who walked by, ground their teeth, and refused to eat. Within a week, though, they adjusted to their new home and were back to their normal behaviors.[272]

As her pregnancy progressed, Moka became hungrier. She dominated mealtime, making it clear to Nikumba that she had the first choice of food. He got the leftovers. Each day, she and Nikumba typically ate three oranges, three apples, two pounds of mixed food from a recipe created by the Philadelphia Zoo, a pound of cooked horse meat, and a pound and a half of kale.[273] They also often ate three pounds of bananas and drank three quarts of milk twice a day mixed with eight raw eggs, a vitamin-mineral compound, and four tablespoons of brewer's yeast. Their bonus snack was seven hard boiled eggs already peeled and salted for them.

Gallagher and the other keepers tried to feed Nikumba separately, but Nikumba refused to eat unless he was with Moka and continued his submissive role at meal times.

The zoo didn't have a scale large enough to weigh the juvenile gorillas, but it was estimated that Nikumba was about 200 pounds, and Moka, at the height of her pregnancy, outweighed him at 250 pounds.

With the baby growing inside her, Moka had no interest in doing anything more than eating and lounging on her back with her swollen feet and ankles propped up against the cage's bars. Nikumba got bored with his playmate's inactivity and began spitting at crowds and keepers with more frequency, stealing the water hose from the keepers, and playing in the water tub. One time, Nikumba touched Moka's breast, and she slapped him on the side of his head. Another time, he was watching her stomach move with the baby inside when he took his long arms and strong hands and drummed on her belly. Moka was not upset, but it stressed the keepers who were watching.[274]

Gorilla gestation lasts 37 weeks. With an anticipated birthdate in either September or October 1961, keepers kept a constant watch on Moka during the day and an hourly check was done overnight. Although a scheduled monitoring plan was in place, no one witnessed the actual birth.

On September 9th, at just before 6 a.m., Night Keeper Melvin Kilby did his hourly check on the gorillas. Everything was normal and Moka was calm. An hour later when he walked by the gorilla cage again, he saw the baby in Moka's arms. She did not seem anxious, but she was not holding the baby close to her body.

Gallagher arrived shortly afterward, and Moka brought the baby to him in her extended arms while he stood on the outside of the barred cage. He congratulated her, pet her, and put her morning vitamins in her mouth. She turned back to the center of the cage, laid the baby down on the concrete floor, and walked back to Gallagher. Nikumba tentatively walked over to the baby, and Moka rushed back to the center of the cage to stand between he and the baby. A short time later, she laid on the hard floor next to the infant, but did not touch her newborn.[275]

Ted Reed arrived, and he and the others consulted about Moka's apparent lack of interest in the baby. They worried the infant was cold and hungry and would suffer from neglect. The pressure to make such a significant decision so quickly was immense. After several brief conversations, they decided to remove the infant from its parents, putting its survival in the hands of humans. The contingency plan was to have Louise Gallagher, the keeper's wife, care for the baby gorilla at their home in a Maryland suburb of D.C. Although Louise Gallagher had no formal zoology training, she was a surrogate mother to a few of the zoo's chimpanzee babies.[276] She already prepared for the gorilla birth by getting an incubator, towels, diapers, and baby formula.

Kilby called Animal Head Keeper Ralph Norris, George Washington University hospital obstetrician James Sites, Associate Zoo Director Lear Grimmer, and Secretary of the Smithsonian Leonard Carmichael to tell them the good news about the gorilla's birth.

The men were eager to check the baby. Using a long-established ritual, Norris greeted Moka and Nikumba from the visitor's side of the outdoor enclosure of the Small Mammal House. The gorillas went right to him, knowing that Norris would give them chewing gum as he did most mornings. With the gorillas outside, the door between the inside and outside enclosures was closed, and Gallagher entered the indoor cage and scooped up the baby from the floor. From a window, Moka and Nikumba could see Gallagher take the baby, but neither one seemed upset.[277]

With the baby wrapped in a towel and sheet, Dr. Stiles and Carmichael, whose work in academia focused on the psychology of primates,[278] examined the baby's vision and physical state. The infant boy gorilla measured 18 inches long with an arm span of 22 inches,[279] and weighed 5 pounds, 4 ounces.[280] They declared the baby normal and healthy. Norris held the infant as he climbed into the back seat of Reed's car. With Reed at the wheel, they drove out of the city and to the Gallagher home. By the time the men arrived at the Gallagher's Prince George's County home, Louise was waiting with a bottle of Bremil baby formula, and the incubator was warmed to 75 degrees.[281]

Soon, the press showed up at the Gallagher home to take pictures of the little ape, which Louise Gallagher dressed in a diaper and infant T-shirt. Reporters wrote articles and took pictures of the baby gorilla's yawning, eating, and cuddling with the Gallagher family for the papers that evening and the next day.[282]

"They need all the love and care you would give your own baby to survive," Louise Gallagher told a newspaper.[283]

Back at the Small Mammal House, Moka ate normally hours after she gave birth, but was quiet. The next day, she refused to eat her regular food, and the keepers offered her a favorite treat—ice cream, which she ate eagerly. By the third day, she was back to her regular appetite and behavior. By the fifth day after the birth, she and Nikumba were mating again.[284]

The Gallagher house was full. In addition to the new baby ape and the humans, the house had a dog, a canary, and a five-month-old chimpanzee named Lulu—a zoo animal that was also being hand-raised by Louise Gallagher.[285] The baby gorilla, however, demanded most of the attention, day and night. Louise Gallagher not only fed and changed the baby gorilla's diapers, she cuddled him and recorded his growth and behavior, which she reported to Reed.

Reed promised Nick Arundel naming rights to the newborn gorilla. In turn, Nick opened the honor to the public. By now he was the owner of Arlington, Virginia-based radio station WAVA. He had purchased the station a year earlier in 1960 when it was the country-music station WARL. Within six months, Nick turned the station into the first long-sustaining, 24-hour news radio station in America.[286] Its success was credited to the Washington, D.C., area's growing demand for breaking news about major events in the 1960s, such as the Vietnam War, the civil rights movement, and the assassinations of President John Kennedy, Martin Luther King, Jr., and Robert Kennedy.

Nick also used the platform to advocate for zoo projects. During one break in the continual news cycle, WAVA held a naming contest for the baby ape. More than 400 names were submitted by listeners, and Tomoka, which had no special meaning, was chosen as the winner.[287]

Louise Gallagher would take Tomoka, dressed in baby clothes, for carriage rides in the neighborhood and on errands around town. One time, she dressed him in a bonnet, sweater, and blanket for a trip to the grocery store. Another customer at the store saw the baby and remarked to a friend, "My God in heaven, I'd love to see what that girl's husband looks like."[288]

Neighbors would stop by to check on the baby ape's progress, and, at one point while hand rearing various zoo animals, the Gallaghers were forced to unlist their phone number in the county phone book to stop the flood of calls from parents asking if they could bring their children over to see the animals.

The baby gorilla was an oddity living in the Maryland suburb, but he was also a curiosity to the greater zoo world. Tomoka was the fourth western lowland gorilla born in captivity in the world and only the second in the United States. Although it was becoming more common for zoos around the world to showcase gorillas and zoos were getting better at understanding their needs, a successful pregnancy seemed hopeless to zoo administrators. That is, until Colo's birth at another zoo.

Colo became the first baby gorilla ever born in captivity a few days before Christmas in 1956 at the Columbus Zoo in Ohio.[289] After Colo's surprise birth, a part-time keeper found the baby laying on the floor, still in its amniotic sac. He broke the sac and gave the infant mouth-to-mouth resuscitation. When the baby started breathing, he wrapped her in towels and took her to the zoo's boiler room to get warm. The baby was cared for by humans until she got large enough to move back to the zoo.[290]

Colo developed into a healthy ape and bore three children. She became a grandmother, great-grandmother, and even great-great grandmother before her death in 2017 shortly after celebrating her 60th birthday.[291] She was the oldest living gorilla ever in captivity, far outliving the 35-year captive life expectancy of gorillas.[292]

Years earlier, Colo's parents, Baron Macomb and Millie Christina, along with a third gorilla, Stephi, had been captured in Cameroon by the gorilla hunter William Said, a resident of the Columbus area and John Biname's mentor. He sold the three gorillas to the Columbus Zoo in 1951.[293] Soon after, the Columbus Zoo sold Stephi to the Basel Zoo in Switzerland.[294]

At the Basel Zoo, Stephi was paired with Achilla, who was also captured in Cameroon. Achilla gave birth on September 23, 1959, to the first gorilla born in captivity in Europe and the second in the world. Achilla appeared to not know how to nurse her baby, so the infant, who the zoo named Goma, was soon taken to the zoo director's home and raised there for the first few years of her life.[295] Remarkably, Goma is still alive, and by the end of 2016, she was 57 years old.[296]

Two years after having Goma, Stephi and Achilla had another baby—a baby boy named Jambo. When he was born, he stayed with Achilla, who was able to care for and raise him. At maturity, Jambo had a baby with his sister Goma, a boy named Tam-Tam, who was raised by Goma.[297]

By the time Jambo was an adult silverback, he was transferred to the Jersey Zoo, also known as Durrell Wildlife Park. The wildlife sanctuary, which works with international groups for the recovery of threatened species, sits on a small island between England and France and is open to the public. While there, Jambo made international news in 1986 when a five-year-old boy fell into the gorilla enclosure. While a horrified crowd looked on, Jambo stood guard over the boy, appearing to protect him from the other gorillas, before the boy could be rescued.[298]

In all, the three gorillas Said captured and sold to the Columbus Zoo in 1951 produced the first three gorillas born in captivity—the start of generations of zoo-born gorillas.[299] Said's violent practices for capturing gorillas now bring feelings of ignominy and regret, but was the origin of successful breeding programs for zoo gorillas.

The fourth gorilla born in captivity—Tomoka, the National Zoo's baby gorilla—was thriving at the Gallagher home, and Louise Gallagher meticulously tracked his development. On his ninth day of life, he smiled, and three days later, he laughed. At a month old, he could pull himself up on the arm of a chair, and after three and a half months, he had the true knuckle walk of a gorilla.

Tomoka and Lulu the chimp were becoming best friends. They wrestled, hugged, and slept together. When Louise Gallagher put her coat on to go outside, both Tomoka and Lulu would cry. But if she put on their coats first, they would be content, knowing they were going along with her. At four and a half months, Tomoka had his first temper tantrum when he tried to get out of his crib and no one came to help him. He got scared and cried when he first saw himself in a mirror. After a few more times seeing his reflection, he would burst into laughter.[300]

The hand-raising of Tomoka was guided by Louise Gallagher's instincts and also on the common practice of that time. Zoo officials followed the Columbus Zoo's example on hand-rearing of Colo. Louise Gallagher became more experienced in raising baby apes. Before she became a surrogate ape mom she believed, "you couldn't treat any animal like a child." But when her husband first brought home a six-month-old chimp, she changed her mind. "Within three days, that was my baby," she said in a Smithsonian newsletter.[301]

Emotions aside, in the early years of infant gorilla care, zoos—mostly American zoos—would not hesitate long before separating mother and baby after the birth. Zoo leaders didn't want to jeopardize the baby's life considering how much money and effort went into getting gorillas. In fact, of the first 15 gorillas born in captivity around the world, 10 were hand-raised by humans. Of the five gorillas that were parent-raised, four were born in European zoos. Another gorilla, Roberta, was born at the Colorado Springs Zoo and died within five days of her birth, but it was unknown if she was ever hand-raised.[302]

When Tomoka was nearly eight months old and 15 pounds, he came back home to the National Zoo. His friend Lulu came along with him, and the two were put in the same cage in the Small Mammal House to help each other with the homesickness.[303] Their cage, next to the zoo's chimpanzees, was not in the same room as Moka and Nikumba. As the Gallaghers said their goodbyes, a diaper-clad Tomoka tugged on Bernard Gallagher's pants and then kissed his hand.[304]

Tomoka struggled with his transition to the zoo and got upset when keepers didn't dress him in diapers and clothes.[305]

"I can well remember the first time that he had his diapers removed on public exhibition. The poor little devil was terribly embarrassed by the whole thing and assumed the classical pose of 'September Morn.' It was rather pathetic to see how he missed his tri-cornered trousers," Reed wrote in a letter years later.[306]

In the same letter, Reed acknowledged Tomoka had "separation trauma" when he moved back into the zoo.

Tomoka and Lulu probably wished they could have stayed with the Gallaghers. The Small Mammal House was loud and odorous, and car traffic still flowed in the middle of the park, right next to the building.

Still, the Small Mammal House was actually quite large and housed nearly 100 species of animals. A 1963 narrative guide boasts that other zoos used the Small Mammal House building as a model for their animal buildings.[307]

A variety of animals lived there in the early 1960s, including a hedgehog, mongoose, porcupine, and a celebrity chimpanzee.[308] On January 31, 1961, Ham, the famous chimpanzee astronaut, was strapped into a Redstone rocket for a 16.5-minute flight into space, traveling up to a speed of 5,857 miles per hour—more than seven times the speed of sound. During the flight, Ham was weightless for more than six minutes. Three months later, Commander Alan B. Shepard operated Mercury 3, the United States' first manned space mission.[309]

In January 1964, Moka and Nikumba had a second baby named Leonard after Smithsonian Secretary Leonard Carmichael, the man who had urged Reed to accept the help of the Friends of the National Zoo and who examined Tomoka shortly after his birth.

Although more than two years separated Tomoka and Leonard's births, Leonard was only the fifth gorilla born in captivity in the world. Although Leonard clung to Moka's belly fur with both hands after his birth, zoo staff removed the newborn gorilla and brought him to Louise Gallagher's house.[310]

Bringing newborn apes to Louise Gallagher became a predict-able and reliable protocol. The baby gorilla got so accustomed to wearing diapers and clothes at the Gallaghers' that when he returned to the zoo eight months after his birth, he tried to hide to cover his nakedness.[311] Leonard, who was bigger and bolder than Tomoka at that age, also screamed in protest at being put in his cage.[312]

While Leonard's birth was a special event, it was overshadowed by the birth of another infant animal at the National Zoo—a rare white tiger. The cub was born just a few days before Leonard to Mohini, also a rare white tiger who arrived at the zoo several years earlier from India.

With her blue eyes, cream fur, and grayish-black strips, Mohini attracted a lot of attention from visitors. She was one of the first white tigers born in captivity in the world and was gifted to the National Zoo in 1960. Although a donor purchased her for $10,000, her value was estimated to be much higher. Soon after her arrival in Washington, she was put in a mobile cage and driven two-and-a-half miles to the White House to meet President Dwight Eisenhower.[313]

After Mohini gave birth to her white cub and two orange cubs in 1964, the tigers' popularity grew even more. A television spe-cial, airing nationally, featured the new family. Zoo visitor counts shot up, with some people staying all day to watch Mohini and her cubs.[314] The white tigers were such a sense of pride for the zoo that Mohini's likeness became the emblem of both the National Zoo and FONZ.[315]

But Mohini ended up being one of the zoo's biggest mistakes. White tigers are born from parents—either white or orange tigers—that have a recessive gene that determines pigmentation. To better the odds of white cub births, zoos and other white tiger owners would breed the white tigers with other known carriers of the recessive gene, triggering many cases of inbreeding. Mohini's litter in 1964 was fathered by Samson, who was both Mohini's uncle and half-brother. Mohini was the offspring of her mother and maternal grandfather.[316]

Ted Reed, as a veterinarian, was uneasy with inbreeding and he asked other prominent zoo directors about the practice. "So I was told that the wild animals were so heterozygous that [there are] five generations of inbreeding before you have any problems. And five generations, we had problems, so we were concerned about it," Reed later told a historian with the Smithsonian.[317]

The inbreeding at the National Zoo and elsewhere was damaging for future litters of white tigers who carried health problems such as shortened legs, crossed eyes, and early deaths.[318] The controlled breeding programs were—at the time—believed by the public and zoo staff to be an important step toward conserving these exotic animals. But because white tigers are not a separate tiger subspecies, they are not part of any tiger conservation programs. The Association of Zoos and Aquariums, which accredits zoos in America that volunteer for the scrutiny and potential credibility, now condemns the intentional breeding of animals with rare genetic traits in order to produce animals with unusual color morphs, including white tigers.

"Even among today's frequently informed and educated zoo visitors, the interest in seeing white tigers, white lions, white alligators, or king cheetahs continues often in preference over the 'normal' looking individuals of the same species," says a 2011 paper from the Association of Zoos and Aquariums.[319]

There was no such drama with inbreeding up the hill at the Small Mammal House. As Tomoka grew older, zoo officials became concerned they wouldn't find a mate for him to continue the family line and for him to have a friend. He was still sharing a cage with

Lulu, but Tomoka was getting aggressive with her by hitting her and pulling her hair.[320] By the time he was three, he was 60 pounds, and the National Zoo was having difficulty finding a same-sized gorilla companion for him.

Lear Grimmer, the zoo's associate director, contacted Antwerp Zoo Director Walter Van den bergh, whom Grimmer called, "more of a gateway for gorilla acquisition than any other single man in the zoo world." Van den bergh promised to help find the National Zoo a female gorilla for Tomoka, but warned the search would not be easy. "They are all exported from the ex-French Congo, where they kill the mothers and hand rear the babies, which are shipped as soon as possible."[321]

Once again, Nick Arundel used his radio station to motivate listeners to help the zoo. This time he held a contest to find someone willing to go on a safari to find a prospective mate for Tomoka. "The person sought should be in good health; he should also be experienced in preparing baby formula, and be prepared to donate the cost of this expedition and the baby," the ad said.[322] Although several people responded, including an airline executive promising free or reduced transportation,[323] no one, it seems, actually went through with the trip. Nick Arundel then quietly offered to donate $3,000 to the zoo toward the purchase of a young gorilla.[324]

The zoo did get its desired young gorilla in January of 1965, but the details of Femelle's origins are unclear. Records show only that she was captured in Cameroon, owned briefly by animal dealer G. Van den Brink from Holland. She was estimated to be between 19 months and three years old when she came to the National Zoo.[325]

WAVA broadcast news of Femelle's arrival at the zoo over the airwaves. "With the gift of this young female, we hope to step up reproduction in captivity of Earth's diminishing gorilla population and enable additional research concerning this animal, important here since there are less than 60 gorillas in captivity in the entire world today," the WAVA report said. "Washington now will have five of them, including a probably unprecedented two couples for its breeding program."[326]

Moka and Nikumba had their third and last baby together in 1967, a girl named Inaki. She was the world's 13th western lowland gorilla born in captivity. Although zoo officials' understanding of gorilla pregnancies and births was improving and there were more successful births, it was still more common at the time to hand raise zoo-born gorillas than to leave them with their mother. Louise Gallagher again stepped in to hand raise the gentle and curious Inaki.[327]

Zookeeper William Blackburne walks Asian elephants Dunk and Gold Dust on zoo grounds in 1898. Dunk and Gold Dust were the first animals at the zoo's Rock Creek Valley location when it opened in 1891. *Smithsonian Institution Archives. Image NZP-0288.*

A young giraffe takes a drink from a raised bucket while on route from Port Sudan during the National Geographic Society–Smithsonian Institution Expedition in 1937. The expedition collected nearly 900 animals for the National Zoo. *J. Baylor Roberts/National Geographic Creative.*

Ten-year-old Nicky Arundel at his Washington, D.C., home writing articles for his neighborhood newspaper *Nicky's News,* which advocated for giraffes at the National Zoo. *Photo taken in 1938. Richard Hewitt Stewart/National Geographic Creative.*

Dr. William Mann, director of the
National Zoo from 1926-1956,
went on several expeditions to
collect wild animals for the zoo
and spent many years trying to
bring gorillas to the National Zoo.
Smithsonian Institution Archives.
Image 76-6169.

Nick Arundel holding
Moka (age 20 months)
in the African Congo
in February 1955.
Nikumba (age 14
months) can be seen in
the lower right corner.
Photo courtesy of Nick and
Peggy Arundel.

Nick Arundel and Moka in the
African Congo in February
1955. This picture is described
in Chapter 1. *Photo courtesy of*
Nick and Peggy Arundel.

Nick Arundel holding Nikumba, left, age 14 months, and Moka, right, 20 months, in the African Congo in February 1955, shortly before bringing the gorillas to the National Zoo. *Photo courtesy of Nick and Peggy Arundel.*

A year after their arrival at the National Zoo, in March 1956, Nikumba, right, had grown from a shy introvert into a hard-playing extrovert. Moka remained tolerant and affectionate. They were never separated. *Photo courtesy of Nick and Peggy Arundel.*

Nick Arundel holding Nikumba at the National Zoo in March 1956. *Photo courtesy of Nick and Peggy Arundel.*

In 1962, zoo director Theodore Reed holds Tomoka, the fourth gorilla born in captivity in the world. Tomoka, the first offspring of Moka and Nikumba, was raised by a zookeeper's wife for the first seven months of his life. *Smithsonian Institution Archives. Image 2003-19493.*

Mohini, a white tiger, rests in her enclosure at the National Zoo in 1973. *Smithsonian Institution Archives. Image 73-9626.*

Ling-Ling, left, and Hsing-Hsing, the first giant pandas at the National Zoo, play together in their outdoor enclosure in 1985. *Smithsonian Institution Archives. Image 96-1378.*

Femelle sits in the outdoor enclosure at the Small Mammal House where the gorillas lived from 1955 to 1981. In 1981, a new Great Ape House was built that gave the gorillas more indoor and outdoor space. *Smithsonian Institution Archives. Acc. 16-065, National Zoological Park, photographs, circa 1955-2005, Box 10.*

Keeper Robert Shumaker and Mandara, in the late 1980s, make eye contact between the laminated glass separating the visitor area and the gorilla habitat in the Great Ape House. *Smithsonian Institution Archives. Acc. 16-065, National Zoological Park, photographs, circa 1955-2005, Box 27.*

Augustus, also known as Gus, strategically built alliances with other gorillas at the zoo to become the leader of the troop. Photo taken between 1987-1995. *Smithsonian Institution Archives. Acc. 16-065, National Zoological Park, photographs, circa 1955-2005, Box 80.*

Mandara, already mother to Kejana, became a surrogate mother to newborn Baraka Ya M'Welu, the offspring of Haloko. Here the threesome stay close in their outdoor enclosure in 1992. *Smithsonian Institution Archives. Acc. 16-065, National Zoological Park, photographs, circa 1955-2005, Box 80.*

M'Geni Mopaya, also known as Mopie, was Nikumba's last offspring. His birth in 1972 to Femelle was the last gorilla birth at the zoo until Kejana arrived in 1991. *Smithsonian Institution Archives. Acc. 16-065, National Zoological Park, photographs, circa 1955-2005, Box 11.*

Nick Arundel visits the outdoor gorilla exhibit during the Friends of the National Zoo's 50th Anniversary Celebration in 2008. *Photo courtesy of Nick and Peggy Arundel.*

Nick Arundel visits with Nikumba, top, and Moka, in his arms, at the National Zoo in 1956, a year after he brought them to the zoo from the French Congo. *Robert F. Sisson and Donald McBain/National Geographic Creative.*

CHAPTER 7

HEALTH SCARES

Reassured that its gorilla population was healthy and expanding, zoo staff wrote reports bragging about the gorilla births. As Nikumba sired his offspring with Moka, he continued developing into a healthy and handsome gorilla. He was long and lean and fit, weighing 325 pounds.[328] In a few years, he would grow the distinguished silver fur on his back that signals adulthood for male gorillas. He was still popular with the tourists, but more importantly to zoo officials, Nikumba proved his value by reproducing the next generation of zoo gorillas.

He was in such good health that keepers were immediately concerned on June 13, 1963, when they noticed Nikumba's breathing suddenly became rapid and his stomach protruded in and out with every labored breath. That day, he did not play as usual, but ate normally. The veterinarian gave him an antibiotic-antihistamine mix. The next morning Nikumba struggled to rise from a seated position. He did not seem to be in pain, but his body was weak, and he couldn't control his legs. The next day, he didn't stand at all.

Doctors determined he was paralyzed in his lower body. But he was still hungry and didn't show any signs of pain. Zoo officials called in the city's leading neurosurgeons to better understand what was ailing Nikumba. Drs. Henry Feffer and Hugo Rizzoli were well-respected local surgeons. Rizzoli was pioneering treatments of lumbar disc herniations and brain surgery. Feffer was an orthopedic surgeon and the go-to guy in the city for complicated spine surgery.[329]

The doctors did a thorough exam on the large ape. First, they worked with the zoo veterinarians to sedate Nikumba and then to restrain him with his back against the cage bars, his arms spread out and tied to the bars. He was pricked numerous times from his toes to his pelvis, but none of the pin pricks caused a reflex or other reaction. The doctors lowered the gorilla's long arms and folded his head between his legs. Attempts to draw spinal fluid failed, and the doctors and zoo officials decided not to collect fluid from the brain for fear that it could lead to permanent damage. Demerol was given to ease any after-exam pain.

Three hours after the exam began, Nikumba was unbound and alert. Although the exam didn't provide all the answers the doctors and Nikumba's caretakers were hoping for, they made a tentative diagnosis of a viral infection of the spinal cord. A combination of antibiotics and Vitamin B complex was prescribed and injected daily using the Cap-Chur projectile syringe.

Nikumba hated the Cap-Chur gun. Before his paralysis, when keepers or other familiar zoo staff approached his cage, he would come forward, his arms stretched out front, looking to give and receive affection. But if he spotted the Cap-Chur gun, he would flee to the far corner of the cage or swing from the horizontal bars at the top of his cage. His darting around the cage made it harder to set the right trajectory for the shot, but as soon as the syringe hit his body, he would become calm and friendly again. Now that Nikumba could not move his legs, it was easier to give him the antibiotics and vitamins, although he still protested vocally.

Five days into treatment, Nikumba was still paralyzed in his lower body but did not seem to be suffering. In fact, he seemed determined to recover and began testing ways to move his sluggish body around his cage by using his powerful and still-compliant upper body. First, he raised his lower body off the floor with his long arms and scooted backward. Then he started to roll. To sit upright, he lay on his back and folded one leg to his chest, using his other leg as a lever to gain momentum.[330] His will and ingenuity to move gave his keepers and Ted Reed hope that the gorilla's legs would recuperate and Nikumba would survive.

As time passed, Nikumba's mobility got more sophisticated. His keeper, Walter Tucker, described how Nikumba began conducting his own physical therapy by exercising his legs until he was exhausted. He would pick up one foot and use his other hand to flex it, front, back, and in circles. He would lower that foot and pick up the other and flex that foot, front, back, and in circles. He did this every day, several times a day.[331] Three weeks after his diagnosis, he was able to flex both feet without the help of his hands.

His keepers elevated his feeding tray so that he had to pull himself up to eat. At first, it was meant to exercise his arms, which were still strong. But later, it also worked to help retrain his leg muscles. Doctors discontinued the antibiotics, but kept giving him cortisone and Vitamin B complex.

Nine weeks after the paralysis struck, Nikumba stood and walked two steps before sitting down again. He walked with his knees flexed and his weight on the outer parts of his feet, toes curled inward. He moved with slow and cautious steps, but the mysterious and sudden paralysis was dissipating.

Eight months after his diagnosis, Nikumba made a complete recovery. He stood erect and was walking flat footed as gorillas should.[332] He was his old self just in time for Leonard's birth. And—continuing to astonish the medical community and zoo officials—Nikumba and Moka had daughter, Inaki, in 1967. The paralysis did not seem to disrupt his long-term potency.

Just as Nikumba was making his recovery, Tomoka started having health problems. Even though Tomoka took some time adjusting from the pampered upbringing in the Gallaghers' home to the barred cages at the National Zoo, he was growing into a healthy and happy ape. He was one of the most popular animals at the zoo because of his playful youth. His only health problem, thus far, was when he was still a baby and he became ill with an intestinal infection. His treatment team consisted of local pediatricians, but when their efforts to make the gorilla better failed, Tomoka went to the city's Children's Hospital for treatment. He was put in the animal research laboratory to treat his fever, diarrhea, dehydration, and stomach cramps. Keepers Bernard Gallagher and Ralph Norris stayed with Tomoka all day and night until he made a full recovery.[333]

Around the time Tomoka was celebrating his fourth birthday, he began showing signs of intermittent lameness in his arms and legs. Zoo staff were unsure of the cause. Two years later, in the fall of 1967, the lameness intensified and was consistent. He stopped growing and became frail. His brown coat began thinning and losing its shine, and his weight dropped to 113 pounds. He seemed to be in constant pain and looked miserable as he rubbed his sore joints. Zoo visitors walked quickly by his cage so they didn't have to look at the morose gorilla that sat in a corner for much of the day.

Throughout the next year, the pain was concentrated in his left foot and then his left hand and wrist. His foot, hand, and wrist were swollen, stiff, hot, painful, and useless to him.[334] Zoo doctors diagnosed the gorilla with arthritis, but he had only temporary relief from the more than 20 medications he was given.[335]

Tomoka was suffering, and he wasn't getting better. Zoo leaders determined he would have to be euthanized. Days before putting him down, zoo officials placed a call to the nearby Arthritis Institute to see if doctors there wanted to examine Tomoka's body post mortem. Absolutely, the doctors said. But first, they wanted to check him before his scheduled death.

Doctors at the Institute examined Tomoka's blood, which showed cell tissues supporting the growth of bacteria. Further examinations revealed that the bacteria were not of the infectious-type and that this certain growth of bacteria seen in Tomoka was similar to that occurring in certain human arthritis patients. The gorilla's immune system was mistakenly attacking his body's tissues. This was unlike the more common osteoarthritis that occurs from wear and tear on the joints and that typically emerges during old age.

In other words, this was the first time doctors had seen human rheumatoid arthritis in an animal. It was an exciting discovery for the doctors because the gorilla, whose DNA closely resembles humans, could be an accurate test model for studies of the disease. "Future studies should include attempts to reproduce the ideas in the gorilla and test therapeutic mechanisms," said one report written shortly after the discovery.[336]

The doctors decided to treat Tomoka as they did human patients. They started him on an intravenous low dose of tetracycline, a type of antibiotic, on a biweekly basis. As expected, Tomoka's condition worsened at first, but then began improving. He gained weight, and after 18 weeks, doctors stopped the treatment, and Tomoka's pain returned and his weight plateaued. Treatment began again a month and a half later, and he gained weight again and appeared more active and comfortable.

The same pattern repeated for the next several years until doctors were able to administer the antibiotic orally, often mixing it with applesauce, one of Tomoka's favorite treats. Five years after the disease was discovered in Tomoka, his doctors declared his rheumatoid arthritis in remission. He was a healthy 315 pounds; his muscles were toned and his coat was thick and lustrous. Doctors at the time said he was the most active gorilla of the zoo's great apes.[337]

His health, however, seesawed between good and bad for the rest of his life. At one point, in 1975, he stopped eating, and his weight dropped to 250 pounds.[338] He recovered after being taken off all his medications.

After rheumatoid arthritis was found in Tomoka at the National Zoo, other zoos realized that arthritis may be ailing their gorillas. In several of the cases, the early onset of rheumatoid arthritis was overlooked as an injury, temporary weakness, or side effect from other health issues, such as pregnancy. The diagnoses were made more difficult because the animals could not talk and describe their ailments. Because of Tomoka's case, zoos that had arthritic gorillas could identify the disease and treat it earlier, leading to more successful recoveries, according to the doctors who treated him.[339] The greatest hope was that all this information would lead to a vaccine that could cure human arthritis.

Another health crisis erupted at the end of the 1960s at the National Zoo. Nearly half of the zoo's primates died of lead poisoning over a 15-year period from the mid-50s to the early 1970s. Lead poisoning was suspected in zoo animals around the world since the 1950s, but it was not until the late 60s and early 1970s that zoos started to understand its damage and take action against it. From 1954 to 1971, there were only six documented and published cases of confirmed animal lead poisoning at national and international zoos, other than reports from the National Zoo, according to officials at the National Zoo.[340]

At the National Zoo, 35 primates died from chewing or licking the lead paint on the walls and bars of their cages. The deaths often occurred suddenly without any warnings that the animals were severely ill, although the poison was slowly causing internal damage.[341] Some sick animals were throwing up, convulsing, or lethargic. Keepers and veterinarians often did not know how serious the animals' illnesses were until they died.[342]

Once officials at the National Zoo made the connection between the sick and dying animals and the lead paint, they made the problem public and took action.[343] Affected animals were moved to lead-free or low-lead cages, or their cage bars were sand blasted down to the metal. The use of lead paint was prohibited.[344]

The problem was embarrassing and costly for the zoo. It spent $9,411 to replace the 35 primates—none of which were gorillas. Additional expenses included diagnosing, treating, and autopsying animals. The zoo's primates weren't the only animals eating lead paint. Ten of the park's parrots died from lead poisoning. The head of pathology vented his frustrations in the zoo's Annual Report from 1971: "It is hoped that other zoos will soon recognize and in turn prevent lead poisoning, for surely it is a disgrace to capture, confine, and then poison our dwindling stocks of wild animals."[345]

Around the same time, several gorillas and orangutans tested positive for tuberculosis. The zoo closed the ape section of the Small Mammal House for three months and set up a great ape clinic to treat and prevent the disease. The sedated animals were X-rayed and TB antigens were injected into their eyelids. Doctors tested the animals' blood and stomach contents.[346]

"We are giving them the most thorough tests ever made in a zoo at one time," Reed told the local *Washington Star* newspaper.[347] Doctors finally determined the apes had only been allergic to the components in the tuberculin tests, and their exhibit was reopened to visitors.[348]

Nikumba's paralysis, Tomoka's arthritis, the lead poisoning, and the brief tuberculosis scare plagued the Small Mammal House during the 1960s and into the 1970s. Articles about these health problems ran in local newspapers, and fans demanded updates on the ailing apes.

For the public, the mental health of the gorillas was also a concern.

"He looks so bored and unhappy," a visitor wrote to Reed of Nikumba. "I feel sorry for him. He just sits in his cage all day and never gets outside. I know I shouldn't be telling you how to take care of the animals but do you think you could make him more happy?"

Toys, swings, and bars would give Nikumba joy and help him stay busy, the visitor suggested.[349]

Reed wrote back that Nikumba was such a powerful animal that any toys left in his cage would be destroyed instantly. "You must not feel sorry for him, as he really is a happy animal. All gorillas have a rather mournful expression, but it does not mean that they are unhappy."[350]

But Nikumba did seem bored and anxious. He started spitting at keepers again and became moody.[351] More visitors noticed his unruliness and took on the mission to make the gorilla less depressed. Several organizations offered to entertain the gorillas by donating televisions to the apes, which were displayed far enough outside of their cages so the gorillas couldn't reach them.

The gorillas didn't pay any attention to the shows. In the 1970s, they had a fleeting interest in "Sesame Street" and "All My Children," but the gorillas remained indifferent, even when they were shown "Search for the Great Apes," a National Geographic special about mountain gorillas.[352]

In the late summer of 1968, Moka suddenly became ill. A few days later, she died. Her death surprised and saddened zoo staff. Moka was always fit, extraordinarily healthy, and she bore three babies. Reed called Moka's death, "the most tragic loss the zoo has ever experienced."

"I hope you realize how hard Moka's death has hit me and I know that it was the same way with you and Nick," Reed wrote to Russell Arundel at the time. "While she was not a young gorilla,

I never dreamed that she would not be with us for many years and many offspring more."[353]

To make matters worse, Reed and the zoo staff couldn't determine the exact cause of Moka's death in the days and weeks after she died. Testing of Moka's red blood cells indicated an infection, and the kidneys weren't functioning optimally, but a necropsy did not offer much information as to why her body broke down. The official cause of her death was listed as non-specific hepatitis,[354] Reed told Russell Arundel.

With Moka's death, the international zoo community lost one of its most prolific dames in captivity. The National Zoo lost its matriarch gorilla and a visitor favorite. Nikumba lost his lifelong friend and lover.

CHAPTER 8

COOPERATION

In the first seven decades after its founding, the National Zoo made slow steps to evolve from its original Victorian-era menagerie. By the 1960s and 1970s, when the zoo was learning how to care for its growing gorillas, it was also ready to mature in many other ways. Several international and national forces helped it move in the right direction.

Caged animals at the National Zoo who, in the past, were viewed as simple curiosities were now earning respect and understanding. Their habitats became bigger and more natural. They benefited from better medical treatments, and zoo staff gained more competence to treat the ailments of their gorillas and other animals with more humane and sophisticated treatments. The National Zoo's reputation as a leader in the national and international zoo community was blossoming.

The "zoological slum" that Zoo Director Ted Reed spoke of in the 1950s was starting to resemble a safe and popular park thanks to efforts made locally through FONZ and the realization of Reed's ambitious plans to improve the zoo. Like no other time in the park's history, the 1960s also marked great change in how zoos acquired and managed their animals. Zoo leaders also began concentrating on the plight of animals outside their park's boundaries.

These early days of the zoo's modernization still faced several obstacles. At the start of the 1960s, competition between zoos remained fierce. Often, if a zoo acquired a wild animal from a dealer, that zoo would make the dealer promise not to bring the same animal to another nearby zoo for a certain period of time.[355] Zoo directors needed to be cunning entrepreneurs, and they were hesitant to share information about animal diets or other proven practices that gave an edge to another zoo.

"It was vicious competition," Reed later said. "There was one-upmanship all over the cotton-picking place."

One time Reed was eager to get more information about caring for two red pandas the zoo acquired. He called Carey Baldwin, director of the San Francisco Zoo that had red pandas that reproduced.

"I called him up and said, 'Carey, I've got a pair of lesser pandas in here. What's the secret of breeding them?'" Reed paused, expecting helpful advice.

"Ted, first thing you do, make sure you got a male and a female. The second thing you do is get lucky," Baldwin said.[356]

This silo mentality started breaking down as zoos became more committed to the survival of certain species, and they needed each other's help to support this overwhelming mission. The days of buying animals from dealers who would drive their trucks onto zoo properties with the animals in the back trailer were ending. So too was the practice of contracting with hunters to acquire any exotic species at whim. For one, it was becoming highly restrictive to capture and take wild animals out of their native habitats, even under the mission of research and conservation.

As never before, the cooperation of animal-interest groups around the planet was growing and the purchasing and trading of wild animals under common rules was becoming the new acceptable standard. While animal protection resolutions or laws like the Convention on International Trade in Endangered Species of Wild Fauna and Flora agreement and the U.S.'s Endangered Species Act were not fully adopted until the early 1970s, predecessor laws and practices in the 1960s started this tectonic shift.

Reputable zoos had to get used to the new way of doing business. Some zoo administrators, however, found it difficult to turn away the opportunity to get a desired animal just because the animal's origins were questionable.

"And it was a hard thing. For example, you might know there were 20 orangutans for sale in Singapore. Well, orangs are not native to Singapore; obviously they had been caught and brought there. But you felt sorry for them, and it was a temptation to say it was better to buy them and give them security and good vet treatments and so on than to leave them in terrible conditions in Singapore. But if you did this, other wild orangs would be caught and subjected to the same merciless process. So you had to stop, period," said Reed in the 1980s while reflecting on the changes that occurred two decades earlier.[357]

While there were always private exchanges between zoos for animals, now zoos started to fully and openly cooperate with each other to balance the supply and demand for animals. A greater emphasis was put on reproduction of certain existing captive animals in order to minimize capturing animals from the wild. Zoos started working together for the benefit of endangered species by creating committees to determine if institutions were duplicating breeding efforts or if there was a neglected need.[358] The National Zoo began to shrink the number of animals caged in isolation in favor of building up family groups of animals in order to encourage reproduction.[359]

During meetings of the Association of Zoos and Aquariums, zoo leaders in the U.S. could look at other zoos' lists of surplus animals and make trades. There were still some cases of resistance and competition, but the efforts at cooperation did level the playing field a bit by making it cheaper to get a desired animal.[360] The National Zoo was under the umbrella of the federal government, however, which meant profits from a sale of an animal to another zoo went to the general fund of the U.S. government.

"The theory on this was, we're a government agency. We have to do things through government purchases," Reed told a Smithsonian historian. Luckily, the purchases did not require bids and the following paperwork. "God, can you imagine writing a bid for a baby elephant? By the time the elephant got through the government red tape, it would be full-grown," Reed said.[361]

Awareness about preserving gorillas was growing internationally, and, in 1967, the Frankfurt Zoo in Germany attempted to document every captive gorilla so it could track individual animals and assess the population for trends and sustainability. Frankfurt Zoo sent its first questionnaire to 400 zoos across the world and only got 120 responses. A second questionnaire sent the following year received a better response rate, and by 1970, every zoo in the world knew how many gorillas lived in each zoo and their ages, gender, offspring, and names.[362]

Reed embraced this new team effort. "The thing that's clear now is that zoo animals don't belong any more to San Diego or Memphis or Washington or wherever the zoo is. They belong to America, to the world," Reed said.[363]

The management of animals housed at the National Zoo also changed dramatically in the 1960s and 70s. Reed started hiring more staff with animal expertise and degrees in zoology. Curators for different classes of animals directed the general care of those groups of animals. The existing keepers, many of whom were under-educated African-American men or veterans of World War II or the Korean War, were being replaced with men, and a few women, who had backgrounds in animal care. The government salaries of keepers began to rise to a level comparable to a carpenter or plumber.[364]

Doc Mann used to tell Reed that if someone could hear lightening and see thunder, he would hire them to work at the zoo.[365] Under Reed's watch, new hires were expected to have a college degree or animal experience or both.

Until this point, keepers were considered by many to be zoo janitors—common laborers whose duties mainly consisted of cleaning cages and feeding animals. But many had long tenures at the zoo and tended to stay at the same animal exhibits, developing an institutional knowledge of the zoo community and forming personal bonds with certain animals. Although they may never have been officially trained in animal husbandry, they knew what their animals liked to play with, who they liked to socialize with, and what annoyed or frightened them. They were fiercely loyal to the zoo and their charges and were threatened by the new personnel. In retaliation, a few of the "old guard" keepers flooded animal cages.[366]

The zoo required keepers to document slight changes in feeding, behavior, sleep, and play. The days of keepers showing human dominance over animals were coming to an end. Instead of squirting animals with water to get them to obey a command or using a shock prod to get a large animal to move, keepers trained animals to comply using reward systems of food or a favorite toy and other positive behavior techniques.[367]

Keepers and head animal managers needed to know the specific animal characteristics of their animals. They paid more attention to animals' natural behaviors and redesigned some exhibits to accommodate certain animals' instinctual habit of scattering fecal matter. They experimented with different flooring and yards to make the hoofed animals comfortable.[368]

Melanie Bond was one of the first female keepers when the zoo hired her in 1973 to care for the apes in the Small Mammal House. The boots she wore on her first day at work were three sizes too big, and when Reed first saw her he muttered, "I guess we're going to have to buy aprons with ruffles." Reed and Bond later became very good friends, and although she and other female keepers found it challenging to break into the male-dominated role of animal keeper, she admired and trusted Reed's devotion and leadership.

Bond came to the zoo with a degree in biology and psychology and an innate love of animals. While working at the Small Mammal House, she studied how the apes ate, slept, and interacted with visitors and each other. She felt sorry for them living behind their small barred cages, sometimes all alone. She was particularly melancholy about Ham, the NASA space chimp. Although visitors were still in awe of the first chimpanzee in space, she could see that Ham was depressed and lonely. When no one was looking, Bond would go near his cage and play with him by sliding her fingers under a metal door. From behind the door, he would push his fingers out, mimicking her.

Her heart went out to the other apes. When Tomoka would let her, she would reach into his cage to feel the heat from the arthritis in his toe. One time after visiting hours, when Bond was cleaning near the gorilla cage, The Jackson 5's "Dancing Machine" played on the radio. She started dancing, sliding her feet across the concrete floor and moving her arms in the air. When she glanced over at Nikumba, she saw him wiggle his arm. From then on, when he wanted to play or something met his approval, he would wiggle his arm when Bond was near. Once, when a show about gorillas was playing on the ape's TV, Bond saw Nikumba's arm wiggle.[369]

Bond and the other keepers kept a predictable schedule for the great apes that began each morning with an individual greeting to each animal. The gorillas would respond with a welcoming grunt. Ham, the space chimp, would excitedly dart about his cage and show his teeth. Bond and other keepers talked to the animals in gentle tones with upbeat pitches and were careful not to let the apes see them stressed or angry. The apes were sensitive to any negative behaviors from humans, which could influence them to become mad or upset.[370]

The attitude of respect and dignity for animals became more commonplace. These animal management practices were supported, in part, by a new scientific research department at the National Zoo, created in the mid-1960s and headed by a resident scientist who became an essential member of the zoo management team.[371] The goals of the department were ambitious. It focused on research that was conservation based. It shunned housing animals used solely for the purpose of medical research because zoo leaders didn't want those animals to be perceived or treated less equally than exhibited animals. The research department hoped to gather a variety of animal scientists, such as pathologists, nutritionists, veterinarians, ecologists, and others so that these professionals could work together to better understand, care for, and protect animals.

Although the activity and science excited him, Reed would tell people, "I hired a scientist to help us solve problems we have. Not only has he not found the answers to our problems, he's come up with more problems we didn't know we had."[372]

The careful analysis and proof-gathering to declare a theory right took time and would often lead to more questions or the discovery of more challenges. Instead of rushing to find absolute answers, the zoo's researchers worked through a process of eliminating all scenarios until the best or correct conclusion emerged. And each discovery could mean a better future for an animal.

"Zoos have been parasitic on wild populations. From now on, the relationship will become increasingly symbiotic," wrote John Perry in 1966, then the zoo's assistant director and a former FONZ president. "Zoo-based research will help in safeguarding endangered species."[373]

The changes at the zoo were largely at Reed's direction, but were also greatly influenced by national and international wildlife protection plans. These conservation conscience efforts were years in the making that were finally gaining traction.

By 1966, Harold Coolidge, Jr. was president of the Brussels-based International Union for Conservation of Nature and Natural Resources (IUCN). Since its inception 20 years earlier, the group made strides in raising awareness around the world about endangered species. Many under-developed countries, however, did not have the funding and manpower to stop demands from foreign poachers for their exotic animals. Terminating the supply of animals for exploitation became of top priority.

One of the people helping protect the world's critters and creatures was Lee Talbot, an American ecologist for IUCN.

When Talbot first began working for Coolidge at the IUCN in the mid-1950s, the organization was known as the International Union for the Protection of Nature. Talbot's first three-year assignment was to collect information about endangered species in parts of Africa, the Middle East, South and South East Asia, with the cost of his research funded by the $8,000 grant Russell Arundel gave to Coolidge.[374]

Though inexperienced for the mission, Talbot possessed the education, passion, and pedigree for the task. Talbot's grandfather, Dr. C. Hart Merriam, was founder and first director of the Biological Survey, which evolved into the U.S. Fish and Wildlife Service. His mother was an ethnologist and naturalist. His father, M.W. Talbot, was a wildlife ecologist who headed the research branch of the U.S. Forest Service and spent his life's work on conservation and science-based management of the nation's forests and ranges.[375] Lee grew up hiking and exploring with his parents. At college, he studied ecology and conservation and then briefly served as a Marine Corps officer. After leaving the military, he set out on a career that mirrored his family's. He started traveling the globe studying and analyzing threats to animals and landscapes.

In 1956, he took a critical expedition to East Africa to survey threats to the wildlife of the recently-established Serengeti National Park and to the white rhinos of Uganda.[376] It was a "young ecologist's dream job," he wrote in an essay several decades later.[377]

"Information about the status of species and of conservation in general was generally unavailable for the developing parts of the world, and it was determined that the only way to obtain it, and develop conservation plans accordingly, was to send someone to get the information directly," Talbot wrote.[378]

His expedition team to the Serengeti included Russell Arundel, wife Marjorie, Nick, and Nick's sister Jocelyn, who also worked for IUPN writing press releases about vulnerable animals. Natives and guides helped the expedition with supplies and logistics.

Just a year earlier, Nick took his first trip to Africa to get gorillas for the National Zoo. Talbot heard that Nick captured gorillas on the earlier trip, but the two men didn't talk much about it.[379] On this trip to the Serengeti, Nick's focus was on filming wildlife and the landscape. He later turned the films into a movie titled, "Africa's Twilight Kingdom," which aired on public television and was shown at professional lectures for several years afterward.[380]

At the time of the trip, Serengeti's border in Tanganyika, a United Nations Trust Territory under the administration of the British, was recently formally adopted but in dispute. There were conflicting interests in the park—to preserve nature and to allow native Maasai tribes rights to their homeland.[381] Talbot and the Arundels went to the Serengeti to survey animals after learning about plans to alter the boundaries of the young park to accommodate the Maasais' use of the land for raising cattle. After several weeks, the group determined the proposed altered boundaries would harm a major migratory path for animals and shrink the Serengeti by thousands of acres.[382] One night, while at their campsite, Talbot and Jocelyn Arundel typed out a petition pushing for an ecological study of the park before any boundary changes were made.

Over the next few months, the group collected signatures from international conservation groups supporting a comprehensive study of the land.[383] After Russell Arundel and Lee Talbot hand delivered the petition to Colonial African officials in London, officials agreed to the study with funding for the research coming from the Fauna Preservation Society.[384] The final recommendations were that the park include the migratory paths of the animals. The Maasai people living in the Serengeti Park were evicted and relocated to the Ngorongoro Crater, which was separated from the national park but made into a special conservation area.[385]

"It would have been the death of the Serengeti had they done it," Talbot said of slicing into the migratory path.[386]

Talbot continued his travels on behalf of IUCN to better understand environmental impacts on wildlife. By the 1960s, he was working with government and non-government groups on an agreement between countries to ensure that the trade of animals and plants did not harm the species' survival.[387] That work evolved into the Convention on International Trade in Endangered Species of Wild Fauna and Flora (CITES), which was agreed to by 80 countries at a meeting in Washington, D.C., on March 3, 1973. It formalized the cooperation and understanding among volunteer member countries that the preservation of certain species depends on careful management of what animals and plants come into and out of each country. Today, there are 183 member countries and 35,000 species of animals and plants under protection.[388]

At the same time Talbot and others were developing plans for the international agreement to protect wildlife, Talbot also focused on helping the U.S. create stricter laws for safeguarding its own vulnerable creatures and to restrict the import and export of certain species. As a scientist with the new President's Council on Environmental Quality, he worked alongside Russell Train, CEQ's first chairman, to strengthen existing federal wildlife protections.[389] On the legislative side, Reps. John Dingell (D–Mich.) and Pete McCloskey (R–Calif.) worked together to co-sponsor a bipartisan bill in the U.S. House of Representatives that would become the Endangered Species Act—the national endorsement of the worldwide effort by CITES to protect species at risk. Congress also took a stand for animal protection by approving the Animal Welfare Act of 1966, which set rules for the care of animals in captivity.

The National Zoo's Ted Reed and John Perry consulted on the drafting of legislation that preceded the Endangered Species Act of 1973.[390] Regulations for the Endangered Species Conservation Act of 1969 listed gorillas from central and western Africa as a foreign species off limits for importation into the U.S. An exception was made for zoological, educational, scientific, or preservation purposes.[391]

Working off of that 1969 law, Talbot knew the next iteration of the Endangered Species Conservation Act needed to be meaningful, impactful, and acceptable to Congress.[392] Its forceful language, which included an endorsement for a worldwide agreement to protect endangered species, was overwhelmingly accepted by Democrats and Republicans, whose constituents grew concerned about oil spills and chemicals harming animal habitats, the shrinking numbers of bald eagles, and other impacts to animals and the environment. Personally, McCloskey became troubled by the damage the chemical DDT was doing to animal habitats and how miners used canaries to determine if toxic gases were in the air underground.[393] The U.S. agreement also created a system to categorize plants and animals into lists of "threatened" or "endangered" species.

On the legislative path toward making the Endangered Species Act a law, Congresswoman Leonor Sullivan, chair of the Committee on Merchant Marine and Fisheries, wrote in a 1973 report: "Throughout the history of the world, as we know it, species of animals and plants have appeared, changed, and disappeared. The disappearance of a species is by no means a current phenomenon, nor is it an accession for terror or panic.

"It is, however, at the same time an occasion for caution, for self-searching, and for understanding. Man's presence on the Earth is relatively recent, and his effective domination over the world's life support systems has taken place within a few short generations. Our ability to destroy, or almost destroy, all intelligent life on the planet became apparent only in this generation. A certain humility, and a sense of urgency, seem indicated."[394]

As the world strengthened protections for at-risk animals, African animals faced chaos closer to home. African countries were in various stages of decolonization from European control. The independence movement in Africa in the 1960s was at its most intense, and in many parts of the great continent, the switch to autonomous rule was disastrous and deadly. Some of the new sovereign nations couldn't protect their people, much less their animals.

The abandonment of certain animal protection plans in Africa was alarming to many across the globe. One group that took action to save animals and their habitats in Africa was comprised primarily of men who enjoyed the sport of hunting the continent's large, exotic creatures.

The African Safari Club of Washington, D.C., was a social club for big game hunters who traded stories about their first big kill, their preferred types of weapons, and what elusive animals they were going to hunt next. For several members, the inspiration for the sport and adventure of hunting came from the late President Theodore Roosevelt. As young kids who dreamt about traveling to faraway lands, some read Roosevelt's post-presidential book "African Game Trails" about his 1909 to 1910 safari through East Africa.[395] Roosevelt's expedition was sponsored, in part, by the Smithsonian Institution and resulted in 23,151 natural history specimens, including the bodies of around 5,000 mammals, many of which were mounted for exhibition at the U.S. National Museum on the Mall in Washington. In support of Roosevelt's expedition in Africa, a local Nairobi man donated still-living lions, cheetahs, a leopard, a warthog, a gazelle, and various birds to the National Zoo.[396]

The D.C. African Safari Club met regularly at the Roma Restaurant, a long-established, family-owned Italian restaurant on Connecticut Avenue, located just a mile from the National Zoo. The restaurant owner's personal collection of stuffed tigers, lions, and other game hung on the walls and perched on tables, their frozen expressions looking over the group and others while diners ate lasagna and linguine with white clam sauce.[397]

Jim Bugg was a member of the club. His first big kill was an African elephant in 1960. On his first safari, he traveled to Somalia, which was at that time a protectorate of the United Kingdom and Italy. Bugg learned how to track elephant herds by touching urine and saliva to see if it was still warm to gauge how close he was to the herd and reading prints left in the dirt to see which direction the elephants traveled. He had never hunted before, and this first trip was to last 28 days. After that, he would run out of money and would need to return home. On the 27th day, he finally had a clear shot of a large elephant and took aim. The great beast fell to the ground. Bugg immediately regretted killing the animal that he had watched and followed for nearly a month.

"It was the beginning and end of my elephant hunting," he said decades later. But he kept the dead elephant's tusks, which weighed about 80 pounds each, displaying them in the study of his Maryland home.

Nick Arundel also was a member of the African Safari Club, telling other members of his trips to Africa and about capturing two baby gorillas by killing their parents. Like Bugg, Nick's gorilla-killing story was punctured with repentance. When Bugg asked Nick for details of his gorilla capture, Nick only said, "It's a sad story."[398]

Russell Train, who would later become head of the Environmental Protection Agency and first president of the U.S. chapter of the World Wildlife Fund, was another member of D.C.'s African Safari Club. He made two hunting trips to Africa in the late 1950s, then never hunted there again.[399]

The three men, along with African Safari Club members Maurice Stans and Kermit Roosevelt, Jr., who was Theodore Roosevelt's grandson, worried about how decolonization in Africa was causing the abandonment of the knowledge and protections of wildlife. The best way to ensure the immediate and long-term future of animals and habitats in Africa was to train Africans to manage their own wildlife resources, the men decided.[400] They sought guidance from Lee Talbot about how they, as Americans who hunted the continent's large beasts, could put their plans into action.[401] The five men broke away from the African Safari Club to form the African Wildlife Leadership Foundation in 1961 and, by the next year, created the College of African Wildlife Management in Mweka, Tanzania, funded with support from other international groups concerned about the declining numbers of certain species.[402]

Over the next decade, the group launched conservation clubs for Kenyan students, contributed to a wildlife management school in Cameroon, established wildlife clubs throughout Africa, built conservation education centers, and supported Dian Fossey's ground-breaking mountain gorilla research in Rwanda by supplying her group with uniforms for guards, camping equipment, and communication devices.[403]

"No one knew or thought much about protecting wildlife and preserving the environment in 1961," Train was quoted as saying in the group's 40th anniversary newsletter. "When we founded AWLF, it was the only international organization significantly working on African conservation."[404]

In the first 15 years of AWLF's creation, about 3,000 young Africans trained in wildlife management at universities in Africa and in the United States.[405] Many of those young Africans rose to senior management positions in Africa's huge park system.[406]

The founders of AWLF weren't opposed to hunting non-threatened animals in Africa, though some found it difficult to explain the difference between hunting some animals while protecting others. Several of the AWLF founders still hunted or supported the practice to varying degrees after founding the group. Sport hunting shouldn't include vulnerable animals, it should have an altruistic purpose and should be done with transparency and within local, national, and international laws, the group agreed.[407] What they sought was responsible animal management with understood guidelines. They wanted to organize wildlife protections and establish natural parks and put that responsibility in the hands of Africans to monitor, regulate, and educate other Africans.

Now called African Wildlife Foundation, the group celebrated its 50th anniversary in 2011. It is credited with helping curb the slaughter of African wildlife and has kept the same strategy used when the group first formed—to partner with local residents and build regional interest and knowledge about protecting animals.

While AWF's mission has expanded since its founding, its collaboration with other like-minded organizations still offers training to rangers, who monitor and protect a variety of at-risk species, including the vulnerable mountain gorillas of the Virunga Heartland.[408]

CHAPTER 9
SATELLITE ZOO

Looking out at the 163 acres of the National Zoo in the center of Washington, D.C., the park that once felt expansive now seemed constraining to Ted Reed. The momentum of the world-wide conservation movement was building, and people were making deeper connections between the exotic animals they saw living in zoo cages and those animals' relatives living in the wild. Reed wanted to put the National Zoo at the forefront of this transition of respect for animals, but first he needed to build the zoo's clout and footprint.

He started by growing the zoo's research and science department with gusto. The zoo scaled down the number of species displayed in order to focus on animals that met specific criteria: visitor appeal, educational value, adaptability to captive management, breeding potential, and value for scientific research. In many cases, these chosen animals were put in bigger and more natural exhibits.[409] Animals that didn't fit these categories were sold and transferred to other parks.

In 1949, about 3,700 animals lived at the zoo. By 1969, there were 3,000 animals, representing 852 species, according to that year's Annual Report of the Zoo to the Smithsonian Institution.[410] By 1978, the animal count at the zoo decreased even more and there were 2,481 animals representing 428 species.[411]

It was a dramatic change in practice for the zoo in the nation's capital. Ever since it was founded, the zoo was accepting of all animals—big and small, memorable and forgettable, valuable and expendable—from the public, including the city's power players. In 1960, Robert F. Kennedy gave the zoo a sea lion gifted to his children that was living in the family's swimming pool in Northern

Virginia.[412] Over the years, area residents gave the zoo numerous snakes, raccoons, and rats. Except for high-profile gifts to the government, the practice of accepting all creatures was slowly coming to an end for the National Zoo as staff put their energy into taking care of at-risk and purposeful animals.

Breeding its own population of animals became the new priority.[413] The U.S. Department of the Interior, which issues importation permits under the Endangered Species Act, was insisting that applicants that wanted to bring foreign animals into the country have a strong plan in place for quality breeding programs.[414]

Zoos from across the country started having their requests for import permits for wild animals denied because their facilities did not support animal breeding programs. Additionally, purchase costs for certain wild animals were exorbitant—about $2,500 per animal or more.[415]

"Zoos are challenged to become net producers rather than net consumers of wildlife," Reed wrote in a 1971 report for the Smithsonian Institution.[416]

The limitations of the National Zoo's urban boundaries stood as an obstacle to these grand plans for breeding certain captive animals. The zoo's D.C. location needed to stay devoted to animal exhibitions for the public. It could not provide the acres of space some animals need to naturally support their social structures and for successful mating and reproduction. Pére David's deer, for example, live in groups that have a dominant male, a group of females, their offspring, and a group of bachelors. If these rare animals that are native to China are too cramped, they get stressed and aggressive.[417]

The National Zoo could not make a significant impact on animal conservation efforts, or improve or build upon the zoo's future generations of animals, without land away from the city and the public, leaders continued to emphasize.

With the approvals of the Endangered Species Act and the Convention on International Trade in Endangered Species agreement, the zoo was ready to make its move to expand beyond the Capital Beltway. The timing became ideal in part because the Smithsonian finally had sole fiscal responsibility and ownership of the zoo. The joint city-federal parenting of the zoo was over. It would have been difficult to convince the District of Columbia government to spend money on an animal park outside city limits. The zoo was also bolstered at this time by those adorable pandas from China that broke attendance records, bringing positive attention and a bump in finances.

Reed traveled to different properties in Virginia and Maryland to find space for a zoo annex, but none fit all his practical and financial demands. His practical demands were pages long and considered topography, climate, infrastructure, access, and more. His financial demands were much simpler. The zoo had no extra money, so Reed was only able to consider property already owned by the federal government.

After 14 years of wishing and many trips to various sites, he finally found what he was looking for in 3,150 acres in Front Royal, Virginia, just 70 miles, or an hour and a half drive, from the National Zoo.

"I'd died and gone to heaven," Reed later said of visiting the property for the first time.[418]

The vast space in Virginia's Shenandoah Valley was montane and ranged from 900 to 1,200 feet above sea level. Rolling hills, steep slopes, open pastures, and thick forests covered the land neighboring the Appalachian Trail. Spring-fed streams naturally hydrated the property.[419] And although the place seemed secluded, it was really only minutes from Front Royal's business district and Route 66, which drew nearly a straight line to Washington, D.C., to the east.

The Front Royal property had, for the previous 70 years, been a lively place for humans and animals. Since 1909, the land owners—the U.S. government—used it as a breeding and training ground for Army horses. The military corps there kept the buildings, fences, barns, stables, and roads in pristine shape. German prisoners-of-war were held on the property during World War II.

After that war, the military no longer needed horses for conflicts, and the property was repurposed as a cattle farm operated by the Department of Agriculture. Angus, Hereford, and shorthorn cattle roamed over hundreds of acres while the Agriculture Research Service office recorded the types of grasses and feeds that were most beneficial to the animals. The Department of State also staked claim to the land, using the property for an Emergency Relocation Site with room large enough for the secretary of state and 700 department staffers to evacuate to in case Washington, D.C., fell under attack or had a crippling natural disaster.[420]

By the middle of 1973, however, the Agriculture and State departments ceased nearly all activities at the Front Royal property. Even though the zoo did not own the property yet, Reed moved quickly and strategically by getting a temporary permit to put animals on the land, staff the operation, build fences, and put up signs. Taking a lesson from his family's military background, he took the high ground and held on to it as if it was the zoo's land all along.[421] He established a strong presence at Front Royal despite having to use non-federal funds to do so.

"There was no question in any of our actions or anything we did that we were just caretakers," Reed said. "We owned the place, and told everybody we owned it, and they believed it."[422]

Still, zoo officials needed formal permission from the federal government to permanently put the property under Smithsonian ownership.[423]

FONZ helped in these efforts. As president of FONZ, Nick Arundel lent support by writing to the area's federal and state legislators and environmental leaders. "We are, as you know, heading into a situation where many of the great species of world wildlife will be known to our children only in picture books. In short, this undertaking is the right thing at the right time," Nick wrote in one letter.[424]

Even though the Smithsonian only had a temporary permit to use the land, the zoo invested so much effort into the property that about a year later, the federal government officially transferred the land rights to the zoo, and the property became known as the Conservation and Research Center.[425] From the start, CRC was part of the National Zoo organization, but it was and always has been closed to the public.

When Chris Wemmer arrived at the rural zoo in October of 1974 as supervisor, he was eager to get the program to full capacity. Wemmer worked for the National Zoo years before as a temporary keeper while earning his PhD in zoology at the nearby University of Maryland. His childhood home in San Francisco was near Cliff House next to the Pacific Ocean, and he fell asleep each night listening to the sea lions bark. From then on, he always wanted to work with wildlife.

He was excited at the chance to pioneer the build-up of CRC. He followed the movement in the zoo community to expand self-sustaining endangered species populations and was energized by efforts to support at-risk animal populations in the wild. Still, when he took the helm of CRC, exactly how to go about saving species was not at all clear.

This new animal conservation movement was developing rapidly in America, and it was up to Wemmer, other National Zoo staff, and like-minded scientists across the country to pioneer practices that would save species. There was no definitive plan that charted the future of conservation at zoos. It was up to Wemmer and many others to develop those plans and, as they got started, a lot of their work was done by trial and error.[426]

His job as head of the new CRC—at least in the beginning—dealt less with animals and more with personnel issues and construction projects, such as renovating buildings and building or fixing 14 miles of fencing around the property to keep the threatened animals in and the unwanted animals and trespassers out. Wemmer, who had Reed's enthusiastic support, never doubted he could grow the CRC operation, but had many frustrations in those early years.[427]

It was a long, slow start to build up the animal population at CRC. A committee discussed the criteria for choosing what animals would live at the Front Royal property, and after much debate it was determined CRC should fill the pastures and woods with threatened or endangered animals whose captive populations were dwindling or difficult to manage.[428] Yet, zoo leaders were hesitant to move animals that were visitor favorites, such as the pandas, from the D.C. zoo to the remote center.

Years later, Reed explained why the pandas didn't relocate to CRC, even though some thought the privacy could have helped their disappointing reproductive record: "We could not put them at Front Royal because the people want to see them. They belong to the people and we've got to meet our obligations to the people. There are a lot of people at the zoo who know full well that we are federal and we're getting our money from the federal government and to hell with the people. But we are still beholden to the public, and if we don't cater to the public, why Congress will soon find out about it and chop us off."[429]

Some of the first animals to live on the Front Royal Zoo property was a herd of Pére David's deer, loaned from zoos in New York,

Chicago, and other places.[430] For three years, zoo scientists and students at CRC observed the deer's behaviors. They steered a four wheel drive vehicle gently through the fields and hills—sometimes with Ted Reed standing against the roll bar—to follow the seasonal changes in the deer's social organizations and communication.[431] They took notes, recorded vocalizations, and filmed social signals, such as the rutting call by the stags.[432] The Pére David's herd at CRC soon became the fourth largest breeding group in the world of a species that no longer existed in the wild. The zoo's behavioral observations of the animals led to improvements in nutrition, including replacements for mother's milk for newborns who could not nurse.[433]

Scimitar-horned oryxes were also among CRC's early residents. The northern African animal, with its brown and white hides and horns reminiscent of fabled unicorns, was quickly becoming extinct in the wild due to climate changes and over hunting. They live in herds of up to 40 animals, and their 35-acre home at CRC allowed them space to move and reproduce.[434]

Other animals filled the fields and barns as well, and Wemmer soon had a problem he and several others had not anticipated— the loss of control over a variety of animals in such a spacious area. "We found our situation to be more like that of farmers in an alien land,"[435] he wrote in a science journal a few years after CRC opened.

By the end of the 1970s, CRC significantly renovated the former Department of Agriculture buildings into animal facilities, a commissary, living quarters for staff, and an observation tower. More importantly, CRC staff was making headway into the study and survival of threatened species.

In 1979, 80 percent of the female Pére David's deer gave birth to healthy babies, and 88 percent of scimitar-horned oryxes bore viable offspring. A variety of animals now lived on the land, and scientists gained confidence in successful reproduction rates, all while continuing to search for more methods to improve the animals' care. Lesser pandas, Eld's deer, Grant's zebra, and Bactrian camels now also occupied the land. CRC also became the home of several at-risk species of birds, including Stanley cranes (blue crane), Rothschild's mynahs (Bali myna), and the Florida sandhill crane.[436]

Students of conservation biology came to the center to gain hands-on experience with wildlife. The eagerness of these students to learn and work and CRC's need for researchers at little or no pay made the training program there flourish, and soon it attracted national and international interns, grant-supported researchers, and doctoral students who assisted in the emerging science behind saving species.

Perhaps the greatest success story of the National Zoo and CRC's early efforts at a coordinated focus on conservation is that of the golden lion tamarin—a monkey with a bushy reddish-orange mane around its dark face. These diminutive, one-to-two pound monkeys with big personalities were quickly disappearing from their shrinking native area in tropical rain forests near the southeastern coast of Brazil.

In 1965, Reed bought two golden lion tamarins for $25 each from a dealer in Leticia, Colombia—a purchase he later regretted. "It was not illegal to buy golden lion tamarins from Colombia, because there were no laws protecting the golden lion tamarin in Colombia, because they didn't have any," he explained years later. "And it was no violation of the law to bring them in from Colombia, because we were not violating any laws of the country where they were shipped from, point of origin. But I knew it was wrong."[437]

Reed wasn't alone in wanting to get the vulnerable animal.

In 1968, the number of golden lion tamarins in captivity peaked because of a rush by zoos and animal dealers to get a hold of the animals before a ban was put on their trade. The American Association of Zoological Parks and Aquariums labeled golden lion tamarins, also known as golden marmosets, as an at-risk species in 1966 and called for the IUCN to classify the monkey as endangered. The next year, the World Zoo Organization asked that its members not import the species.

Reed was so contrite about his rush to get these animals that he vowed to put the National Zoo in the leadership for saving this species and asked scientists at the Washington, D.C., zoo to update him regularly on their research. Zoo staff visited Brazil to coordinate conservation programs and to monitor the animal's population. The zoo worked with the Wild Animal Propagation Trust—an organization of American zoos dedicated to saving certain species—to create a Golden Marmoset Committee. Committee members set protocols for caring for the monkeys and negotiated loan agreements between zoos for the best possible breeding scenarios.

The National Zoo hosted a "Saving the Lion Marmoset" conference in 1972, which brought 28 European, American, and Brazilian animal biologists together to create long-term animal care practices and research and conservation priorities. The experts who gathered agreed to collect and share information about each and every golden lion tamarin in captivity, including when and where they were born, where they had lived, and any offspring they had. They would use this studbook data to make decisions about transferring animals between zoos and sanctuaries in order to match animals together for the best possible chances for reproduction.[438]

It was an ambitious and pioneering effort for the zoos and sanctuaries involved who had, only a few years before, worked against each other to stay competitive.

Scientists at the National Zoo put their resources and hearts into solving the demise of these small monkeys. Led by the National Zoo's first female scientist, Devra Kleiman, research on the animals was extensive. The animals' behaviors at the D.C. zoo were recorded, as were their reactions to changes in their diets, exhibits, social groups, and play. The zoo's scientists continuously analyzed the data, looking for tweaks to improve the animal's future.

But year after year, even with all the time and attention the monkeys received, their reproductive rates were depressing. Not only that, the animals fought and hurt each other and were very temperamental. They were quick to catch colds and other illnesses that were sometimes fatal. By the end of 1975, only 83 golden lion tamarins existed at 16 institutions outside of Brazil. Kleiman, especially, seemed defeated. She began to worry that the monkeys would never have a future in a zoo or in the wild.[439]

The scientists, using data from the studbook, applied more stringent methods to deciding the who and when of pairing young animals. Kleiman also figured out a simple, yet critical factor for reproduction; these animals were monogamous.[440] Moving them around to different partners lowered their reproductive potential. The animals also needed to remain with their families as youngsters so they could interact with their younger siblings to practice being around and caring for babies.

"Some zoos used to pull youngsters out of the family group at weaning," Kleiman said in a 1978 zoo press release. "We found the experience of interacting with infants is essential to becoming normal parents. These juveniles had no experience of raising kids, so when they became parents, they would abuse and kill their babies."[441]

The collaboration among zoos that housed golden lion tamarins and the adherent practices for managing the animals proved successful, and by 1978, the National Zoo celebrated the 100th birth of a golden lion tamarin at the zoo. It was a significant milestone, as it was estimated that only 200 existed in the wild.[442] The animal's birth and longevity rates continued to climb at the National Zoo, CRC, and elsewhere. Those institutions that had growing populations of golden lion tamarins agreed to loan the animals to other zoos that promised to follow the same management protocols for the monkeys.

It was an unusual practice at that time to loan animals to other zoos rather than sell the surplus animal outright. But by doing so, control and responsibility was kept with the zoo owning the animal and with the core group of experts who made decisions about each animal's potential to reproduce successfully. It was the first time that management and authority of creatures owned by a variety of American zoos would fall to a central oversight committee. This agreement became the model for future Species Survival Plans organized by the Association of Zoos and Aquariums.[443]

Seeing the success in the growing population, the institutions holding the monkeys put even more restrictions and rules on the care and reproductive management of the animals. They started considering genetic diversity in reproduction by looking at the underrepresented genes from the first members of the captive population—those that came from the wild—and increasing the chances that those animals and their offspring would reproduce. By 1991, most of the institutions around the world that owned golden lion tamarins agreed to transfer ownership of the animals to the Brazilian government, although the animals still remained in their care.

Working collaboratively, 41 zoos and other institutions moved 146 of the captive monkeys to protected reserves in Brazil between 1984 and 2001 with hopes that those animals would repopulate the wild habitat.[444]

As of 2008, only 1,000 golden lion tamarins lived in protected reserves in Brazil, but the species' conservation status was down listed from critically endangered to endangered on the IUCN's Red List of Threatened Species, in part because of the decades of conservation efforts at the National Zoo.[445]

Kleiman and other researchers at the zoo accomplished another subtle, home-grown feat—they sparked an intensive research mentality in all National Zoo staff caring for animals. For decades, Ted Reed encouraged keepers to take notes about animal births, changes in diet, or social settings.[446] Now, it became mandatory and more organized. In essence, staff and volunteers became recorders of the daily habits of zoo animals that had never before been so studied. The scientists and keepers exchanged information about particular animals and ways to improve their care.

The bevy of data on a variety of animals helped National Zoo scientists make a not-so-surprising discovery about reproduction, but one being ignored by many; breeding between related animals led to increased mortality in young animals and reduced fertility in adults not only with captive animals, but also in wild populations.

Evidence of the dangers of inbreeding was seen years earlier with the white tiger Mohini and her offspring. But after National Zoo scientist Katherine Ralls, along with others at the park, analyzed extensive and detailed animal reproductive records, they wrote a paper about the detrimental effects of inbreeding in dorcas gazelle, a type of antelope from Northern Africa.[447] That report was soon followed with another paper finding similar problems of inbreeding in a variety of species.

There were many skeptics, including Ted Reed, who pushed Ralls to investigate other possibilities that brought infant mortality, early deaths, or deformities to these animals. But the data, which was just beginning to become computerized, was clear that the main factor was inbreeding. Reed became convinced.[448]

It was the first statistically valid study of inbreeding at zoos, according to Reed.[449] "It kind of shocked the zoo world," Reed said a few years later.[450]

It took some time for zoos to accept the fact that their birth rate successes among related animals were detrimental to those animals' offspring. After all, with their ability to get certain animals from the wild now limited, zoos would now need to cooperate with each other to introduce non-related animals into their own populations.

When William Conway, director of the Bronx Zoo and an early zoos-as-conservation-centers advocate, reviewed the records at his zoo and found the same problems with inbreeding, he endorsed the National Zoo scientists' report and attitudes of zoo leaders started changing.[451]

The studies exposed damaging past animal management practices at the National Zoo under Ted Reed's watch, but Reed praised the publications in the zoo's 1979 Annual Report: "This study has elicited considerable discussion in zoos around the world, and should help formulate cooperative breeding plans and programs for captive-animal conservation. Its application to the wild is also significant. Shrinking habitats have caused many wild animal populations to withdraw into discrete clumps, literally genetic islands. These islands may in the future force inbreeding, with deleterious effects on wild populations."[452]

The early years of CRC did have some growing pains. One of the zoo's biggest embarrassments was a proposed public deer hunt on the CRC property in the fall of 1982. White tailed deer lived freely on the land, and their numbers were controlled by hunting long before the National Zoo took ownership of the thousands of acres. But when the zoo took over in 1974, Reed banned hunting out of fear that hunters would shoot an exotic hoofed animal by mistake.

Within five years, however, the wild deer population exploded and became a threat to some of the zoo's endangered animals. Native deer were eating most of the zoo's annual crop of alfalfa hay, much of which was shipped to the zoo in D.C. for animals to eat.[453]

Wemmer consulted with the Virginia Commission of Game and Inland Fisheries and national and international game experts who visited CRC in order to find solutions to the deer problem. Higher fences were built and graduate students studied the deer population by tagging and tracking the animals. Zoo staff held a deer drive where they lined up side-by-side and walked toward the deer. The advancing wall of humans forced nearly 100 deer off the property.

A two-day controlled public hunt took out 126 deer in the fall of 1981. Three more deer drives in March of 1982 forced another 159 deer off the property.

It wasn't enough. The area's habitat could handle about 130 deer, yet at least 1,000 deer were living on the zoo's land by the summer of 1982.[454] The zoo's hay crop continued to get smaller.[455]

And there was a mysterious death. One Bactrian camel worth $4,500 succumbed to lungworm, believed to have originated from a deer. A zoo pathologist began examining deer feces for parasites, and a zoology student surveyed slugs and snails to see if they were carrying the parasite. The zoo blamed the parasite-carrying white-tailed deer for causing the deaths of $30,000 worth of threatened animals, including scimitar-horned oryxes.[456]

One night, after Reed and Wemmer ate dinner at a restaurant near Front Royal, Reed asked about the alfalfa supply. Wemmer said he would need money to buy hay because the deer were still eating much of the zoo's crop. Reed was furious. "Dammit, you get on the line with Fish and Game and get the deer under control," he yelled at Wemmer.[457]

When another public controlled deer hunt, using shotguns and bows and arrows, was planned for the fall of 1982, people began protesting. How could the National Zoo and the Smithsonian Institution, which touted its efforts in conservation of species, organize the methodical killing of indigenous creatures right in its backyard, the protestors challenged. FONZ opposed the hunt, and Wemmer got hate mail. A Congressional subcommittee called for a hearing on Capitol Hill and demanded Wemmer testify about the hunt. With Reed by his side, he was joined by a panel of witnesses who both supported and protested the hunt.

"Our primary responsibility is the care, maintenance, and propagation of exotic animals whose numbers have dwindled to the point where their only hope is in survival centers such as we have established at Front Royal. The loss to science and to the community of these rare animals would have far-wider and longer-term ramifications than the slight but effective reduction of a more plentiful species," Wemmer told the House Subcommittee of the Department of Interior's Appropriations Committee.

An alternative solution to a deer hunt would be to build a higher fence that the deer would have difficulty jumping over. The cost would reach $350,000 or more—a significant expense for CRC, whose annual budget for 1982 was $1.7 million.[458]

One protester and animal welfare reporter, Ann Cottrell Free, begged the Committee to cancel the hunt and fund the cost of the higher fence: "The price, Mr. Chairman and members of the Committee, would be far less than the dreadful cost a strongly stubborn Smithsonian Institution has already incurred in loss of face and loss of faith among its many admirers and supporters."[459]

In the end, Congress gave the zoo money for the fence, and the public hunt was cancelled. That next spring, Wemmer counted 42 emaciated carcasses of white tailed deer at CRC, likely victims of starvation.[460]

Although the number of deer on CRC property decreased, the problem wasn't completely solved. Deer still found their way onto zoo land at non-gated sections, as well as during the winter when snow piled high against the fences. Wemmer said state game experts would discretely hunt the deer to keep the population manageable.

"There was no simple solution," he said years later.[461]

The challenges of the deer management at CRC did not over-shadow the excitement around the booming animal population at CRC and the discovery of strategies aimed to help the populations of at-risk animals flourish. The breakthrough research on the golden lion tamarins gave zoo leaders confidence that they may find more clues to help the recovery of other species, including the zoo's western lowland gorillas.

CHAPTER 10
NEW HOME

Life on the landscape of the Virginia countryside was not the same as wandering through their dry African savannah homeland for the scimitar oryx. The Appalachian mountain range could not duplicate the native southern China swamplands for the Pére David's deer. But these havens for vulnerable animals at the National Zoo's Conservation and Research Center in Front Royal, Virginia, were quiet, safe, and spacious.

And to the delight of Ted Reed and the CRC staff, the animals were doing exactly what everyone hoped for—making lots of babies. Reed joked that he was, "The only guy left in the government that could be totally in favor of sex and unrestricted reproduction."[462]

More seriously, Reed said years later, "I really think that Front Royal will mean more to the survival of many animals who are breeding in our scientific research programs than we could possibly do down at the zoo, and certainly more than many zoos are capable of doing. Of course, that's our mission—for the advancement of science, education, and recreation of people. We don't have any people out here to educate or recreate, but we sure advance science. And, of course, we consider that breeding animals is a science, too."[463]

Zoo staff weren't just keeping eyes on the number of births at CRC in Front Royal. Scientists and veterinarians at the zoo's D.C. location watched and recorded animal mating patterns and borrowed successful interventions developed at CRC.

The births of future generations of its captive endangered animals became the priority at the National Zoo. The pandas Ling-Ling and Hsing-Hsing weren't procreating, and all efforts were made to make their habitat—an indoor den and spacious outdoor play yards—as welcoming and comfortable for copulation as possible. FONZ volunteers worked in shifts to watch for any signs of a panda pregnancy.[464]

To encourage animals to mate—and for health reasons—the zoo made the unpopular decision of prohibiting the feeding of animals by visitors. All the peanuts, popcorn, marshmallows, and even lollipops guests gave animals, especially the bears, hippos, and gibbons, caused gastrointestinal problems and unthrifty hair coats, zoo veterinarian Mitchell Bush wrote to a zoo supervisor.[465]

The "Monday morning diarrhea problem" became a big concern. Tackling the problem with a scientific-mindset, zoo staff, collected data on what types of food people gave the animals and how often. Then they consulted with the Smithsonian secretary for solutions. The feeding of certain animals, such as the gorillas and sea lions, by visitors was stopped years earlier, and FONZ and the zoo no longer sold food marketed for feeding the animals. Other animals, however, were being fed food by the guests that was originally meant for the guests.[466]

"People lined up along the rail tossing peanuts and the elephants standing there begging, sticking their trunks out. The monkeys would have their hands out of the cages. Everybody was interested. The bears were very intent on the people," Reed recalled years later. "When we stopped that, why then they are oriented on themselves—more sex, more babies, and more social interaction among the animals, which is what we want. We don't want to have our animals be beggars. Although the people enjoy feeding them, believe me. The people enjoy it."[467]

In the Small Mammal House, Nikumba did his best to perpetuate his lineage, even after Moka's death. Femelle, who was originally supposed to be Tomoka's mate, and then Leonard's mate, had bonded sexually with Nikumba instead—often and in full view of visitors.

She became pregnant in mid-1971, and her pregnancy was non-eventful until one day, Nikumba slapped Femelle hard with the back of his hand. Femelle, a confident and stoic gorilla, was alright, but it scared the keepers, and the two were immediately separated.[468]

FONZ volunteers worked in shifts to watch for any signs of a birth or any other out-of-the-ordinary activity. But the indolent Femelle was not so exciting to monitor, and the volunteers' minute-by-minute hand-written logs show more fascination with tracking the mice and cockroaches moving through the gorilla cages.

"Twas the night before Sunday and all through the cell, all the creatures were stirring except for Femelle," one observer wrote in the pregnancy log.[469]

Another wrote: "Pregwatchers, pregwatchers, a tip of the hat to all of you. For your time and devotion to watch Femelle's view. I have baby sat for a tortilla before, but gosh, never for a gorilla. Femelle, do hope you have a good birth and increase your family in a short time so I can end this silly rhyme."[470]

On May 29, 1972, a very calm Femelle gave birth rapidly, but afterward, she seemed confused and irritated.

For several months before the birth, zoo visitors were kept away from the gorilla area, leaving her area of the Small Mammal House isolated and quiet. Now, keepers and scientists crowded around her cage, talking to her and each other.[471]

The zoo's veterinarians, Clint Gray and Mitchell Bush, stood in the background. They needed to be nearby in case there was an emergency, but they knew that if they got closer to her cage, Femelle would get stressed. The vets were typically the ones to dart the gorillas with the Cap-Chur guns. The gorillas associated the veterinarians with that pain, and when they would see the men, they would scream and run around. Some would throw their feces at the doctors. Bush and Gray did not want any additional tension in the Small Mammal House that day.[472]

Bernard Gallagher saw Femelle sit on the infant "looking as though she were trying to push it back up into her vagina," he recalled in a report about the birth. Bush saw Femelle try to pass the baby to Nikumba in the cage next to hers. "The head got caught as she tried to pull it back," Bush said, according to the report.

Hoping to ease Femelle's frenzy, most of the observers moved to another room to watch the mother and baby on a television monitor. But when Femelle saw a keeper, who stayed near the cage, she ran and threw herself against the bars. She also started dragging the infant by the arm with her walking arm.

A half hour after the birth, employees decided to remove the baby from Femelle.[473] The little male was unharmed and healthy, weighing 5 pounds, 10 ounces. Nikumba's fourth offspring was named M'Geni Mopaya, who zoo staff nicknamed "Mopie."

Like the other newborn gorillas before him, Mopie was brought to Louise Gallagher's house, where the surrogate mother bottled-fed him on demand in the first few weeks and gradually gave him more freedom to explore, climb, and try new foods.[474] He grew rapidly in the Gallaghers' care, hitting developmental milestones earlier than his half-brothers and half-sister. Mopie grew faster and heavier than the other gorillas the Gallaghers raised.[475]

A few months after Mopie's birth, Femelle was pregnant again, but she miscarried the baby on New Year's Eve 1972.[476] When Mopie came back to the zoo soon after Femelle's miscarriage and seven months after his own birth, there was new excitement in the Small Mammal House as the youngster "visited" for hours at a time in a cage by himself before going back home to the Gallaghers.

Then, abruptly it seemed to the keepers, it was decided Mopie would move to the Bronx Zoo to live alongside a juvenile female so he could eventually do what his father had done so successfully—carry on the family genes.

After Mopie's birth and even after Femelle's miscarriage, the zoo's great ape managers did all they could to help the gorilla couple produce another baby. Zoo staff debated leaving Nikumba and Femelle together all day and all night, which had never been done and they eventually decided not to do.

Stuffed toys were put in Femelle and Nikumba's cages to see how they would react. Nikumba just watched as Femelle juggled, dropped, and sniffed the toys.[477] On a few occasions, a female zoo employee sat outside Femelle's cage breast-feeding her own baby to demonstrate the maternal duty for the gorilla.[478]

Other zoos were consulted, and National Zoo staff read the papers of field researchers, including George Schaller and Dian Fossey, whose studies of mountain gorillas in the wild taught others about the animals' social intelligence, tender attitudes, and daily routines. That information influenced zoos to adopt more natural conditions for captive gorillas, such as their need to live in the company of other gorillas and to gather branches and leaves to make nests each night to rest.[479]

And zoo staff analyzed what went right and wrong with Mopie's birth. Of particular concern was the decision to remove the infant so quickly. Femelle did seem aggressive toward Mopie by dragging him, but the gorilla caretakers wondered if they overreacted by removing the newborn too soon.

"Clearly this was not adequate, but whether (1) it was harmful and (2) Femelle might have shown greater maternal responsiveness had she been less excited, is open to question," says a 1973 gorilla birth plan from the zoo. The plan, which gave examples of gorilla births at other zoos where the mother successfully raised her baby, recommended that if the National Zoo had another gorilla birth, the mom and baby should stay together unless there was strong evidence the baby could be seriously hurt. "Where it was thought that adequate maternal responsiveness was present, it is clear that mothers may examine and manipulate their young extensively, often in a manner that appears harmful to humans,"[480] the plan said.

Mopie's transfer to the Bronx Zoo and the loss of the unborn baby was a double-blow to keepers. Years before Mopie was moved, Nikumba and Moka's babies Leonard and Inaki also were transferred from the National Zoo soon after living at the Gallagher home during their early months. Leonard was sent to the Riverside Zoo (now known as the Toronto Zoo). Inaki moved to Yerkes Primate Center, a research center in Georgia, in exchange for an orangutan the National Zoo wanted. "The young animals involved all seem quite happy with this arrangement," the 1968 National Zoo report reads.[481]

The shuffling of gorillas was meant to protect the species and perpetuate their lineages by placing the non-related successful breeders together. But the moves, coordinated among individual zoos, were still difficult for zoo staff who would disagree on the timing or reasoning behind some of the transfers. The keepers, some of whom had worked at the zoo for decades, knew their animals well, and some were frustrated at the loss of decision-making for an animal's future.

One such caretaker was Bernard Gallagher. For nearly two decades, he was revered as the most knowledgeable ape caretaker. The apes trusted him, as did zoo staff, including the veterinarians, who tried to schedule medical procedures on the primates while Gallagher was on shift, knowing the animals would be more calm if Gallagher was nearby.

Now, as more degreed keepers joined the staff and veterinarians, scientists and others questioned his decisions or overrode his suggestions, Gallagher probably felt marginalized. He was reaching a breaking point.

On a warm summer morning in 1973, an associate curator of the Reptile House walked along the main walkway past the Small Mammal House. Gallagher was leaning against the building smoking a pipe, as he typically did before the zoo buildings opened to visitors for the day. When the man walked by, Gallagher called out his name, and the man came closer. The two zoo staffers had been cordial for several years, but today, Gallagher was upset over a memo the man had sent him asking that the Small Mammal keepers not put any stray turtles found on zoo grounds into a pond outside the Reptile House. The associate curator wanted to make sure the stray turtles were a good fit with the other animals in the pond.

The two argued, and their voices grew louder. Their shouting escalated, and suddenly, Gallagher moved forward, and with an open pocket knife in his hand, he stabbed the curator just below the man's heart. Pressing his hand against his wound, the man backed away, and without any other words spoken, the curator walked up the hill to the Elephant House, where another keeper called for an ambulance.

At the Washington Hospital Center, doctors performed exploratory surgery to check for internal damage. When the man woke up from surgery, Ted Reed was in his room along with a zoo police officer and a Smithsonian lawyer. Reed was surprised and upset that Gallagher snapped, but grateful that the curator was recovering and that no permanent trauma was done. The assistant curator declined to press criminal charges, and Gallagher was asked to resign from the zoo and never return to zoo property again.[482]

Bernard Gallagher had fed, bathed, nurtured, and nursed

Nikumba, Moka, and other gorillas and apes for more than 15 years. He and his family raised Nikumba and Moka's newborns and a half a dozen other zoo infants in their home, cuddling them in the middle of the night, calming them as they transitioned back to the zoo.[483] As the gorillas grew up and lived out their lives at the National Zoo, their bond with Gallagher, who they saw nearly every day, continued.

But by the early 1970s, the culture of the folksy zoo Gallagher had joined many years earlier was evolving into a science-based, conservation-focused institution. Simply having a love of animals no longer qualified someone to care for them. And because of a fit of rage, Gallagher's career with the National Zoo and his time with the gorillas came to an abrupt end.

As zoo staff worked to improve the practices of animal management, they changed the design and purpose of several animal houses to match the transition of prioritizing the humane treatment of animals. Several renovations to the 1937 Small Mammal House's cages over the years gave more room to the gorillas that lived behind the steel bars and plate glass in their elevated cages.

For decades, zoo officials talked about creating larger, modern, and more natural exhibits for its animals, and in the mid-1970s, a building boom occurred. Nearly every major building was renovated between 1974 and 1976 with the intent to conceal views of buildings and maximize safety for the animals and visitors. New buildings were constructed partially underground or into natural hillsides. Existing animal exhibits were shed of barred cages as much as possible.

For the reptiles, a new "jungle scene" with plants and pools livened up their space. Bigger pools and more rocks were put into the seal and sea lions' habitat. The Bird House got more water features to allow natural nesting conditions, and the grizzly and polar bears' habitats got moats and rocks. Larger exhibits allowed the zoo to showcase families of species and in some cases, multiple species in one habitat.

The dark and poorly ventilated Monkey House, built in 1906, smelled so strongly of urine, feces, and animal sweat that many visitors avoided it, and at least one child threw up once she entered. It, too, was updated with bigger cages that were easier to clean.[484]

Even zoo administrators got a new, low-profile building with grassy, sloped sides that sat right along the main visitor walkway near the main entrance of the park on Connecticut Avenue. The 1820s Holt House hidden on zoo property that the administrators moved out of was so badly deteriorated that it was abandoned entirely by 1988.[485]

The highest profile construction upgrade was the lion exhibit. The 1893 Lion House was the zoo's first permanent structure for animals, housing hundreds of disparate animals over the past nine decades. Extensive renovations were constructed over time that led to a schizophrenic design featuring intricate stonework with boulders from Rock Creek Valley on one side of the building and a barren wooden facade on the other end.

Still, the structure held a lot of sentimental memories for zoo staff and visitors who came to watch the birds, snakes, hippos, and other beloved creatures who resided there over time, including N'Gi, the zoo's first gorilla.

Someone mentioned starting a petition to save the building, but before Reed even secured funding for new construction, he ordered the demolition of the structure. He didn't want the antiquated building declared historic and all the restrictions for renovations that would follow.

"A lot of people loved that old Lion House. I loved it. I thought it was great. We spent a couple of years trying to figure out what we could do with it, and there was nothing we could do with it. Any remodeling would just be a gerrymandered deal. It would look like a bird house that was a lion house at one time," he said years later.[486]

There may have been another reason Reed was eager to tear down the building; it was the physical memory of little Julie Ann Vogt's mauling death by a zoo lion, one of Reed's lowest moments in his otherwise admired and productive zoo career.

The new three-acre outdoor lion and tiger habitat allowed visitors to walk a full quarter-mile circle around a wide, deep river moat.[487] The moat surrounded three separate, grassy yards with tiered platforms. Zoo visitors could peer down or at eye-level to watch lion and tiger families play and sleep.

Across from the lion and tiger yards and under the visitor walkway, offices were built for researchers and other zoo staff. Late one night, soon after the exhibit was completed, Judith Block, the registrar who organized the records of each animal at the zoo, sat at her desk working. A tiger, who was likely curious about the light from the window, swam right up to her office, and the two became startled as their eyes met through the thick glass.[488]

At the very end of the construction schedule was a new Great Ape House just for the gorillas and orangutans. For decades, zoo staff knew the space in the Small Mammal House was inadequate for gorillas.

"As you know, Ted and I are most anxious to either re-design the present clock of cages, move the gorillas to where the gibbons are now with completely new facilities, or some way wangle a new primate house, which is not only desirable but almost necessary when you consider the hazards of the present position against the pricelessness of their possession," Lear Grimmer, associate zoo director, wrote to Nick Arundel nearly two decades before in 1959.[489]

Over the years, the public also grew more concerned about the gorilla's tiny living spaces. Some complained the cages were dirty, although the cages were cleaned twice a day.[490] Hay laid down for the comfort and entertainment of the gorillas made the cages seem messy and clogged the water drains. Keepers were concerned with the safety and functionality of the cages. These intelligent apes could find weaknesses in the bars and break some sections off.[491]

At one point, Nikumba damaged a door between two cages. "Something should be done to the doors on the shift cage. One has to be operated by hand and the other will not operate at all," Bernard Gallagher wrote in a daily report in 1972. "This condition has existed for seven to eight months. The doors have to be chained and locked with a pad lock (sic) to keep the gorilla from escaping. This is very dangerous for the man who has to lock and unlock the door as the gorilla is excited and mad and can easily grab the man."[492]

By 1979, a new building for the apes was very overdue from an aesthetic, logistic, and emotional standpoint. Nikumba, now a handsome silverback, was again behaving erratically. He was grinding his teeth. He pounded on the walls in the back of his cage. Although he had always been a spitter, both when he was acting playfully with keepers and when he was irritated, his spitting took on a new intensity, and the precision of his aim was so accurate, it both impressed and scared the keepers. "He could spit around corners and hit you in the eye," keeper Melanie Bond warned other zoo staff.[493] The journal where keepers recorded each animal's daily activities became water stained with Nikumba's saliva.[494] Visitors were protected from the projectile spit as they stood behind plate glass in front of the gorilla cages.

Nikumba hardly ever took his aggression out on Femelle, but they rarely mated anymore and never did have another baby, even after Femelle started fertility drugs. It was theorized that the animals' lack of intimacy was due to boredom. "The environment is not socially or physically stimulating enough to result in normal sexual behavior," a curator wrote to Reed.[495]

One gynecologist who reviewed Femelle's records concluded Femelle was "terminally infertile."[496]

On the other end of the temperament scale was Tomoka. Except when he was in pain, he was calm, peaceful, and predictable. He sometimes showed his dislikes by simply squinting his eyes.[497] Humans raised him when he was a baby and rescued him from near death when he was battling arthritis. His only non-human friendships were with Femelle, and when he was younger, Lulu, the chimpanzee. For many years before a new Great Ape House was constructed, zoo leaders considered moving Tomoka to another zoo.[498] Maybe a new female would make him happier, they wondered.

Instead, they brought a female to Tomoka.

M'wasi, a chubby, happy, and aloof gorilla, was born in Africa and lived at the Bronx Zoo before coming to the National Zoo. While at the Bronx Zoo, she gave birth to a stillborn baby, but never had a successful birth.[499] When she was paired with Tomoka, he was 18 years old, had never sired a baby, and was unpracticed sexually. Still, zoo officials were optimistic that a new, spacious Great Ape House could increase the procreation possibilities of their two pairs of gorillas.

The apes' new home would be built right next door to the Small Mammal House and on the same slice of land that once held the 1891 elephant shed for Dunk and Gold Dust. The new building replaced an area along the main visitor walkway that featured the "short line," a row of pre–World War II individual cages. Those wooden structures with bars on one side held an ever-changing conference of animals—dogs, Barbary apes, young tigers—and other animals that were in limbo at the zoo.

When construction began in 1979 for the new multi–million dollar great ape home, it was one of the most expensive projects in the Smithsonian Institution that year and one of the most exciting for zoo staff and visitors.[500]

The architects sought a minimalist design so the building itself wouldn't distract from the focus on the animals.[501] Zoo officials also favored the easier–to–clean concrete and brick, Brutalist–style design because they were still highly concerned about tuberculosis outbreaks among the apes and the possibility of infections being passed between apes and visitors.[502]

Miles Roberts, the zoo's curator of mammals, worked with the design team to plan the new ape house. The group considered the building's visitor flow, caretaker needs, and animal accommodations, but forefront on Roberts' mind was the safety of keepers and visitors.

He knew how dangerous it could be if humans and gorillas got too close. One time when he was hosing down Nikumba and Femelle's cage in the Small Mammal House, he entered the smaller, barred shift cage through the cage's doorway that connected directly to the keepers' aisle. The shift cage was enclosed and surrounded by the larger gorilla living space. He forgot that Nikumba was resting on a platform above the shift cage. As Roberts washed the floor, Nikumba jumped down, reached one powerful arm between the bars of the cage and grabbed Roberts by the shoulder. A frightened Roberts lifted his hand that held the water hose in an attempt to defend himself. The water from the hose splashed Nikumba directly in the face, surprising him. He released Roberts and walked away. There was no doubt in Roberts' mind Nikumba would have killed him had he not been hit with the water. Roberts never wanted another keeper to have that near–death experience.[503]

The space for the gorillas in their new building was much larger than what they had in the Small Mammal House. Even so, zoo staff knew they couldn't let all the gorillas live together in the same enclosure. Although Tomoka and Nikumba were father and son, they may violently attack each other because they never lived together in the same cage before. Keepers would still need to alternate the times the gorilla couples spent outside. In other words, the gorillas' freedom would still be tightly restricted.

Inside the gorilla enclosures, sections of the hard, concrete floors were heated, and other sections featured pools of water that were constantly replenished. Concrete and fiberglass climbing structures filled the living spaces. The fiberglass trees and concrete floors obviously didn't come close to the jungle landscape of the African tropical rainforest. Zoo staff, however, say it was the best way to keep the area hygienic. It had only been 26 years since Nikumba and Moka first came to the zoo from Equatorial Africa. Since then, through careful planning and luck, four baby gorillas were born healthy, and the zoo's gorillas were maturing into older adulthood. Many more generations of gorillas would follow, it was hoped. Planners were careful not to change their habitat too dramatically.

The gorillas could move through four separate, but connected spacious indoor areas that rose two stories high with some rooms having floor-to-ceiling glass fronts. The 1¼-inch thick, laminated glass allowed visitors to walk right up to the gorillas' enclosures and, if a gorilla so wanted, sit on the other side of the glass. Humans and apes now could stand face-to-face only inches apart, with nothing but glass in-between them. And if the visitors or other gorillas got to be overwhelming, several privacy areas gave the apes options to hide.[504]

Reed seemed indifferent to the aesthetics of the new building and was far more focused on creating a functional, safe, and healthy space for the apes. "Are we exhibiting fake nature or are we exhibiting animals? I think that we're exhibiting animals. I think if the cage physiologically and biologically suits the animal—that is, if an animal is a brachiator, you've got to give him a jungle gym, whether it's pipe, wood, fake trees, fake swinging trees, and he can swing on those. Does he really care whether it looks like a tree that he's never seen? People like it, but then, you know, you've got to meet the physiological and psychological needs of the animals. Fish got to swim, birds got to fly, monkeys got to swing, and directors sit at their desk,"[505] he said years later.

Behind the new Great Ape House was a large outside play yard. Dry moats hidden behind concrete walls kept the animals confined but within the sight lines of visitors. Their grassy 6,000-square-foot yard, which was 12 times larger than the concrete outdoor yard the gorillas used at the Small Mammal House, was filled with rocks and plants.[506]

For the first time in his 26 years at the zoo, Nikumba would be able to walk on grass.

CHAPTER 11

MISMATCHES

A new, grassy and spacious yard was just steps away, yet the gorilla foursome—Nikumba, Tomoka, Femelle, and M'wasi—were cautious about the new freedom. Nikumba was especially apprehensive. When the electronic gate between the outside and inside areas opened for the first time and Nikumba was free to put his feet on the spongy ground, he tried to pull the gate closed. The media, keepers, and visitors watched and wondered why he wasn't more excited to go outside. Did he not want to step out into the hot July day because he preferred the air-conditioned interior?[507] Or did he fear entering unfamiliar territory? For hours, the gate was left open, and everyone patiently waited for him to go outside. Finally, he stepped through the door and into the sunny, humid open space.

"Went well," was the entire summary in the gorillas' daily log book that day.[508]

Just six months after the Great Ape House opened in 1981, two new gorillas joined the group. Sylvia, a 17-year-old people lover, was captured in Cameroon when she was a baby in 1964. Hercules, a handsome but moody 15-year-old silverback, was captured in Cameroon just two years later in 1966, although the two were not thought to be related. Both were brought to the Baltimore Zoo in Maryland, as young gorillas by animal dealer G. Van den Brink, the same man who transported Femelle to the National Zoo.[509]

Baltimore zoo keepers gave Sylvia and Hercules a lot of attention and affection, and as they grew, they continued to live and play together.[510] In 1976, when Hercules was 10 and Sylvia was 12, the two were separated with the hope that a later-date reunion would spark sexual interest. But when they were reunited, they fought viciously, and Sylvia was wounded. For the next five years, the gorillas stayed in separate, nearby cages. They could hear and smell each other, but could not see or touch each other.

The National Zoo's socialization plan for Sylvia and Hercules was first to introduce Sylvia to Femelle and M'wasi and then individually to Nikumba, Tomoka, and Hercules and hope she would choose a mate naturally. Hercules would also meet the females individually and choose a favored partner.

"The goal of this program was to have both Hercules and Sylvia enter the breeding population and leave wild-caught genes in the founder population," according to an animal management plan for the National Zoo gorillas in 1985.[511]

The match-making of gorilla pairings maximized the chances of a pregnancy, prevented any one gorilla from living alone for an extended time, and allowed researchers to document the idiosyncrasies of each relationship.[512]

But all the pairings failed to produce a baby or even regular sexual activity. Hercules and Sylvia did not copulate at all with each other or any of the other gorillas, although Sylvia would often masturbate or solicit her favorite male keepers.[513]

For 184 hours over a four-month period in the mid-1980s, Dr. Benjamin Beck, a research primatologist at the National Zoo, organized observations of these pairings. He wanted to understand what behavioral or environmental factors were interfering with successful pregnancies and births in the National Zoo's gorillas.[514]

Before coming to the National Zoo, Beck spent more than a decade as a researcher and curator of primates at the Chicago Brookfield Zoo. His biggest challenge was understanding why captive gorillas were having a hard time breeding. He knew that gorillas naturally have slow reproductive rates. If zoo gorillas weren't breeding, or if most of the births came from a limited number of

gorillas, zoos would not be able to sustain the entire captive population for future generations, he predicted.

Beck considered all the possible obstacles, including the new
theory that young gorillas needed to be with other gorillas to learn
socialization skills that would help them when they became of
breeding age. At one point, Beck thought that the sexual incom-
patibility was due to the shape of gorillas' noses, but his theory
fell apart, and he and every other captive gorilla expert remained
perplexed over the reproductive failures.[515]

After weeks of watching and recording who the National Zoo
gorillas groomed, rested near, copulated with, or showed aggression
toward, Beck still didn't have the answers he hoped for.[516]

"The gorillas at NZP are afflicted with a variety of physiological and psychological problems that make it unlikely that they will
reproduce naturally," Beck wrote to the zoo director.[517]

What zoo staff could control—the gorillas' weight and daily
diet, their toys, and their physical activity—they did. They even
removed all the television sets near the gorilla cages, hoping to
emphasize the gorillas' natural routines and behaviors. Plus, the
keepers were becoming increasingly frustrated with visitors asking
if the apes watched Redskins games and if they had a favorite local
newscaster.[518]

Zoo staff also focused on the physical health of the gorillas.
Medical procedures for all animals were becoming more safe, reliable, and sophisticated. Zoos, including the National Zoo, used
preventative exams and medications more frequently, helping to
diagnose and prolong the vitality of ill animals who were more
likely to hide a sickness as not to appear weak or vulnerable.

When veterinarian Mitchell Bush began treating animals at the
National Zoo in 1972, he used the Cap-Chur gun to anesthetize his
patients. He'd aim the gun carrying the syringe of anesthetic, and

when the animal was immobilized or unconscious, he never was sure when the animal would become alert again or if the drug was too powerful or too weak. If the animal patient didn't get enough of the drug, it could wake in a panic while being examined or under surgery. If the drug was too strong, the animal could die in the middle of a procedure intended to save it. Reliable anesthetic monitoring was just developing. Bush stressed over this level of uncertainty, especially when he used newer drugs and his patient was an endangered 400-pound gorilla.

Bush was passionate about comparative medicine as it related to the field of clinical research of zoo species. He liked learning about the cause and effect of certain mysterious ailments and their treatments. He began documenting dosage amounts for various drugs used on different animals and the range of effects the drugs would have. He learned, for example, that if snakes were given too much of certain antibiotics and too often, their kidneys could fail.

He focused on the ideal dosages of anesthetics after seeing too many animals die from incorrect amounts. Death rates for some complex animals, such as giraffes, undergoing anesthesia were high, and Bush wanted to push those numbers down.[519] By the late 1990s, he succeeded in lowering the anesthesia mortality rate for National Zoo animals from 20 percent to less than one percent.[520]

The expanding scientific techniques at zoos spread to many different animal management practices. In the 1980s, zoos started experimenting with the use of contraceptives for certain animals. Female oral contraceptives were becoming safer for humans, and zoos discovered that apes and monkeys especially took well to the pregnancy prevention pills.[521]

In the past, when zoos wanted to prevent unplanned pregnancies and an overpopulation of some animals, the institutions would simply separate certain males and females. But that didn't work well, especially for gorillas, because it left those apes in isolation or sexually inept when it was their turn to "perform." Zoos also used vasectomies or hysterectomies, but those procedures were invasive, expensive, and non-reversible. In the time since, scientific discoveries and advancements have given zoos more control over the reproductive fates of their animals, including artificial insemination and genome banking.[522] Zoos still give fertile female gorillas birth-control pills.[523]

Overpopulation of the National Zoo's gorillas in the 1980s, however, was never a worry. The concern was the lack of pregnancies.

Zoo doctors, researchers, administrators, and keepers continued to do all they could to understand the problem. There was even discussion about establishing a primate facility at the zoo's Conservation and Research Center in Front Royal, Virginia, at a construction cost of $1 million, to give the gorillas space and privacy, but it was never built.[524]

Instead, staff continued to tackle the issue at the zoo's main campus in Washington, D.C. They examined sperm counts and sperm movement in the male gorillas. They analyzed hormone levels and estrus cycles in the females. They developed three phases of different couplings of gorillas toward the goal of having a successful pregnancy, with each phase becoming more intense and invasive, including the suggestion of electrojaculation and artificial insemination by immobilizing a male and a female gorilla repeatedly and shutting down the Great Ape House temporarily.[525]

Staff hired to help perpetuate animals' family lines worked diligently. Even the zoo's beloved pandas—Ling-Ling and Hsing-Hsing—did not mate for the first 10 years they lived at the zoo, and staff and outside panda experts were searching for reasons why.[526]

Publicly, Reed had a simple explanation for those who kept asking him when the National Zoo would have baby pandas and gorillas. "I have come to the conclusion that, unlike humans, most animals will not breed if they don't like each other," Reed said.[527]

As frustrating and disappointing as all this was to zoo staff, they were steadfast in the belief that the tweaks they made to improve the gorillas' physical and mental health were meaningful. For Lisa Stevens, the great ape curator at the time, small changes such as laying soft hay on the indoor floors, giving gorillas toys they could maneuver and manipulate, and providing browse—food the gorillas foraged for—could lead to the biggest rewards; happy gorillas who would eventually have babies.[528]

The National Zoo wasn't the only zoo having trouble breeding gorillas.

"Current analyses suggest that the situation is critical. Few captives over 20 years of age have reproduced, and 38 percent of the North American captive population are over 20 [years old]. Many of the younger animals are unlikely to reproduce due to physiological or behavioral problems. The North American population is decreasing at three to four percent per year, and the rate of decrease is predicted to accelerate as proven wild-caught breeders age," according to the zoo's gorilla management plan in the mid-1980s.[529]

Another reason for the urgency in solving the birthing problem also nagged at National Zoo staff and other zoos that housed gorillas. They started carrying more of the burden of responsibility for the wild populations of gorillas, along with conservation groups. It was becoming clearer that the plight of all subspecies of gorillas in Africa was worsening.

Many international and national groups were attempting to protect these great apes, including the African Wildlife Leadership Foundation, now called African Wildlife Foundation; the Wildlife Conservation Society, which began at the turn of the 20th century as the New York Zoological Society; the World Wildlife Fund of which Russell Train was president and chairman in the 1980s; the Digit Fund, which began from Dian Fossey's work to preserve mountain gorillas; and many more African local government agencies, indigenous groups, international non-government organizations, and universities.[530]

Even though it was now illegal to kill or capture wild gorillas, the species was still being slaughtered for its valuable bushmeat and in an effort to capture young gorillas to sell.[531]

The wild gorillas' fate only grew dimmer as political upheaval left these animals with fewer guardians in the jungles. Profiteers started moving further into the gorillas' hidden rainforest habitats, building roads to log timber or to hunt the animal, bringing humans and wild apes closer together and shrinking the gorillas' homeland.[532]

At the National Zoo, there were still no gorilla births by the mid-1980s. Zoo staff decided to start from scratch. They transferred several gorillas in and out of the Great Ape House, hoping new relationships would lead to breeding successes. But their decisions on which animals to move were based on new criteria. They stopped depending on the availability of gorillas at a nearby zoo or the personal connections staff had with gorilla caregivers at other zoos. The old way of breeding management—randomly mixing animals and hoping to "get lucky"—was not working, at least for the gorillas at the National Zoo.

In its place came the methodical, data-driven, match-making process of coupling gorillas. Just as was done for the golden lion tamarins, the American Association of Zoos and Aquariums created an oversight committee guided by the newly created Gorilla Species Survival Plan.

The plan, first developed in 1982 and updated annually, started dictating gorilla transfers in American zoos and eventually set uniform management practices and "mini goals" for every gorilla in captivity.[533] This not only took into consideration the breeding potential of each gorilla, but also its personality, age, past relationships, and other factors, including the size of the gorilla habitat at each zoo. The careful arrangement of compatible animals, in the right environment and at the ideal time, was a fairly new concept in zoos, but one the National Zoo and a few other zoos practiced informally for many years for certain species.

With this formal level of cooperation, the gorilla population in American zoos essentially became part of one national zoo with the common mission to strengthen the survival rates of captive gorillas.

The new Gorilla Survival Species Plan also attempted to create generations of captive gorillas who were genetically diverse. The evils of inbreeding were now accepted by the greater zoo community. Zoos needed to prevent the genes of the prolific breeders from overpopulating the captive gorilla community.

"What we must do, and what we in fact do now, is examine the relationship of animals in various zoos. We might send a beautiful animal to be exhibited at some other zoo, some zoo where they will not breed with him. Because we do not want the stock of the world's animals to become too restricted in their genetic material. This is something to think of. It is not just a question of a magnificent tiger, but of what genes he has to pass on; so you want to keep the widest assortment of genetical material background alive in zoo tigers," Reed told the *Washington Post* at the time.[534]

Nikumba's bloodline was adequately represented in the captive gorilla population. His genetic profile was particularly attractive to zoo managers because he was born in the wild and assumed to be unrelated to the other wild-caught gorillas in the captive population. He also sired healthy babies. Of Nikumba's four offspring, three—Tomoka, Inaki, and Mopie—were still living. Nikumba and Moka's second son, Leonard, who went to the Riverside Zoo (now known as the Toronto Zoo), died at the age of four from an infection.[535] Although zoo leaders vacillated about Tomoka's potential as a sire because of his health problems, his sister Inaki and his half-brother Mopie were vibrant and young enough to carry on the family's wild-caught genes.

With the great apes in their own building and many other zoo animals in upgraded habitats, Ted Reed was finally content with the park he once called a "zoological slum." He was particularly proud of the creation of CRC in Front Royal, Virginia, and the fiscal health of the zoo. When he started as zoo director in 1956, the budget was $669,000, and there were about 125 employees.[536] By 1984, the budget was up to $10.6 million and the zoo employed 316 people.[537]

In 1983, Reed retired after 27 years at the zoo. Like Doc Mann before him, he transformed the zoo but always remained restless at the slow pace of progress. Reed credited the pandas from China for helping to boost zoo finances and the numbers of visitors.

His favorite animals were the pandas and the white tigers, although he intimately knew the characteristics of hundreds of other animals living at the zoo. He still mourned the sudden deaths of Moka and a favorite Komodo dragon. Privately, he told friends that his least favorite animal was the chimpanzee because one took a bite out of his hand when he got too close to the cage. Bernard Gallagher came to Reed's rescue by fighting the chimp's jaws away from Reed's hand, but the bite was bad.[538] For the rest of his life, Reed couldn't fully close his right hand.[539]

By the time he retired, Reed shaved his crimson beard, was nearing 60, and walked with a cane due to a recent hip replacement. He still had a contagious passion for the zoo. He was tough on his staff, always telling them to tuck in their shirts and to answer visitors' questions. He was gruff and demanding, but never nasty. He carried no sympathy for employees who were alcoholics or philanderers. His staff didn't always agree with his decisions, but they trusted him, admired his honesty, and always knew the zoo's results-centered reputation was his top priority.[540]

Upon reflection many years after his retirement, with time to ponder what he and others at the zoo accomplished and what he wished he could have done differently, he hinted at remorse for the mistakes made to the earlier generations of zoo animals—the ones who lived alone in small cages. As the zoo's director, he orchestrated the shift in attitudes that put the dignity and respect for animals to the forefront. He tried to re-dedicate the National Zoo to the conservation mission that was the zoo's origin when it was created in 1889, but had struggled for so long to make meaningful impacts to animals' lives in the wild and in confinement.

"Now zoos are viewed as the last hope for many, many animals, birds, and reptiles that are not going to make it into the next century without zoo breeding," Reed told a Smithsonian historian several years after his retirement. "And we've got to keep a diversity of genes, we've got to have good, healthy stock, we've got to have animals that can eventually, we hope, be returned to the wild."[541]

Reed's replacement was Michael Robinson, a quiet and cautious leader. Robinson, a Brit, was educated as a zoologist and had a natural excitement for studying animals in their native habitats. Before becoming zoo director, he spent 18 years conducting animal behavior research, including prey versus predator relationships at the Smithsonian Tropical Research Institute along the Panama Canal. He carried on Mann's and Reed's tradition of bringing zoo animals to Capitol Hill budget meetings. He even kept a few unusual pets in his house, such as an otter and giant rat.[542]

Despite continued funding problems at the National Zoo, Robinson pushed to connect visitors with scientific discoveries by open-ing zoo laboratories to guests and explaining the science behind understanding animal relationships and routines and how conser-vation efforts helped certain species.[543] Many guests enjoyed the exposure to the work behind preserving and improving the lives of zoo animals and their wild habitats, but others simply just wanted to watch the animals play.[544] Robinson would lead the zoo for the next 16 years and into the 21st century.

With no successful pairings in the Great Ape House, Femelle, M'wasi and Sylvia were transferred out and replaced by new gorilla residents. Femelle went to the Milwaukee Zoo. A year after arriving, she gave birth to a stillborn male.[545] The zoo let her hold her dead baby for six days, hoping the mournful bonding would prepare her for a successful mother-baby union in the future.[546] In 1992, at the older gorilla age of 30, while still at the Milwaukee Zoo, she had a healthy female baby.[547] She was an attentive and caring mom to her baby girl. As she aged, she still tenderly cared for younger gorillas by giving them rides on her back. She died at the zoo in 2016 at the age of 54.[548]

M'wasi moved to the Topeka Zoo, where she died in 1998 with-out having any offspring.[549] Sylvia also never bore any babies after moving to the Columbus Zoo, but she was a supportive surro-gate mom to at least one infant gorilla until her death there in 2004.[550] Keepers who cared for her said her selflessness in caring for the younger gorillas and her socialization with other gorillas was a major accomplishment considering her unusual attachment to humans in her youth.[551]

In their places at the National Zoo came a male, two-year-old Kuja, and a female, three-year-old Mandara. Both were born in captivity and were coming from the Milwaukee Zoo.[552] When they arrived in D.C., National Zoo staff placed the youngsters with

Tomoka, the zoo's most tolerant and tender gorilla.

Mandara's first meeting with Tomoka did not go well. Having only lived with Kuja, she was clueless about gorilla social etiquette. Tomoka showed off his authoritative status to Mandara by beating his chest and strutting around the enclosure. Instead of being intimidated, she thought it was playtime and chased him. Tomoka picked up her small body, put her face down on the floor, and placed his teeth on her back. After a few seconds, he got off her and walked away, concluding his lesson on gorilla hierarchy at the National Zoo. From then on, Tomoka looked after Mandara and Kuja as a loving father-figure.[553]

In 1987, floppy-eared and energetic six-year-old Augustus "Gus" arrived. As an infant, he had received his food and care from humans, but he had spent his days and nights with other baby gorillas. His mixed upbringing gave him the ability to work well with both his human caretakers and gorilla cage mates. He was highly intelligent socially, and as he grew bigger and older, he strategically built alliances with other gorillas at the National Zoo by spending one-on-one time with each, providing and accepting favors, before moving on to bond with another gorilla. Like a skilled politician, he patiently calculated his path to leadership among the troop.

The male leadership role should have gone to Tomoka. He was bigger, older, and a senior resident of the Great Ape House. But Tomoka shied from conflict, and Gus dominated the less confident Tomoka. Each taunt and tease made Tomoka's health and spirits worsen. Gus also overpowered Kuja, who became withdrawn.[554]

To keep the male-to-female ratio and gorilla personalities in proportion, the Gorilla Species Survival Plan coordinators suggested the National Zoo acquire Mesou, a senior female from the Milwaukee Zoo. Just like Nikumba, she was born in the Congo and brought to an American zoo in 1955 as a baby. But unlike him, she lived at several zoos during her life and the transfers deflated her spirits. By the time she got to the National Zoo in 1987, she was cranky and struggled to get along with any of the gorillas or keepers.[555] National Zoo staff wanted her to be a companion to Nikumba, but the time the two gorillas spent together was tense, and they were eventually separated. Nikumba was lonely again, and the keepers put three young colobus monkeys into his enclosure to keep him company.

"Suffice to say, it has been a resounding success, for keepers, gorilla, and colobus," wrote keeper Melanie Bond in a newsletter for gorilla keepers.[556]

Hercules moved out in 1989 and was sent to the Pittsburgh Zoo and then later to the Dallas Zoo, where he became a popular animal with visitors, but temperamental in the eyes of keepers. One morning in late 1998, when a door between cages of his gorilla habitat was accidentally left opened, he attacked and severely injured a keeper.[557] He died in Dallas in 2008 from cardiac arrest while being treated for back pain from spinal disease, never having had any offspring.[558]

Haloko, a sweet, gentle, and quiet female, was the last addition to the gorilla section of the National Zoo's Great Ape House in the 1980s. She bore two healthy baby gorillas and one stillborn baby in the early 1980s while at the Bronx Zoo. She was estimated to be 22 years old by the time she moved to the National Zoo. As a young gorilla, she was captured in Africa, the exact whereabouts unknown.[559] She would be the last gorilla the National Zoo acquired who was born in the wild.[560]

By 1990, Nikumba was slowing down. At 37 years of age, he was one of the oldest gorillas in a zoo. He remained an intense animal, still grinding his teeth and still apprehensive of strangers. He reserved his warm, goofy, and playful side for zoo staff or volunteers who he trusted.[561]

On a hot July afternoon that year, he was enjoying one such playful moment with Robert Shumaker, one of the keepers on duty. Although the door to the outside play yard was open, Nikumba choose to stay in the cool building. His wide, silver-haired back sat against the wire mesh in the rear of the exhibit as Shumaker stood on the other side of the mesh in the keepers' aisle, tickling Nikumba's backside through small openings in the barrier. The two reveled in the moment, with Nikumba laughing with each touch and Shumaker appreciating the connection with the animal he grew up watching while on visits to the zoo as a child and now had the privilege of working with every day.

"I'm going to get you some food," Shumaker told Nikumba after the lengthy tickle session, and he walked away for less than a minute. When Shumaker returned with the treats, Nikumba still had his back against the mesh, his body tilted forward slightly. Shumaker could not see Nikumba's face, and he thought the gorilla was still playing. But when he called out Nikumba's name, there was no response. Shumaker pushed slightly on Nikumba's back, and there was still no response. Shumaker knew he was gone.

He called Mitchell Bush who quickly arrived at the Great Ape House and formally determined that Nikumba passed away. As Shumaker, Bush, and other zoo staff discussed how to move Nikumba's massive body, visitors gathered in front of the glass enclosure. From the other side of the exhibit, Shumaker could see the confusion and worry on the visitors' faces. The staff briefly wondered if they should close the building. The scene could scare and sadden the adults and children who were gathered. The staff decided to leave the doors open. Death is a part of life, and Nikumba lived a long, full life. They didn't want it to appear as if something wrong occurred. The visitors should have the opportunity to mourn and appreciate Nikumba, the staff determined.

With visitors watching, zoo staff moved Nikumba's body to the keepers' aisle and called the other gorillas over. They wanted the gorillas to see Nikumba's body and understand he died and would not be coming back.[562]

An Associated Press article about Nikumba's death appeared in newspapers across the country, honoring his origins in the wild and his siring of Tomoka, one of the first zoo-born gorillas in the world.[563] Zoo staff who worked with Nikumba throughout the years and affectionately called him "Nick" or "Nicky" can name more accomplishments other than his breeding record, including that his life, purpose, and placement at the National Zoo left a profound impact on understanding, caring, and respecting the lives of captive gorillas.[564]

His life began at a time in history when it was acceptable—even heroic—to capture gorillas in the wild, often by violent methods, and then house them in solitude in small clinical cages. By the time of Nikumba's death, more was understood about the natural behavior and needs of gorillas and zoos were recognizing their responsibility of housing these intelligent, endangered animals. Respectable zoos were improving the dietary, physical, social, and emotional needs of their zoo-born and zoo-raised gorillas.

In D.C., zoo supporters mourned Nikumba's death. Nick Arundel especially took the news of Nikumba's death hard, telling friends and family about the gorilla's death. The next year, at Nick Arundel's urging and financial support, the zoo renovated the gorillas' outdoor play yard and put a small plaque among the plantings in honor of Nikumba and Moka.[565]

Nikumba's death left six gorillas at the National Zoo—the males Gus, Tomoka, and Kuja and females Mandara, Haloko, and Mesou. Aside from Mesou, the females were at the ideal age, health, and temperament to conceive. But Tomoka was old and sick and Kuja was finicky and inexperienced. All hope for a baby gorilla at the National Zoo was left to Gus.

CHAPTER 12

FAMILY LEGACY

Summer passed, and when the crowds thinned, the National Zoo staff was eager to fill the vacancy in the Great Ape House that Nikumba's death left. They asked that Mopie—Nikumba's son and the zoo's last born gorilla—return to Washington, D.C.[566]

When Mopie left D.C. as an infant, he went to the Bronx Zoo to live with another male his age. About the time he became an adolescent, the Bronx Zoo did not have room for him. He transferred to the San Antonio Zoo, where zoo administrators and keepers there planned to find him a mate or at least a companion. Instead, he lived alone for the seven years he stayed in Texas.

There were opportunities to pair a reproductive female with Mopie, but those gorillas were instead sent to zoos with males who were recorded sires. There were hopes that an older, non-breeding female would join Mopie in San Antonio, but those gorillas moved to zoos to be companions to older males.

"Mopie was a victim of a Catch-22 situation. He couldn't have a mate because he was unproven as a breeder and he couldn't demonstrate his breeding potential because he was alone," wrote a San Antonio zoo curator in a zoo newsletter.[567]

When Mopie returned to the National Zoo in late 1990, he was 18 years old. Keepers noticed immediately the attractive and burly resemblance to Nikumba. But Mopie was much larger than Nikumba. His tall and massive body held 600 pounds, which was nearly all bone and muscle.[568] He was placed in an enclosure with Mesou. She was still moody from time to time, but became happier as she settled into her life of consistency at the National Zoo. Mopie and Mesou seemed content to be together rather than alone.[569]

The relationships between the other gorillas oscillated between tension and tranquility. Gus emerged as a trusted protector and peacemaker—the true silverback leader of his group. He continued to push the submissive Tomoka from authority and demonstrate his power over the quirky and awkward Kuja. And if this wasn't enough to damage Tomoka's ego, Gus would copulate with Mandara and Haloko in front of Tomoka.[570]

Mandara was only seven when zoo staff suspected she may be pregnant. A urine test confirmed her condition for the gorilla caretakers who were at first elated and then nervous. It had been nearly 20 years since Mopie's birth at the zoo. Over those years, about 150 gorillas were born in North American zoos, an accomplishment built on the growing experience of housing gorillas in captivity and field research of gorilla behaviors in the wild.[571]

With the anticipated birth, zoo staff wondered what they could do to ensure a successful outcome. Should they move Gus to another room in the habitat? Should the Great Ape House become off limits to visitors? How could they physically and mentally prepare Mandara for the birth?

As the May 1991 due date approached, the anticipation and anxiety grew. No one at the zoo wanted the birth to be a failure. Under the calm and level-headed guidance of the zoo's primate expert, Benjamin Beck, and Great Ape Curator Lisa Stevens, the staff decided not to change the routine or social setting of Mandy, as some keepers affectionately called her. They vowed to let Mandara keep her baby for as long as possible, until it seemed Mandara's life or the baby's life would be in jeopardy. Even if alarming, but not dangerous, scenarios took place, zoo staff overseeing the pregnancy and birth pledged not to intervene, although they set up contingency plans to deal with a variety of possible emergencies. If, after all their careful planning, the birth was in some way a failure and if something did go terribly wrong, letting Mandara deal with the situation without human intervention would help set the stage for a future birth, the staff concluded.[572]

"We weren't going to do anything new," wrote keeper Robert Shumaker in a 1994 article for the *Gorilla Gazette.* "We wanted Mandara to feel as though nothing abnormal was happening. The less disruption the better. The other important factor to remember was that Mandara, Gus, Kuja, and Tomoka had never been around babies either. We couldn't predict how they would react, but we had faith in them and hoped for the best."[573]

Beck, who studied gorilla breeding for decades, co-wrote a paper a few years earlier based on research of captive gorillas in North America stating that mother-reared male and female gorillas were more successful reproductively than hand-reared gorillas. This was likely because a very young gorilla's exposure to his or her mother and other gorillas can lead to better social development. If those ape social skills are lacking at an early age, it can be harder for a gorilla to find and breed with a mate, Beck and his co-author wrote.[574] It was an acknowledgement that zoos' past practices of hand-rearing gorillas in isolation from their species may have hurt those gorillas' future breeding potential. The hand-raised baby gorillas may have been well-fed and nurtured by humans, such as Louise Gallagher, but their social needs weren't being met.

Many zoos, like the National Zoo, regularly removed newborn gorillas from their mothers in the 1960s, 70s, and into the 80s. But as more successful captive births occurred and more was known about gorilla behaviors in the wild, protocols from the Gorilla Species Survival Plan were developed to keep babies with their mothers.

Zoo leaders were encouraged to wait longer—at least 72 hours— for nursing to begin before separating the mom and baby. Training programs for pregnant gorillas were held to help prepare the mother. And if hand-rearing was necessary, zoo administrators were urged to reintroduce the young apes to their mothers as soon as possible and to get them familiar to the sounds and smells of the ape house.[575]

Beck and his co-author also concluded that a new mother gorilla's competency wasn't based on whether that mother was hand-reared or mother-reared or was born in the wild or in captivity.[576] That conclusion—that captive, hand-reared female gorillas can be caring moms, just like mother-reared gorillas—was a relief to those working with captive gorillas.

Still, even with all this anecdotal and research-based information, it was difficult for some zoo staff to believe that the young, inexperienced Mandara, who was removed from her mother and hand-raised as an infant, could know how to properly care for her newborn. Because they had worked so hard and waited so long for a gorilla birth at the zoo, they began considering worst-case scenarios.[577]

In the early morning of May 10, 1991, Mandara gave birth to a healthy son. It quickly became clear that the behind-the-scenes worrying was for nothing and that perhaps, the relaxed attitude the keepers and staff projected boosted Mandara's self-possession.

When keepers arrived that morning, Mandara was holding her baby boy close and nursing him with ease. The rest of the troop was calm but protective about its newest member. Kejana, as the infant was called, was healthy, and as he clung to his mother, she lovingly patted his small body. Although Mandara herself was still so young, she naturally took to motherhood, even following her nightly routine of picking a favorite resting place to sleep, her hands embracing her infant.[578]

The excitement of the newborn, the pride of watching Mandara excel at motherhood, and the astonishment of Kejana's rapid development, masked the concern in the Great Ape House about Tomoka's fading stamina.

He was removed from the troop, too weak to deal with any tense social dynamics. He ate normally but continued to lose weight, and he spent most days sitting in one spot with his head in his hands. Medical tests showed some dental problems and an enlarged colon but nothing to explain his rapid weight loss and inactivity. Painkillers were removed from his various medications because of a concern with his elevated liver enzymes. But he continued to deteriorate, losing 46 pounds in one month.[579]

Nearly a year after Kejana's birth, Tomoka was struggling to live. The zoo staff decided he needed to be euthanized.[580]

Tomoka's birth as the fourth gorilla in captivity—the offspring of Nikumba and Moka—was a slight miracle that was celebrated across the globe. His life was a series of second chances and opportunities to improve compassion and care for great apes in captivity. His death, unlike his life, should be as painless as possible, his caregivers decided. They asked Mitchell Bush to put the sleep-inducing drug into Tomoka's favorite food instead of using the Cap-Chur gun. The gun was the more precise method of administering the chemicals to bring a large animal into unconsciousness, but it would have been stressful and upsetting to Tomoka. After Tomoka ate the food and entered a deep sleep, Bush injected the death-inducing medicine into his weak body.

The very last moments of Tomoka's life were peaceful and comfortable as keepers stood around him, quietly paying tribute to a gorilla that had given so much to the zoo community.[581] Even though zoo staff knew his suffering would end, they were heartbroken. They were trained not to get too attached to the animals because the animals get transferred or eventually die, but some human caregivers can't easily turn off that emotion. Tomoka was the zoo's first baby gorilla, his health see-sawed his entire life, and then just as he was becoming a father figure to young Mandara and Kuja, Gus pushed him to the lower ranks of the gorilla hierarchy. He was the zoo's underdog whose plight carried an emotional and pervasive attraction from staff and the public who pitied and supported him. Now he was gone. Even today, 25 years after Tomoka's death, some former zoo employees who knew him still have a hard time talking about his death.[582]

Only a few months after Tomoka's death, the unexpected happened—another baby gorilla was born in the Great Ape House. It was Saturday, April 11, 1992, and as the zoo was closing for the day, Haloko walked over to an off-exhibit area. According to visitors who strained to see what was happening through the doors of the Great Ape House, about 15 minutes after Haloko went out of sight, Mandara appeared holding both 11-month-old Kejana and Haloko's newborn gorilla.

When curator Lisa Stevens got to the Great Ape House that night, Mandara was nursing both the newborn and Kejana; Haloko was laying on the floor, recovering from the birth.[583] No one knows if Haloko gave the baby to Mandara or if Mandara just took the baby from Haloko. Either way, Haloko did not attempt to get her infant back, and Mandara deftly took responsibility for feeding both youngsters.[584]

The newborn, who the zoo named Baraka Ya M'Welu, was healthy and continued to get all his love and nutrition from Mandara.

A few weeks after Baraka's birth, Mandara started weaning Kejana and making him walk instead of riding on her back. He was miffed and continued his demands for attention, but Mandara was firm. Kejana sought out the only other available mother figure—Haloko.

"Whether she was planning on it or not, Kejana became her

new shadow. He constantly pursued interactions with her, and even though she rarely responded, Kejana was not deterred," wrote Shumaker in the *Gorilla Gazette*.

Slowly, Haloko started becoming more receptive to Kejana, and the mothers and the babies settled into their new roles.[585] Mandara would have five more healthy babies at the National Zoo over the next two decades,[586] earning her the nickname of "Super Mom." Haloko never had another baby, but was an attentive aunt to Mandara's other children.[587] Eventually, the National Zoo's gorillas merged into more natural family troops and bachelor groups as the younger males aged and could either breed with new females, or wait their turn. The zoo was finally building the gorilla family units that it had spent four decades trying to coordinate.

Nikumba and Moka were the origin of this blended family balance at the National Zoo even though neither of their genes carried on into a third generation. Leonard had died at a young age at the Riverside Zoo.[588] Inaki—Moka and Nikumba's only daughter—moved from the Yerkes Primate Center to Busch Gardens in Tampa, Florida, where she lived until her death in 2013.[589]

The great ape staff hoped to breed Mopie with Mandara. But again, timing and placement were not in Mopie's favor. He couldn't breed with Mandara because her successive offspring were too young to be introduced to Mopie. Opportunity passed him by as he waited his turn with Mandara.[590] He died at the National Zoo in 2006, never having had any offspring.[591]

Mopie's death was a lost opportunity to carry on Nikumba's wild caught genes, and zoo staff mourned that too. Each baby gorilla born at a zoo was greater insurance that the species could survive and build on the population of captive gorillas. Mopie did not have a chance to contribute to that.

In that sense, Nikumba and Moka's capture from the wild and

move to the zoo in Washington, D.C., served no purpose since none of their offspring had descendants. Since their bloodlines ended with their offspring, what was the point of taking them from their families in the wild and forcing them to live in a zoo?

For the keepers, veterinarians, researchers, and other zoo staff who cared for and studied them, Nikumba and Moka weren't disappointments or mistakes. Their lives at the National Zoo provided the world with critical information about caring for confined gorillas and led to improvements that set the stage for the breeding success for gorillas in zoos around the world.[592] In essence, these first-generation zoo gorillas taught zoos the right and wrong ways to raise these animals in captivity. Decades of increasing compassion and respect for captive gorillas and through science and persistence, zoos helped create the healthy population of captive gorillas living today and into the future.[593]

What zoologists later learned about captive gorilla reproduction was that male and female gorillas that grow up together from babyhood rarely copulate with each other once they reach sexual maturity.[594] This behavior is likely nature's way of avoiding inbreeding between siblings. So the odds were against Moka and Nikumba from the start, yet they stayed by each other's sides since they were young apes in Africa, grew up together at the National Zoo, and produced three healthy gorillas that were among the first baby gorillas born in captivity in North America.

Nikumba and Moka's legacies as ambassadors for their species helped zoo visitors better understand western lowland gorillas' existence in Equatorial Africa, say those who knew the gorillas.[595] Zoo staff hoped visitors would leave the Great Ape House knowing about the work being done to help the shrinking population of wild western lowland gorillas and would care enough to support efforts to save the species. By extension, they would become more interested in protecting and preserving other species as well.

The relationship between animals and zoo guests should not be undervalued. Although seeing an endangered species in a zoo does not necessarily lead visitors to engage in activism for preserving that animal, there is an incalculable amount of emotional connectivity for humans. Just as Lucile Mann was so mesmerized by watching N'Gi, the zoo's first gorilla, visitors remain in awe of the size, strength, and human resemblances of these great apes.

There's a bench and concrete steps in front of one of the glass-fronted gorilla indoor enclosures in the Great Ape House at the National Zoo inviting people to sit and watch the gorillas. When the Great Ape House opened in 1981, keeper Melanie Bond repeatedly told observers not to knock on the glass or to stare at the gorillas. Like humans, gorillas feel threatened if stared at by strangers, she told visitors.[596] Guests would sit for long periods of time watching the great apes. Young children would walk right up to the glass to get the best view. From the other side of the glass, the gorillas periodically became interested in the humans, it seemed. As a result, the apes and humans would inevitably make eye contact and a connection would be made.

In 2001, Chris Wemmer was still leading the National Zoo's Conservation and Research Center in Front Royal, Virginia. It had been 25 years since the center opened, when Wemmer's job consisted mostly of hiring staff and recommending which at-risk animals should live at the rural Virginia property. Over the past two and a half decades, the center gradually built a worldwide reputation of advancing animal research with a conservation focus.

CRC scientists, veterinarians, researchers, and fellows were specializing in molecular genetics, migratory bird research, and assistive reproduction techniques, in addition to supporting breeding and conservation priorities of the Species Survival Plans. Populations of threatened animals like the golden lion tamarin, black footed ferret, Asian elephant, desert tortoise, kit fox, and several species of endangered Hawaiian birds and cranes, benefited from research and interventions by CRC staff, who guided or contributed to animal conservation initiatives around the world. CRC staff also initiated a wildlife conservation training program for developing countries and created an environmental education curriculum for Northern Virginia school teachers.

Funding was always precarious, and while fiscal support from Congress was steady, the zoo's scientists and researchers relied more and more on grants and donations to pay for their ambitious projects—a fundraising skill many weren't trained for. The science departments at the zoo's Washington, D.C., and CRC locations reorganized several times and eventually merged to balance their priorities with the funding realities.[597] The consistent juggling was a necessity, but a distraction for Wemmer and staff in Front Royal and in Washington, D.C., who kept tackling challenging animal preservation issues, knowing that saving animal species was a mission that's not easily or ever accomplished.

Wemmer was ending a late-day staff meeting in April 2001 when he left the conference room to take a call from then–Zoo Director Lucy Spelman. When Wemmer hung up the phone, he returned to the staff meeting. "You won't believe what Lucy just said," Wemmer told those still gathered.[598]

As part of the federal government's proposed Fiscal Year 2002 budget, Smithsonian Secretary Lawrence Small suggested closing CRC to save about $2.5 million a year from maintaining the vast property.[599] Some researchers and scientists would lose their jobs; others would transfer to the zoo's Washington, D.C., property or other locations. All the animal science programs would move to the D.C. zoo.

Although Small said the Smithsonian's research efforts would become stronger with consolidation, to Wemmer, the proposal felt like an assault on the work the National Zoo's scientists did to care for and preserve wild and captive animals. To close CRC would be a devastating blow to conservation research at the National Zoo and its national and international partners. Without the space and numbers of animals in Front Royal to study, the institution's contributions to animal welfare would suffer, Wemmer worried.[600]

The lack of confidence from the Smithsonian leader for what CRC was accomplishing—the "advancement of science" that was at the core of the zoo's founding in 1889—shocked and hurt Wemmer. He could protest quietly, hoping to salvage whatever role the zoo would offer him once CRC closed, but he decided to fight his boss' boss for the organization he had spent the last 25 years building.[601]

Within a week, it wasn't only Wemmer and National Zoo staff opposing the proposal. Pleas to keep CRC open streamed in from federal and Virginia state lawmakers, national and international wildlife experts, scientists, veterinarians, environmentalists, and zoo leaders in America and around the world. The protests were so vocal and numerous that a few weeks later, Small withdrew the proposal, and the Board of Regents created a commission to study the scientific activities throughout the Smithsonian.[602]

The threat of closure and its salvation only made CRC stronger as Washington power players made commitments to support the Smithsonian's role in wildlife conservation efforts nationally and internationally. The center's name changed to the Smithsonian Conservation Biology Institute in 2010 as it assumed the role of vanguard for the Smithsonian Institution on preserving wild and captive animals and ecosystems.[603]

Today, National Zoo scientists contribute to a variety of conservation efforts and research studies about gorillas.[604] Several other zoos and conservation groups are leading the coordinated efforts to preserve the wild population.[605]

While zoos were improving breeding and management techniques of captive gorillas, the wild population kept shrinking. The status of the western gorilla species, which includes the western lowland gorillas that live at zoos and the cross river gorillas, moved from vulnerable to endangered on the International Union for Conservation of Nature's Red List of Threatened Species in 1996 because of hunting and the Ebola virus.

By 2007, the outlook grew worse and the animals were classified as critically endangered, putting its conservation status one step away from being extinct in the wild. At the time, the IUCN said wild populations of western gorillas had declined by 60 percent since the 1980s and cited hunting and disease as reasons for the losses, even in protected areas in Africa created to keep the animals safe.[606]

It was Nick Arundel who introduced the first family of gorillas to the National Zoo, allowing millions who visited the zoo in Washington, D.C., to get close to the majestic and hidden apes from Africa. He never did waver on the story that he personally captured Nikumba and Moka in Africa, though he continued to deflect questions about the details of the captures to those who asked.

In 2011, Nick Arundel died in his sleep at his Virginia farm at the age of 83. Outside his bedroom and down the hall hung a framed collage of the pictures of Nick with Nikumba and Moka taken days after he first met them in the French Congo. The frame also included pictures of the young gorillas playing in their barred cage in their first few days at the National Zoo. Outside Nick's bedroom window, overlooking his farm, was the half-acre of bamboo he had planted to feed the zoo's animals, including the pandas.[607]

An hour's drive from the Virginia farm, in the nation's capital, the zoo no longer displays giraffes—the animal that eight-year-old Nicky had persuaded it to showcase. They were displaced several years ago by a re-build of the 1937 pachyderm house to give a larger herd of elephants more indoor and outdoor space. Current zoo leaders hope to bring a giraffe family back one day in the future.[608]

Down the hill from the zoo's renovated elephant house is the Great Ape House. The same pictures of Nick, Moka, and Nikumba attached to the wall in Nick's farm house hung, until recently, on a wall in the basement of the Great Ape House where keepers cook and clean for the current gorilla groups.

Over the years, some keepers would throw the photo collage in a nearby trash bin next to the washer and dryer, saying they didn't want a reminder of the time when gorillas were stolen away from their families in the African jungle, as they believed Nick Arundel had done.

But other long-time keepers, those who remember the days of the small, steel bar cages and practices of human dominance over animals, would dig the photos out of the garbage and hang the frame back on the wall, convinced that if people like Nick Arundel didn't capture wild gorillas, there would be no gorillas to learn from, care for, and appreciate.[609] And eventually, there would be no gorillas anywhere.

Epilogue

The Countdown

A sign titled "Past Mistakes" hangs on the wall next to the glass-fronted gorilla exhibit in the National Zoo's Great Ape House in Washington, D.C. The paragraph that follows explains the former practice of removing newborn gorillas from their mothers so that humans could "safely" raise those infant apes. Human caretakers like great ape keeper Bernard Gallagher and his wife, Louise, comforted, loved, and protected the infant gorillas that they brought to their Maryland home, but the mistake was that they couldn't give the young gorillas the social skills the apes needed for finding a mate to breed with and eventually raise their own offspring.

Other signs on the wall read, "Recent Successes" and "Hope for the Future." These are the National Zoo's attempt to explain the discovery of needing to keep young gorillas with other gorillas and the collective effort by zoos to breed unrelated gorillas. It's also a promise to keep pursuing these practices to build a healthy population of critically endangered western lowland gorillas in captivity.

Anyone reading these signs can shift their eyes slightly and look through the clear, laminated glass to view the zoo's current troop of gorillas, including a 36-year-old Mandara. The "Super Mom" of the house and her offspring still residing at the zoo are the palpable examples of the evolution of change that modernized the National Zoo.

The outlook for all captive gorillas in North America is propitious. Across North America, about 350 gorillas live in 49 institutions that participate in the American Association of Zoos and Aquariums' Western Lowland Gorilla Species Survival Plan.[610] Other regions around the world coordinate similar efforts to build up and safeguard generations of captive gorillas.[611]

A leading measurement of health and sustainability for the North American group of confined western lowland gorillas is the present and future levels of genetic diversity among the animals. AZA's goal—for all species that have survival plans—is the maintenance of 90 percent genetic diversity for 100 years. The current gorilla captive population in North America far exceeds standard management goals with a nearly 99 percent genetic diversity rate.[612] Additionally, the gorilla population is projected to have 95 percent gene diversity for 150 years and 90 percent for 400 years.[613]

Sustaining that level of success will take a lot of effort, cooperation, money, and luck. Less than 100 years ago, humans began to capture gorillas from Equatorial Africa to display them in zoos, malls, and circuses. Only in the last four decades have strict rules prevented the exportation of gorillas out of Africa, forcing zoos to learn how to build stable groupings that produce many generations of offspring.

Western lowland gorillas in the wild, on the other hand, face a moribund future. Survey data show an 18.7 percent population decline for these critically endangered animals from 2005 to 2013. Poaching, even in legally-protected sites, is driving this decline. So, too, is the Ebola virus. Outbreaks of this infectious disease caused massive gorilla die-offs in the past and are feared to occur again at the same time the population struggles to rebound, according to the 2016 update to the International Union for Conservation of Nature's Red List of Threatened Species for western gorillas.[614]

At the current rate of poaching, virus, and habitat erosion, the population of western lowland gorillas could decline 80 percent or more over the next three generations—from 2005 to 2071. In other words, their population would plummet from an estimated 200,000 to 40,000.[615]

In the most recent conservation status update, IUCN added another human-caused threat not seen in previous Red List summaries for gorillas—climate change. Climate predictions say the central African tropical forests will get drier, causing changes in forest growth and elevating the risk of forest fires.[616] Even without the man-made threats of poaching and habitat loss, just surviving in their native forests and swamplands will become a daily struggle for western lowland gorillas.

The 2016 Red List update also increased the threat status of eastern gorillas to critically endangered. Now, for the first time, all four subspecies of gorillas are one step away from becoming extinct in the wild.[617]

Steven Monfort began his lifelong career at the National Zoo as a veterinarian intern in the mid-1980s, when the science behind caring for animals was blossoming. Now, he heads the Smithsonian Conservation Biology Institute in Front Royal, Virginia. He's been through all the zoo's highs and lows of the past three decades—the fickle federal funding cycles, the threatened closure of the zoo's Front Royal location, the release of several captive species back into their native habitats, and the animal protection victories brought about by global cooperation.

What has remained consistent in his time at the zoo is the burden to save species. While still holding on to an awe and gratitude of where his life's work has taken him and what he's witnessed as a leader in the conservation movement, that responsibility to save animals fills every moment of his busy life. He often gets emotional when speaking about protecting species from extinction. Whether he's in Bangladesh to help protect tigers, in Kenya to consult on animal migratory routes, or riding around the 3,000 acres in Front Royal to check on the threatened animals living at SCBI, he worries that not enough work is being done fast enough.

"Zoos will be the firewall against extinction, and like it or not, we won't be prepared," Monfort often says.[618]

Zoos also are at risk of becoming a dying breed. There is anxiety among zoo professionals that they won't be able to perpetuate the future populations of endangered animals at their zoos and an even more overwhelming responsibility to continue to try to save species in the wild—every single one of them.

Zoos also face a demanding public who want to better understand the relevancy of keeping wild animals confined. About 183 million people visit accredited zoos and aquariums each year to see cute and rare animals.[619] On their trips, zoo guests will hear and see messages about the zoo conservation practices and how animals in the wild are benefiting. Savvy zoo visitors know accredited zoos are dedicated to animal conservation practices, but will still ask probing questions about whether animal enclosures are big enough, if zoos are taking animals from the wild, if zoo animals live longer than ones in the wild, and what happens to the animal's body once it dies.[620]

Other people, however, hate seeing animals confined, especially cognitively complex animals like gorillas, elephants, and dolphins. These opponents wish zoos would be the entities that become extinct. Protestors say zoos can never replicate the natural habitat of large, exotic animals and that captivity can lead to irregular behavior such as primates that eat their own vomit, elephants that repeatedly sway back and forth, and lions and tigers that continually pace around the perimeter of their habitats.[621]

Some animal parks have listened to these challenges and are making changes. SeaWorld announced in early 2016 that it's ending its orca breeding program.[622] Ringling Bros. and Barnum & Bailey Circus stopped using elephants in shows in 2016 and will cease all performances in 2017.[623] With these two corporations agreeing to no longer showcase the animals that they built their reputations with, that were featured on their logos and were the reason many guests visited their parks and performances, some wonder what other changes the future holds for large and intelligent wild animals in captivity.

★★★

Early morning on a mild summer day is the ideal time to visit the National Zoo, although the park is open every day except Christmas. If you time it right, you'll see large, recently awakened animals shake off the sleep, devour their morning meal and go to their outside enclosure to play. Several active species will stretch, swim, and roam while keepers hose down their interior rooms.

Soon, the parking lots will fill to capacity with cars full of families who traveled from nearby neighborhoods or as far away as the west coast. Parents will examine zoo maps along the main walkway to find the locations of their child's favorite animal and the zoo's flagship species—the pandas, lions, elephants, and gorillas.

The pandas and elephants each live in recently renovated buildings that leave far more room for the animal residents than for the human guests. Interactive displays and pictures in the panda house explain how difficult a panda pregnancy and birth can be and just how miraculous it was when the National Zoo's first panda to live beyond the first few days of infancy was born in 2005.

When the panda house opened to visitors for the first time after the zoo's newest baby panda—Bei Bei—was born in 2015, guests stood in line for hours in the cold, just to get a quick glimpse of the tiny mammal who slept through most of the commotion. Six million people accessed the zoo's webcam to watch the first few months of the baby cub's life.[624]

A few years earlier, when Bei Bei's sister Bao Bao was born, her early life was also broadcast on the zoo's webcam until the day the federal government shut down because Congress couldn't agree on a budget. News outlets around the country carried stories about the public uproar over losing their panda-viewing rights, and National Zoo staff rushed to reassure everyone that the pandas and other animals would still be fed and cared for even while most of the zoo's federal employees were forced to stay home without pay.

In the upgraded elephant house, visitors can test their strength and weight compared to a typical Asian elephant. Tubes of elephant urine and poop are displayed for those curious about the massive daily output of elephants. The elephants also have a popular webcam.

The Great Ape House, built in 1981, feels antiquated compared to the panda and elephant buildings. Signs talk about "Past Mistakes" and "Hopes for the Future" and keepers and FONZ volunteers are always present to teach about the captive population or their wild cousins, but visitors can expect to learn little else from visual displays about the lives of gorillas except that they are native to Africa and are critically endangered.

A National Zoo 2008 Master Plan suggests demolishing the Great Ape House and using current surface parking lots for animal exhibits. It's an ambitious plan that still needs approval, funding, and alignment with the zoo's focus on the science behind saving species.[625]

There is no webcam for the gorillas so you'll have to visit in person. Stand in front of the glass-plated exhibit and perhaps Mandara or one of the other gorillas will slowly saunter over to the glass from the other side. If a gorilla comes closer to the glass, other visitors will move forward too, trying to get a better look at the animal's short black hair, long, muscular arms, protruding forehead, and deep set eyes. The gorilla will likely gaze at people it doesn't deem threatening—a child who is trying to get the ape's attention or an adult sitting on the concrete steps. Eventually, the two species—gorilla and human—may awkwardly look directly into each other's eyes; one species that is in confinement thousands of miles away from its native land and the other who is trying to save the animals from extinction and, at the same time, causing the wild gorillas' demise.

ENDNOTES

[1] Moka Case History, by Nick Arundel, Feb. 24, 1955, Nick Arundel personal files; also letter to Robert Yerkes from William Mann, March 22, 1955, Smithsonian Institution Archives RU326, Box 80.

[2] "Gorilla Birth at National Zoological Park Washington," Theodore H. Reed, Bernard F. Gallagher, *Der Zoologische Garten* (Germany), Oct. 21, 1961, page 279; also "Paraplegia in Male Lowland Gorilla at the National Zoological Park," C.W. Gray, *International Zoo Yearbook*, 5 (1965), pp. 186-189, Smithsonian Institution Archives, RU326, Box 30; also "International Gorilla Studbook for Gorilla, Gorilla, Gorilla," Frankfurt Zoological Garden, Dec. 31, 2010; also "Moka Case History," by Nick Arundel, Feb. 24, 1955, Nick Arundel personal files; also letter to Robert Yerkes from William Mann, March 22, 1955, Smithsonian Institution Archives RU326, Box 80.

[3] "Gorilla Squeeze," Nick Arundel notes, date unknown, likely between 2001-2009, Nick Arundel personal files.

[4] Nick Arundel, day book entries, Feb. 13-20, 1955, Nick Arundel personal files.

[5] "Paraplegia in Male Lowland Gorilla At the National Zoological Park," C.W. Gray, *International Zoo Yearbook*, 5 (1965), page 186, Smithsonian Institution Archives, RU326, Box 30.

[6] Nick Arundel, day book entries, Feb. 13-20, 1955, Nick Arundel personal files; also "Gorilla Squeeze," Nick Arundel, date unknown, likely between 2001-2009, Nick Arundel personal files.

[7] "Family Portrait," Jocelyn Arundel, *Spots and Stripes*, Friends of the National Zoo newsletter, Sept. 1964, Nick Arundel personal files.

[8] Article about Leonard the Gorilla, *Spots and Stripes*, newsletter of the Friends of the National Zoo, Jocelyn Arundel, September 1964, Nick Arundel personal files; also "Gorilla Squeeze," Nick Arundel, personal notes, date unknown, likely between 2001-2009, Nick Arundel personal files.

[9] "Gorillas for Washington Zoo," *New York Herald Tribune*, Feb. 23, 1955.

[10] "Nikumba Case History," Nick Arundel, Feb. 24, 1955; also "Moka Case History," Nick Arundel, Feb. 24, 1955, Nick Arundel personal files; also letter to Robert Yerkes from William Mann, March 22, 1955, Smithsonian Institution Archives, RU326, Box 80.

[11] "Doc Mann's Wish Is Doubly True," photo by Wellner Streets, Washington Daily News, Feb. 25, 1955, Smithsonian Institution Archives, RU365, Box 50.

[12] World Wildlife.org, http://www.worldwildlife.org/species/gorilla, accessed Nov. 30, 2016.

[13] "International Gorilla Studbook. Mainlist," Dec. 31, 2010, By Thomas Wilma, Frankfurt Zoo, 2011, pages 88 and 89.

[14] *FONZ at Fifty*, Friends of the National Zoo, 2008.

[15] National Zoological Park Historical Note, Smithsonian Institution Archives, RU74, https://siarchives.si.edu/collections/siris_arc_216681, accessed Jan. 15, 2017; also Organic Act of 1871, 41st Congress, 3rd Session, Feb. 21, 1871, Pages 419-429, Library of Congress online, http://memory.loc.gov/cgi-bin/ampage?collId=llsl&fileName=016/llsl016.

db&recNum=456, Accessed Sept. 13, 2016.

[16] History of the District of Columbia, Encyclopedia Britannica, http://www.britannica. com/EBchecked/topic/636322/Washington/282689/Manufacturing#ref1046225, accessed July 22, 2014; Also U.S. Constitution, Article 1, Section 8, Clause 17.

[17] "A Brief History of Pierre L'Enfant and Washington, D.C.," Kenneth R. Fletcher, *Smithsonian Magazine*, online version http://www.smithsonianmag.com/arts-culture/a-brief-history-of-pierre-lenfant-and-washington-dc-39487784/?no-ist, accessed Sept. 15, 2016.

[18] Mann, William, M., "Wild Animals In and Out Of the Zoo." Smithsonian Scientific Series, Volume 6, New York, 1930, page 166, Smithsonian Institution Archives, RU365, Box 36, Folder 17.

[19] "Time Line of the American Bison," U.S. Fish and Wildlife Service Website http://www. fws.gov/bisonrange/timeline.htm, accessed March 2014.

[20] Bechtel, Stefan, *Mr. Hornaday's War - How a Peculiar Victorian Zookeeper Waged A Lonely Crusade For Wildlife That Changed The World*, Chapter 5, page 36.

[21] Bechtel, Stefan, *Mr. Hornaday's War - How a Peculiar Victorian Zookeeper Waged A Lonely Crusade For Wildlife That Changed The World*, Chapter 8, page 87.

[22] Bechtel, Stefan, *Mr. Hornaday's War - How a Peculiar Victorian Zookeeper Waged A Lonely Crusade For Wildlife That Changed The World*, Chapter 13, page 135.

[23] Board of Regents Annual Report, Smithsonian Institution, 1889, page 4, Smithsonian Institution Archives.

[24] Board of Regents Annual Report, Smithsonian Institution, 1889, pp. 4, 25, Smithsonian Institution Archives; also Smithsonian Institution Archives website http://siarchives.si.edu/ collections/siris_arc_216681, accessed March 2014.

[25] "A Brief History of the Zoo," William Mann, *The Scientific Monthly*, November 1946, pp. 350-358, Smithsonian Institution Archives, RU7293, Box 12; also National Zoological Park Historical Note, Smithsonian Institution Archives, RU74, https://siarchives.si.edu/ collections/siris_arc_216681, accessed Jan. 27, 2017.

[26] HR 11810, U.S. Congress, became law March 2, 1889; also "The Smithsonian Institution Documents Relative to Its Origin and History," 50th Congress to 55th Congress, Vol. II, 1887-1889, https://books.google.com/books?id=ug9HAQAAIAAJ&pg=PA1337&lpg=PA1 337&dq=%22Congressional+Record%22+%22zoological+Park%22+1889&source=bl&ots= XyXITvCTfB&sig=53zTwyk20D6L39e0ZseUjksCZsg&hl=en&sa=X&ved=0ahUKEwijkra p94fMAhVM4yYKHQYPBf4Q6AEIHDAA#v=onepage&q=zoological&f=false. Retrieved April 11, 2016.

[27] Board of Regents Annual Report, Smithsonian Institution, 1981, page 22, Smithsonian Institution Archives; also Annual Report of the Central Park Menagerie to the Department of Public Parks, City of New York, 1890, April 8, 1891, page 3, New York City Department of Parks and Recreation online, https://www.nycgovparks.org/news/reports/archive, accessed Oct. 22, 2016.

[28] DCA Normals, Means and Extremes, National Oceanic and Atmospheric Administration, weather.gov, http://www.weather.gov/lwx/dcanme, accessed Jan. 15, 2017.

[29] "A Brief History of the Zoo," William Mann, *The Scientific Monthly*, November 1946, pp. 350-358, Smithsonian Institution Archives, RU7293, Box 12.

[30] Board of Regents Annual Report, Smithsonian Institution, 1900, page 44, Smithsonian

Institution Archives.

[31] Mann, William, M., "Wild Animals In and Out Of the Zoo." Smithsonian Scientific Series, Volume 6, New York, 1930, pp. 126-127 Smithsonian Institution Archives, RU365, Box 36, Folder 17.

[32] Mann, William, M., "Wild Animals In and Out Of the Zoo." Smithsonian Scientific Series, Volume 6, New York, 1930, pp. 74-77, Smithsonian Institution Archives, RU365, Box 36, Folder 17.

[33] Mann, William, M., "Wild Animals In and Out Of the Zoo." Smithsonian Scientific Series, Volume 6, New York, 1930, page 127, Smithsonian Institution Archives, RU365, Box 36, Folder 17.

[34] Board of Regents Annual Report, Smithsonian Institution, 1892, page 29, Smithsonian Institution Archives.

[35] Board of Regents Annual Report, Smithsonian Institution, 1891, page 22; also Board of Regents Annual Report, Smithsonian Institution, 1892, pp. 29, 45, Smithsonian Institution Archives.

[36] Board of Regents Annual Report, Smithsonian Institution, 1892, pp. 34, 70, Smithsonian Institution Archives.

[37] Board of Regents Annual Report, Smithsonian Institution, 1896, page 62, Smithsonian Institution Archives.

[38] Board of Regents Annual Report, Smithsonian Institution, 1895, pp. 68-69, Smithsonian Institution Archives.

[39] Board of Regents Annual Report, Smithsonian Institution, 1896, page 62, Smithsonian Institution Archives.

[40] Board of Regents Annual Report, Smithsonian Institution, 1892, pp. 29-39, Smithsonian Institution Archives.

[41] "A Brief History of the Zoo," William Mann, *The Scientific Monthly*, November 1946, pp. 350-358, Smithsonian Institution Archives, RU7293, Box 12.

[42] Board of Regents Annual Report, Smithsonian Institution, 1892, page 45, Smithsonian Institution Archives.

[43] Board of Regents Annual Report, Smithsonian Institution, 1894, page 69, Smithsonian Institution Archives; also Board of Regents Annual Report, Smithsonian Institution, 1896, page 22, Smithsonian Institution Archives.

[44] *FONZ at Fifty*, Friends of the National Zoo, 2008.

[45] Board of Regents Annual Report, Smithsonian Institution, 1899, pp. 57-58, Smithsonian Institution Archives.

[46] Board of Regents Annual Report, Smithsonian Institution, 1925, page 100, Smithsonian Institution Archives.

[47] Board of Regents Annual Reports, Smithsonian Institution, 1926, 1927, 1928, Smithsonian Institution Archives, 08-061.

[48] "The Wild Animals in My Life," William M. Mann, *National Geographic Magazine*, April 1957, pp. 497, 499, Smithsonian Institution Archives, RU7293, Box 14.

[49] "The Wild Animals in My Life," William M. Mann, *National Geographic Magazine*, April

1957, pp. 499, Smithsonian Institution Archives, RU7293, Box 14.

[50] Mann, William M., *Ant Hill Odyssey*, Little, Brown and Company, 1948, Chapter 2, page 35.

[51] Smithsonian Institution Oral History with Lucile Mann, Interviewed by Pamela Henson, July 20, 1977, page 168, Smithsonian Institution Archives, RU9513

[52] "The Funniest Man in the Zoo," Milton Lehman, *Saturday Evening Post*, Feb. 25, 1950, Smithsonian Institution Archives, RU7293, Box 14.

[53] Mann, William M., *Ant Hill Odyssey*, Little, Brown and Company, 1948, Chapter 5, pp. 84–106.

[54] "The Wild Animals in My Life," William M. Mann, *National Geographic Magazine*, April 1957, page 497, Smithsonian Institution Archives, RU7293, Box 14.

[55] Smithsonian Institution Oral History with Lucile Mann, Interviewed by Pamela Henson, page 54, Smithsonian Institution Archives, RU9513.

[56] *FONZ at Fifty*, Friends of the National Zoo, 2008.

[57] "The Funniest Man in the Zoo," Milton Lehman, *Saturday Evening Post*, Feb. 25, 1950, Smithsonian Institution Archives, RU7293, Box 14.

[58] "The Wild Animals in My Life," William M. Mann, *National Geographic Magazine*, April 1957, page 497, Smithsonian Institution Archives, RU7293, Box 14.

[59] Board of Regents Annual Report, Smithsonian Institution, 1937, page 69, Smithsonian Institution Archives, 08–061.

[60] Board of Regents Annual Report, Smithsonian Institution, 1901. page 43, Smithsonian Institution Archives.

[61] Board of Regents Annual Report, Smithsonian Institution, 1903, page 21, Smithsonian Institution Archives.

[62] Board of Regents Annual Report, Smithsonian Institution, 1937, pp. 69-70, Smithsonian Institution Archives, 08–061.

[63] Nicky Arundel's personal notes, November 1937.

[64] Nicky Arundel's personal notes, November 1937; also *Nicky's News* Vol. 1, No. 1.

[65] *Nicky's News*, Vol. 1, No. 1; also "Children Get Out Weekly Paper," *The Sunday Star*, March 7, 1937, DC Public Library, Washingtoniana section, Feb. 22-March 9, 1937, Reel 799.

[66] *Nicky's News*, Vol. 1, No. 1.

[67] *Nicky's News*, Vol. 1, No. 12.

[68] *Nicky's News*, Vol. 1, No. 1.

[69] "Children Get Out Weekly Paper," *The Sunday Star*, March 7, 1937, DC Public Library, Washintoniana section, Feb. 22- March 9, 1937, Reel 799.

[70] *Nicky's News*, Vol. 1, No. 4.

[71] *Nicky's News*, Vol. 2, No. 18.

[72] "Editor of *Nicky's News*, Aged 9, Bewails Zoo's Lack of Giraffes," *Washington Herald*, April 25, 1937, DC Public Library, Washingtoniana section, April 1-30, 1937, Reel 306.

[73] "The Biography of Russell Moore Arundel," Marjorie Sale Arundel, Arthur Windsor Arundel, and Jocelyn Ann Alexander, 1978.

[74] "FDR's Court-Packing Plan: A Study in Irony," Richard Menaker, History Now: The Journal of the Gilder Lehman Institute, New Deal Essays, The Gilder Lehman Institute of American History, https://www.gilderlehrman.org/history-by-era/new-deal/essays/fdr's-court-packing-plan-study-irony, accessed Sept. 21, 2016.

[75] "Editor-in-Chief, 9, Attends 'Supreme' Court Hearing," Associated Press, March 29, 1937.

[76] "Nicky 'Covers' Court Hearing," *The Washington Times* photo caption, March 30, 1937, DC Public Library, Wahsingtoniana section, Feb. 16-March 31, 1937, Reel 333).

[77] "Editor-in-Chief, 9, Attends 'Supreme' Court Hearing," Associated Press, March 29, 1937.

[78] Kara Arundel interview with Jocelyn (Arundel) Sladen, Dec. 11, 2013.

[79] Arundel, Russell M., *"Everybody's Pixillated — A Book of Doodles,"* Little, Brown and Company, 1937.

[80] Arundel, Russell M., *"Everybody's Pixillated — A Book of Doodles,"* Little, Brown and Company, 1937.

[81] "Editor of *Nicky's News*, Aged 9, Bewails Zoo's Lack of Giraffes," *Washington Herald*, April 25, 1937, DC Public Library, Washingtoniana section, April 1-30, 1937, Reel 306.

[82] "Children Get Out Weekly Paper," *The Sunday Star*, March 7, 1937, DC Public Library, Washingtoniana section, Feb. 22-March 9, 1937, Reel 799.

[83] *Nicky's News*, Vol. 1, No. 14.

[84] "Modern Noah's Ark Returns with Rare Animals for Uncle Sam's Zoo," National Geographic News Bulletin, Oct. 18, 1937, Smithsonian Institution Archives, RU7293, Box 12.

[85] "Zoo Chief Joins Nicky in Desire to Get Giraffes," *The Washington Post*, April 26, 1937, DC Public Library, Washingtoniana section, April 14-May 2, 1937, Reel 553.

[86] "Zoo Chief Joins Nicky in Desire to Get Giraffes," *The Washington Post*, April 26, 1937, DC Public Library, Washingtoniana section, April 14-May 2, 1937, Reel 553.

[87] "Around the World for Animals," William M. Mann and Lucile Q. Mann, *National Geographic Magazine*, June 1938, page 713 and photo caption page 699, Smithsonian Institution Archives, RU 007293, Box 12.

[88] Smithsonian Oral History with Lucile Mann, interviewed by Pamela Henson, July 14, 1977, page 107, Smithsonian Institution Archives, RU9513.

[89] "The Wild Animals In My Life," William M. Mann, *National Geographic Magazine*, April 1957, page 505, Smithsonian Institution Archives, RU 7293, Box 14.

[90] "Around the World for Animals," William M. Mann and Lucile Q. Mann, *National Geographic Magazine*, June 1938, page 713, Smithsonian Institution Archives RU7293, Box 12.

[91] "Around the World for Animals," William M. Mann and Lucile Q. Mann, *National Geographic Magazine*, June 1938, photo caption page 699, Smithsonian Institution Archives, RU 7293, Box 12; also William Mann notes for film presentation, 1949, Smithsonian Institution Archives, RU 7293, Box 12.

[92] "Around the World for Animals," William M. Mann and Lucile Q. Mann, *National Geographic Magazine*, June 1938, Smithsonian Institution Archives, RU 007293, Box 12.

[93] Nicky Arundel's personal notes, November 1937.

[94] Nicky Arundel's personal notes, November 1937.

[95] Smithsonian Institution Board of Regents Annual Report, 1958, page 167, Smithsonian Institution Archives, 08-061.

[96] Board of Regents Annual Report, *Smithsonian Institution*, 1958, page 167, Smithsonian Institution Archives, 08-061.

[97] "Nicky Wins Out In Crusade For Zoo Giraffes," column by Nicky Arundel, *Washington Herald*, 1937, date unknown.

[98] Nicky Arundel's personal notes, November 1937.

[99] *Nicky's News*, Vol. 2, No. 16; also *Nicky's News*, Vol. 3, No. 20.

[100] Board of Regents Annual report, *Smithsonian Institution*, 1940, p. 71 (illustration and text), Smithsonian Institution Archives, 08-061.

[101] Smithsonian Institution Board of Regents Annual Report, 1938, pp. 67-68, Smithsonian Institution Archives, 08-061.

[102] National Zoo Animal Acquisition Record, Gorilla, N'Gi, Dec. 5, 1928, Smithsonian Institution Archives, RU386, Box 3.

[103] Mann, William, M., "Wild Animals In and Out Of the Zoo." Smithsonian Scientific Series, Volume 6, New York, 1930, pp. 22-24, Smithsonian Institution Archives, RU365, Box 36, Folder 17.

[104] "Man's Closest Counterparts," William Mann, *National Geographic Magazine*, Aug. 1940, page 220, Smithsonian Institution Archives, RU365, Box 14.

[105] Mann, Lucile, Q., *From Jungle to Zoo*, Dodd, Mead & Company, 1934, page 15.

[106] Mann, Lucile, Q., *From Jungle to Zoo*, Dodd, Mead & Company, 1934, page 15.

[107] Mann, William, M., "Wild Animals In and Out Of the Zoo." Smithsonian Scientific Series, Volume 6, New York, 1930, page 25-26, Smithsonian Institution Archives, RU365, Box 36, Folder 17.; also Animal Acquisition Record, Feb. 24, 1955, Smithsonian Institution Archives, RU 386.

[108] Mann, William, M., "Wild Animals In and Out Of the Zoo." Smithsonian Scientific Series, Volume 6, New York, 1930, pp. 25-26, Smithsonian Institution Archives, RU365, Box 36, Folder 17.

[109] "History of the National Zoo," Sybil Hamlet, unpublished, 1973, page 147, Smithsonian Institution Archives, 12-086, Box 1.

[110] "Man's Closest Counterparts," William Mann, *National Geographic Magazine*, Aug. 1940, page 213, Smithsonian Institution Archives, RU365, Box 14.

[111] Letter to Julian L. Buck from William Mann, Jan. 8, 1929, Smithsonian Institution Archives, RU 74, Box 75.

[112] Lucile Mann Oral History, interview by Pamela Henson, July 20, 1977, page 208, Smithsonian Institution Archives, RU 9513.

[113] Mann, Lucile, Q., *From Jungle to Zoo*, Dodd, Mead & Company, 1934, page 15.

[114] Mann, Lucile, Q., *From Jungle to Zoo*, Dodd, Mead & Company, 1934, page 15-16.

[115] Physical Characteristics, Gorillas, SeaWorld Parks and Entertainment, https://seaworld.

org/animal-info/animal-infobooks/gorilla/physical-characteristics, accessed Jan. 15, 2017.

[116] World Wildlife Fund, Gorillas, http://www.worldwildlife.org/species/gorilla, accessed April 26, 2016; also Berggorilla & Reginald Direkthilfe e.V. http://www.berggorilla.org/en/gorillas/, accessed Sept. 18, 2016.

[117] "Iconicity and Ape Gesture," Marcus Perlman, Nathaniel Clark, and Joanne Tanner, The Evolution of Language: Proceedings of the 10th International Conference, 2014. http://www.gorillagestures.info/D_PUBS.htm

[118] Mann, William, M., "Wild Animals In and Out Of the Zoo." Smithsonian Scientific Series, Volume 6, New York, 1930, pp. 26-28 Smithsonian Institution Archives, RU365, Box 36, Folder 17.

[119] William M. Mann letter to Walter Chrysler, Dec. 7, 1928, Smithsonian Institution Archives, RU 74, Box 75.

[120] Mann, William, M., "Wild Animals In and Out Of the Zoo." Smithsonian Scientific Series, Volume 6, New York, 1930, page 21, Smithsonian Institution Archives, RU365, Box 36, Folder 17.

[121] Western Lowland Gorilla (gorilla gorilla gorilla) 2013 North American Regional Studbook, Roby Elsner, Knoxville Zoo, July 31, 2013.

[122] Martin and Osa Johnson Safari Museum, Chanute, Kansas. http://www.safarimuseum.com/research/imagevue-galleries-2/africa-1929-1931/

[123] Johnson, Martin, *Congorilla: Adventures With Pygmies and Gorillas In Africa.* Brewer, Warren & Putnam, 1931, pp. 204, 229.

[124] Board of Regents Annual Report, Smithsonian Institution, 1932, page 51, Smithsonian Institution Archives, 08-061; also National Zoo Animal Acquisition Record, Sept. 17, 1931, Smithsonian Institution Archives, RU386, Box 3.

[125] National Zoo Animal Acquisition Record, Sept. 17, 1931, Smithsonian Institution Archives, RU386, Box 3.

[126] "History of the National Zoo," Sybil Hamlett, unpublished 1973, page 162, Smithsonian Institution Archives, 12-086, Box 1.

[127] "Man's Closest Counterparts," William Mann, *National Geographic Magazine*, Aug. 1940, page 229, Smithsonian Institution Archives, RU365, Box 14.

[128] Board of Regents Annual Report, Smithsonian Institution, 1932, pp 56-57, Smithsonian Institution Archives, 08-061; also National Zoo Animal Acquisition Records, RU 386, Box 3.

[129] "Animals: The End of N'Gi," Time Magazine, March 21, 1932, http://content.time.com/time/magazine/article/0,9171,743400,00.html, accessed Jan. 12, 2017.

[130] "History of the National Zoo," Sybil Hamlett, unpublished, 1973, page 162 Smithsonian Institution Archives, 12-086, Box 1.

[131] "Around the World for Animals," William M. Mann and Lucile Q. Mann, *National Geographic Magazine*, June 1938, Smithsonian Institution Archives, RU 7293, Box 12.

[132] Annual Report to the Board of Regents, Smithsonian Institution, 1941, Smithsonian Institution Archives, 08-061.

[133] Smithsonian Institution Archives, online Zoo History Summary, Smithsonian Institution Archives, RU 74, http://siarchives.si.edu/collections/siris_arc_216681, Accessed

Aug. 23, 2016.

[134] Convention Relative to the Preservation of Fauna and Flora in Their Natural State (1933). International Environmental Agreements Database Project, University of Oregon, http://iea.uoregon.edu/treaty-text/1933-preservationfaunafloranaturalstateentxt, accessed Jan. 15, 2017.

[135] International Studbook for the Western Lowland Gorilla, Zoo Frankfurt, 2010, page 87.

[136] Letter to Ministre de la France d'Outre-Mer from Alexander Wetmore, July 3, 1947, Smithsonian Institution Archives, RU 74, Box 175.

[137] Letter to William Mann from Louis van den Berghe, March 8, 1948, Smithsonian Institution Archives, RU 74, Box 164.

[138] Letter to William Mann from Louis van den Berghe, March 8, 1948, Smithsonian Institution Archives, RU 74, Box 164.

[139] Letter to William Mann from Louis van den Berghe, Jan. 26, 1949 Smithsonian Institution Archives, RU 74, Box 164.

[140] Letter to A. Urbain from William Mann, June 2, 1952, Smithsonian Institution Archives, RU 74, Box 175.

[141] Letter to Lucien Blancou from Harold J. Coolidge, June 11, 1952 Smithsonian Institution Archives, RU 74, Box 175.

[142] "Wanted – One Giant Gorilla" by Harold J. Coolidge Jr. Sportsman 4, No. 5, 1928; also Annual Report of the Director of the Museum of Comparative Zoology at Harvard College, 1927-28, page 7, Biodiversity Heritage Library.

[143] Coolidge Jr, Harold Jefferson, "A Revision of the Genus Gorilla," Memoirs of the Museum of Comparative Zoology at Harvard College, Aug. 1929, page 375, Museum of Comparative Zoology, Harvard University, Biodiversity Heritage Library.

[144] Coolidge Jr, Harold Jefferson, "A Revision of the Genus Gorilla," Memoirs of the Museum of Comparative Zoology at Harvard College, Aug. 1929, pp. 295-303, Museum of Comparative Zoology, Harvard University, Biodiversity Heritage Library.

[145] Coolidge Jr, Harold Jefferson, "A Revision of the Genus Gorilla," Memoirs of the Museum of Comparative Zoology at Harvard College, Aug. 1929, page 375, Museum of Comparative Zoology, Harvard University, Biodiversity Heritage Library.

[146] Gorilla Species Survival Plan, About Gorillas, Gorilla SSP Website, http://www.gorillassp.org/aboutGorillas.html

[147] International Gorilla Conservation Programme, Frequently Asked Questions, http://igcp.org/gorillas/faq/, accessed Jan. 14, 2017.

[148] "Life Goes on a Gorilla Hunt," Life Magazine, Nov. 19, 1951, pp. 175-180, online at https://books.google.com/books?id=hVQEAAAAMBAJ&q=Bill+Said#v=snippet&q=Bill%20Said&f=false, accessed Oct. 27, 2016.

[149] Letter to William Mann from John L. Biname, Dec. 12, 1952, Smithsonian Institution Archives, Box 157.

[150] Letter to William Mann from John L. Biname, March 17, 1953, Smithsonian Institution Archives, RU 74, Box 157.

[151] Letter to William Mann from John L. Biname, March 17, 1953, Smithsonian Institution Archives, RU 74, Box 157.

[152] Letter to John L. Biname to William Mann, June 4, 1953, Smithsonian Institution Archives, RU 74, Box 157.

[153] Memo to American Embassy in Madrid from W.M. Randolph for the U.S. Department of State, October 15, 1953, Smithsonian Institution Archives, RU 74, Box 157.

[154] Memo to U.S. Department of State from the Amercian Embassy in Madrid, R.R. Rubottom, Jr, commercial attache. Oct. 26, 1953, Smithsonian Institution Archives, RU 74, Box 157.

[155] Memo to U.S. Department of State from American Embassy in Madrid, R.R. Rubottom, Jr., commercial attache, Dec. 1, 1953 Smithsonian Institution Archives, RU 74, Box 157.

[156] Theodore Reed Oral History, interview by Pamela Henson, Sept. 14, 1989, page 35, Smithsonian Institution Archives, RU 9568.

[157] Kara Arundel interview with Bill Xanten, April 29, 2014.

[158] Arundel, Marjorie, *England To America: A Family History*, self-published, 2001.

[159] Harold Jefferson Coolidge, Jr. (1904-1985), By Lee Talbot and Martha Talbot, https://cmsdata.iucn.org/downloads/h_j_coolidge_biography.pdf

[160] *Harold Jefferson Coolidge Jr. is Thomas Jefferson's great-great-great-grandson on his mother's side.* "Genealogical and Personal Memoirs Relating to the Families of the State of Massachusetts," Vol. 4, William Richard Cutter and William Fredrick Adams, 1910; also New World Encyclopedia International Union for the Conservation of Nature. http://www.newworldencyclopedia.org/entry/International_Union_for_Conservation_of_Nature

[161] Hornaday, William T., "Eight Fascinating Years," an unpublished autobiography, page 33. Library of Congress. William T. Hornaday Papers, Addition II, Box 112.

[162] "The First Five Years," By John C. Phillips and Harold J. Coolidge, Jr., American Committee for International Wildlife Protection, Dec. 1934, page 5 and 9, https://babel.hathitrust.org/cgi/pt?id=mdp.39015079999960;view=1up;seq=1, accessed June 5, 2016.

[163] "The First Five Years," By John C. Phillips and Harold J. Coolidge, Jr., American Committee for International Wildlife Protection, Dec. 1934,https://babel.hathitrust.org/cgi/pt?id=mdp.39015079999960;view=1up;seq=1, Accessed June 5, 2016.

[164] Kara Arundel interview with Lee Talbot, Jan. 13, 2014 and Feb. 24, 2015.

[165] PepCom Company booklet, 1982, Nick Arundel personal files.

[166] "The Biography of Russell Moore Arundel," Marjorie Sale Arundel, Arthur Windsor Arundel, and Jocelyn Ann Alexander, 1978.

[167] Nick Arundel personal diary Jan. 17, 1955.

[168] International Gorilla Studbook for Gorilla Gorilla Gorilla, Dec. 31, 2010; also letter to M. P. Bourgeon from William Mann, Dec. 17, 1954, Smithsonian Institution Archives, RU326, Box 80.

[169] Letter to William Mann from R. Bourgeon, the Inspector-General of Game and of the Protection of the Fauna of the Ministry of France Overseas, Dec. 9, 1954, translation, Smithsonian Institution Archives, RU 326, Box 80.

[170] Letter to John Biname from William Mann, Dec. 28, 1954, Smithsonian Institution Archives, RU 74, Box 157.

[171] Letter to William Mann from Russell Arundel, Jan. 19, 1955, Smithsonian Institution

Archives, RU 326 Box 80.

172 Wilson, H.S., "African Decolonization," Edward Arnold, A member of the Hodder Headline Group, 1994.

173 Kara Arundel interview with Lee Talbot, Feb. 24, 2015.

174 Nick Arundel personal notes, Jan. 21 – Feb. 25th, 1955; also Arundel, Marjorie Sale, "*England to America: A Family History*," self published, 2001.

175 Nick Arundel interview with Cecil Currey, April 2, 2001, Nick Arundel personal files.

176 Kara Arundel interview with SSM member Rufus Phillips, Feb. 27, 2015 and Nov. 11, 2016.

177 Kara Arundel interview with Rufus Phillips, Nov. 11, 2016.

178 Kara Arundel interview with Rufus Phillips, Feb. 27, 2015 and Nov. 11, 2016.

179 Commonplace notes to my family about the Vietnam Operation, Nick Arundel, March 4, 2010, Nick Arundel personal files.

180 Kara Arundel interview with Rufus Phillips, Nov. 4, 2016.

181 Commonplace notes to my family about the Vietnam Operation, Nick Arundel, March 4, 2010, Nick Arundel personal files.

182 Memo from Edward Lansdale to Secretary Robert McNamara, "A Cold War Win," Aug. 1, 1961. Declassified in part May 19, 2014, Page 11, declassified in part May 2014.

183 *Nick Arundel's name and some of his activities with the Saigon Military Mission were disclosed through the release of the Pentagon Papers in 1971. A more detailed account of the month-to-month operations of the first year of the CIA Saigon Military Mission was declassified in part in May of 2014*; also Commonplace notes to my family about the Vietnam Operation, Nick Arundel, March 4, 2010, Nick Arundel personal notes; also Neil Sheehan and the *New York Times*. *The Pentagon Papers*. Bantam Books, 1971, Chapter 1, pp. 57-62; also Memo from Edward Lansdale to Secretary Robert McNamara, "A Cold War Win," Aug. 1, 1961. Declassified in part May 19, 2014; also Kara Arundel interview with Rufus Phillips, Nov. 4, 2016.

184 "Cheers for Outer Baldonia! No Wedding or Farm Woes," The Dallas Morning News, April 17, 1956, page 1.

185 "Our Town" column, *The Washington Daily News*, April 24, 1952, DC Public Library, Washingtoniana section, April 1-30, 1952, Reel 192.

186 "A Short History of an Island Nation," Vernon Doucette, *Atlantic Coastal Kayaker*, December 1994.

187 "Grand Deception…9, Outer Baldonia vs. Soviet Russia," William Bancroft Mellor, *The Washington Daily News*, April 11, 1956, DC Library, Washingtoniana section, April 1-30, 1956, Reel 241.

188 "The State of Baldonia," L. Chernaya, *Literaturnaya Gazeta*, Oct. 25, 1952. Translation by Canadian Embassy (Washington, D.C.).

189 "Mirth of a Nation," Vernon Pizer, *Esquire*, January 1954, page 82.

190 "'Come to My Isle of Hush Up,' State Man Tells Soviet Lady," *Wilmington Sunday Star*, Dec. 13, 1953, page 1.

191 "Bird Kingdom: Arundel to Deed 'Outer Baldonia' as sanctuary," Sudbury (Ontario) Star, 1973.

[192] Nick Arundel personal notes, Jan. 21 - Feb. 12, 1955, Nick Arundel personal files.

[193] Nick Arundel personal notes, Feb. 13-14, 1955, Nick Arundel personal files.

[194] Nick Arundel personal notes, Feb. 15, 1955, Nick Arundel personal files; also "Two Rare Gorillas In Zoo Spotlight; Dr. Mann Proud of His New 'Babies,'" Harry Bacas, The *Washington Star*, Feb. 27, 1955, DC Public Library, Washingtoniana section, Feb. 16-28, 1955, Reel 1320.

[195] Nick Arundel personal notes, Feb, 16, 1955, Nick Arundel personal files.

[196] Nick Arundel personal notes, Feb. 16-20, 1955, Nick Arundel personal files.

[197] Nick Arundel personal notes, Feb. 24, 1955, Nick Arundel personal files.

[198] "Gorillas for Washington Zoo," New York Herald Tribune, Feb. 25, 1955, page 1.

[199] "Two Baby Gorillas Make Bows at Zoo," *The Washington Post* and Times Herald, Feb. 25, 1955, Smithsonian Institution Archives, RU365, Box 50.

[200] "Zoo Arrivals" photo caption, The *Washington Star*, Feb. 25, 1955, Smithsonian Institution Archives, RU365, Box 50.

[201] "'Be Safe on Safari' is Africa's New Slogan," Washington Daily News, Feb. 26, 1955, DC Public Library, Washingtoniana section, NP2019, Reel 227.

[202] Smithsonian Institution Board of Regents Annual Report, 1955, page 106, Smithsonian Institution Archives, 08-061.

[203] "'Little Lost Lambs' Getting New Haven at the Zoo," Mary V. R. Thayer, *The Washington Post* and Time Herald, June 26, 1955, DC Public Library, Washingtoniana section, Reel 943; also Nick Arundel personal notes, Jan. 21 to Feb. 20, 1955, Nick Arundel personal files.

[204] Interviews with about a dozen relatives and friends of Nick Arundel; also "Gorilla Squeeze" notes by Nick Arundel, Dec. 14 2010, Nick Arundel personal files.

[205] Kara Arundel conversation with Nick Arundel, 2001 or 2002.

[206] "Gorilla Birth at the National Zoological Park," Theodore Reed and Bernard Gallagher, *Der Zoologische Garten*, Oct. 21, 1961, page 280-281, Smithsonian Institution Archives, RU 326, Box 81.

[207] "Gorilla Birth at the National Zoological Park," Theodore Reed and Bernard Gallagher, *Der Zoologische Garten*, Oct. 21, 1961, page 279, Smithsonian Institution Archives, RU 326, Box 8; also memo to William Mann from Nick Arundel, Dec. 26, 1955, Smithsonian Institution Archives, RU 326, Box 80.

[208] Memo to William Mann from Nick Arundel, Dec. 26, 1955, Smithsonian Institution Archives, RU 326, Box 80.

[209] National Zoological Park Summary, Smithsonian Institution Archives, RU74, online summary, http://siarchives.si.edu/history/national-zoological-park, accessed Oct. 6, 2016.

[210] United State Department of Agriculture, Forest Service, "History of Smokey Bear," USDA Website, http://www.fs.usda.gov/detail/r3/learning/history-culture/?cid=FSBDEV3_021636;

also Smithsonian Program and Activities Annual Report, 1977, page 60, Smithsonian Institution Archives, 08-061.

[211] National Zoological Park Summary, Smithsonian Institution Archives, RU74, online at

http://siarchives.si.edu/collections/siris_arc_216681, accessed Aug. 24, 2016; also Theodore Reed Oral History, interview by Pamela Henson, April 14, 1989, pp. 75-77, Smithsonian Institution Archives, RU9568; also "Treatment of Captive Animals Using an Automatic Projectile Type Syringe," James F. Wright, Veterinary Medicine, Vol. 54, Jan. 1959, pp. 32, 33, Smithsonian Institution Archives, RU74, Box 255, Folder 11.

[212] "A Zoo For All Seasons: The Smithsonian Animal World," Smithsonian Exposition Books, 1979, page 84, Smithsonian Institution Archives, RU 365, Box 36.

[213] Board of Regents Annual Report, Smithsonian Institution, 1958, page 170-171, Smithsonian Institution Archives, 08-061.

[214] Board of Regents Annual Report, Smithsonian Institute, 1956, page 132, Smithsonian Institution Archives, 08-061.

[215] Theodore Reed Oral History, interview by Pamela Henson, April 11, 1989, page 13, Smithsonian Institution Archives, RU9568.

[216] Comments by Mark Reed at National Zoo Symposium, May 21, 2014; also, Theodore Reed Oral History, interview by Pamela Henson, April 11, 1989, page 39, Smithsonian Institution Archives, RU 9568.

[217] Board of Regents Annual Report, Smithsonian Institution, 1956, page 134. Smithsonian Institution Archives, 08-061.

[218] Board of Regents Annual Report, Smithsonian Institution, 1956, page 160, Smithsonian Institution Archives, 08-061.

[219] Memo to Theodore Reed from William Mann, Dec. 15, 1955, Smithsonian Institution Archives, RU 74, Box 196.

[220] Theodore Reed's Oral History video transcript, interview by Pamela Henson, Sept. 25, 1990, page 3, Smithsonian Institution Archives, RU 9568.

[221] "Helping to Build the Ark; A History of the Friends of the National Zoo, 1958-1983, Montgomery Bradley, edited by Sally Tongren, page 1, Friends of the National Zoo; also Theodore Reed Oral History, interview by Pamela Henson, April 13, 1989, page 68, Smithsonian Institution Archives, RU 9568.

[222] Theodore Reed's Oral History video transcript, interview by Pamela Henson, Sept. 25, 1990, page 8, Smithsonian Institution Archives, RU9553.

[223] Kara Arundel interview with Bill Xanten, April 29, 2014 and March 31, 2016.

[224] Theodore Reed's video interview transcript with Pamela Henson, Sept. 25, 1990, page 3, Smithsonian Institution Archives RU9553; also "Helping to Build the Ark; A History of the Friends of the National Zoo, 1958-1983, By Montgomery Bradley, edited by Sally Tongren, page 1 and 2, Friends of the National Zoo.

[225] "Helping to Build the Ark; A History of the Friends of the National Zoo, 1958-1983, By Montgomery Bradley, edited by Sally Tongren, page 2, Friends of the National Zoo.

[226] "The Crisis At Our National Zoo," Friends of the National Zoo, 1960, Smithsonian Institution Archives, RU 365, Box 12; also Annual Report of the Board of Regents, Smithsonian Institution, 1956, page 160, Smithsonian Institution Archives, 08-061.

[227] "Helping to Build the Ark; A History of the Friends of the National Zoo, 1958-1983, By Montgomery Bradley, edited by Sally Tongren, page 1, Friends of the National Zoo.

[228] "Helping to Build the Ark; A History of the Friends of the National Zoo, 1958-1983,

By Montgomery Bradley, edited by Sally Tongren., page 2, Friends of the National Zoo; also, Theodore Reed Oral History, interview by Pamela Henson, April 12, 1989, page 61, Smithsonian Institution Archives, RU9568.

[229] "Helping to Build the Ark; A History of the Friends of the National Zoo, 1958-1983, By Montgomery Bradley, edited by Sally Tongren, page 3, Friends of the National Zoo.

[230] "Helping to Build the Ark; A History of the Friends of the National Zoo, 1958-1983, By Montgomery Bradley, edited by Sally Tongren, page 3, Friends of the National Zoo.

[231] *FONZ at Fifty*: Friends of the National Zoo, 2008, page 8., Friends of the National Zoo.

[232] Julie Ann's name is spelled as Julia Ann in several news articles "Child Mauled to Death By Lion in District Zoo, *The Evening Star*, May 17, 1958, Smithsonian Institution Archives, RU74, Box 212; also, Harry Jackson's deposition Oct. 1, 1959, Smithsonian Institution Archives, RU 365, Box 20.

[233] Theodore Reed Oral History, interview by Pamela Henson, April 13, 1989, page 66, Smithsonian Institution Archives RU 9568.

[234] "Child Mauled to Death By Lion in District Zoo," *The Evening Star*, May 17, 1958, Smithsonian Institution Archives, RU74, Box 212.

[235] "Tragic Death Spurs Plea for Overhaul," Jerry O'Leary, Jr., Sunday Star, June 1, 1958, Smithsonian Institution Archives, RU74, Box 212.

[236] "Four Zoo Houses Closed to Visitors," Jerry O'Leary, Jr., *The Evening Star*, September 29, 1958, Smithsonian Institution Archives, RU74, Box 212; also "Tragic Death Spurs Plea for Overhaul," Jerry O'Leary, Jr., Sunday Star, June 1, 1958, Smithsonian Institution Archives, RU74, Box 212.

[237] "Safety Survey Begun at Zoo," *The Washington Post*, May 18, 1958; also "Zoo Lion Which Killed Child Expected To Be Spared," *The Washington Daily News*, May, 17, 1958, DC Public Library, Washingtoniana section, May 1-31, 1958, Reel 266.

[238] Theodore Reed Oral History, interview by Pamela Henson, April 13, 1989, page 70, Smithsonian Institution Archives, RU 9568.

[239] Annual Report of the Board of Regents, Smithsonian Institution, 1958, page 178, Smithsonian Institution Archives, 08-061.

[240] Theodore Reed Oral History, interview by Pamela Henson, April 13, 1989, page 71, Smithsonian Institution Archives, RU 9568; also "Julia Ann Vogt" summary of events, Smithsonian Institution Archives, RU365, Box 20.

[241] Theodore Reed Oral History, interview by Pamela Henson, April 13, 1989, page 71, Smithsonian Institution Archives, RU 9568.

[242] Annual Report of the Board of Regents, Smithsonian Institution, 1959, page 179, Smithsonian Institution Archives, 08-061.

[243] National Zoological Park Environmental Description, 1972, pp. 12-13, Smithsonian Institution Archives, 12-086, Box 12.

[244] "The Crisis At Our National Zoo," Friends of the National Zoo, 1960, Smithsonian Institution Archives, RU 365, Box 12.

[245] Theodore Reed Oral History, interview by Pamela Henson, Sept. 25, 1990, page 2, Smithsonian Institution Archives, RU 9568; Similar wording also in Theodore Reed Oral History, interview with Pamela Henson, April 12, 1989, page 62, Smithsonian Institution

Archives, RU 9568.

[246] Theodore Reed letter to Remington Kellogg, "Admission Fees for the National Zoological Park," Dec. 9, 1959, Smithsonian Institution Archives, RU 326, Box 66.

[247] "Helping to Build the Ark; A History of the Friends of the National Zoo, 1958-1983, By Montgomery Bradley, edited by Sally Tongren, page 7, Friends of the National Zoo.

[248] "Helping to Build the Ark; A History of the Friends of the National Zoo, 1958-1983, By Montgomery Bradley, edited by Sally Tongren, page 7, Friends of the National Zoo.

[249] Summary of National Zoological Park, 1887-1966, Smithsonian Institution Archives, http://siarchives.si.edu/collections/siris_arc_216681

[250] "Helping to Build the Ark; A History of the Friends of the National Zoo, 1958-1983, By Montgomery Bradley, edited by Sally Tongren, page 7, Friends of the National Zoo; also, National Zoological Park Annual Report, Smithsonian Institution, 1970, page 1, Smithsonian Institution Archives, 08-061.

[251] "Helping to Build the Ark; A History of the Friends of the National Zoo, 1958-1983, By Montgomery Bradley, edited by Sally Tongren, page 8, Friends of the National Zoo.

[252] S. 3230, approved by Senate and House of Representatives, Nov. 6, 1966, http://uscode. house.gov/statutes/pl/89/770.pdf. Accessed June 7, 2016.

[253] "Helping to Build the Ark; A History of the Friends of the National Zoo, 1958-1983, By Montgomery Bradley, edited by Sally Tongren, page 13, Friends of the National Zoo.

[254] "Helping to Build the Ark; A History of the Friends of the National Zoo, 1958-1983, By Montgomery Bradley, edited by Sally Tongren, page 8-14, Friends of the National Zoo.

[255] "Helping to Build the Ark; A History of the Friends of the National Zoo, 1958-1983, By Montgomery Bradley, edited by Sally Tongren, page 15, Friends of the National Zoo.

[256] Friends of the National Zoo Annual Report, The *Zoogoer*, Volume 5, No. 6,1976-77, Nick Arundel personal files; Also, FONZ Annual Board Meeting, speech by Nick Arundel, Oct. 27, 1976, Nick Arundel personal files.

[257] Kara Arundel interview with Mark Reed, June 8, 2016; Also Kara Arundel interview with Bill Xanten, June 10, 2016; Also Theodore Reed Oral History, interview by Pamela Henson, August 24,1989, page 8, Smithsonian Institution Archives, RU9568.

[258] Theodore Reed Oral History, interview by Pamela Henson, Aug. 24, 1989, page 8, Smithsonian Institution Archives, RU9568.

[259] "When Panda-Monium" Swept America," By Christopher Klein, History.com, Jan. 9, 2014, http://www.history.com/news/when-panda-monium-swept-america. Accessed June 7, 2016.

[260] From a variety of NZP and FONZ documents including, *FONZ at Fifty*: Friends of the National Zoo, 2008, page 15, Friends of the National Zoo; also FONZ Annual Report, The *Zoogoer*, Vol. 5, No. 6, 1976-77.

[261] "Helping to Build the Ark; A History of the Friends of the National Zoo, 1958-1983, By Montgomery Bradley, edited by Sally Tongren, page 17, Friends of the National Zoo.

[262] Nick Arundel letter to Carolyn Jarvis, Zoological Society of London, Oct. 11, 1965, Nick Arundel personal files; Also Arundel letter to Chief, China Desk, U.S. Department of State, Nov. 4, 1966, Nick Arundel personal files.

[263] Treasury Department License No. B-81178, May 8, 1967, Nick Arundel personal files.

[264] Nick Arundel letter to Albert Edgar Ritchie, Ambassador of Canada, July 21, 1971, Nick Arundel personal files; also Arundel letter to Embassy of the People's Republic of China (Canada), Aug. 16, 1971, Nick Arundel personal files.

[265] Nick Arundel personal notes, Panda Project, April 20, 1967.

[266] "When Panda-Monium" Swept America," By Christopher Klein, History.com, Jan. 9, 2014, http://www.history.com/news/when-panda-monium-swept-america; also, "Ailing Musk Oxen No Trade for Pandas," North American News Alliance, published by the Sarasota Journal, May 10, 1972, page 6.

[267] FONZ Annual Board Meeting, speech by Nick Arundel, Oct. 27, 1976, Nick Arundel personal file; also, "Helping to Build the Ark; A History of the Friends of the National Zoo, 1958-1983, By Montgomery Bradley, edited by Sally Tongren, page 19, Friends of the National Zoo.

[268] *FONZ at Fifty*, Friends of the National Zoo, 2008, page 15-16, Friends of the National Zoo.

[269] Memorandum for FONZ Board of Directors from Nick Arundel, May 18, 1976, Nick Arundel personal files; also "Working Understanding Between The Friends of the National Zoo and the National Zoological Park," June 1976, Nick Arundel personal files.

[270] "Gorilla Birth at the National Zoological Park," Theodore Reed and Bernard Gallagher, *Der Zoologische Garten*, Oct. 21, 1961, page 280-281, Smithsonian Institution Archives, RU 326, Box 81.

[271] Board of Regents Annual Report, Smithsonian Institution, 1956, page 136, Smithsonian Institution Archives, 08-061.

[272] "Forced Into Luxurious Home, Couple Rebels," Jerry O'Leary, Jr., *The Evening Star*, March 22, 1961, DC Public Lirary, Washingtoniana section, March 16-31, 1961, Reel 1466.

[273] *The Zoological Society of Philadelphia created a diet for certain captive wild animals called Philadelphia Diet A.* Adequate Diets for Captive Wild Animals, Penrose Research Laboratory Bulletin, Oct. 1956, Smithsonian Institution Archives, RU365, Box 12.

[274] "Gorilla Birth at the National Zoological Park," Theodore Reed and Bernard Gallagher, *Der Zoologische Garten*, Oct. 21, 1961, page 280-282, Smithsonian Institution Archives, RU 326, Box 81.

[275] "Gorilla Birth at the National Zoological Park," Theodore Reed and Bernard Gallagher, *Der Zoologische Garten*, Oct. 21, 1961, page 282, Smithsonian Institution Archives, RU 326, Box 81; also "Baby Gorilla in New Home," *The Sunday Star*, Jerry O'Leary, Jr., Sept. 10, 1961, DC Public Library, Washingtoniana section, Sept. 1-15, 1961, Reel 1477; also "Zoo's Youngest Star Is A Sleepyhead," *The Washington Post*, Sept. 10, 1961, DC Public Library, Washingtoniana section, Sept. 1-15, 1961, Reel 1477.

[276] "To Zoo's Apes, 'Mother' Means Louise Gallagher," Mary M. Krug, The Smithsonian Torch, June 1969, page 2, Smithsonian Institution Archives, RU 371, Box 1; also Smithsonian Institution Archives, http://siarchives.si.edu/sites/default/files/pdfs/torch/Torch%201969/SIA_000371_1969_06.pdf

[277] "Gorilla Birth at the National Zoological Park," Theodore Reed and Bernard Gallagher, *Der Zoologische Garten*, Oct. 21, 1961, page 282-283, Smithsonian Institution Archives, RU 326, Box 81; also, "Baby Gorilla in New Home," *The Sunday Star*, Jerry O'Leary, Jr., Sept. 10, 1961, DC Public Library, Washingtoniana section, Sept. 1-15, 1961, Reel 1477.

[278] Leonard Carmichael 1898-1973, Smithsonian Institution Archives, http://siarchives.

si.edu/history/leonard-carmichael

[279] "Gorilla Birth at the National Zoological Park," Theodore Reed and Bernard Gallagher, *Der Zoologische Garten*, Oct. 21, 1961, page 283, Smithsonian Institution Archives, RU 326, Box 81.

[280] "5-lb. Gorilla Born at Zoo, 4th Such Birth in Captivity," Jerry O'Leary, Jr., *The Evening Star*, Sept. 9, 1961, DC Public Library, Washingtoniana section, Sept. 1-15, 1961, Reel 1477.

[281] "Baby Gorilla in New Home," *The Sunday Star*, Jerry O'Leary, Jr., Sept. 10, 1961, DC Public Library, Washingtoniana section, Sept. 1-15, 1961, Reel 1477.

[282] "Baby Gorilla in New Home," *The Sunday Star*, Jerry O'Leary, Jr., Sept. 10, 1961, DC Public Library, Washingtoniana section, Sept. 1-15, 1961, Reel 1477; also "5-lb. Gorilla Born at Zoo, 4th Such Birth in Captivity," Jerry O'Leary, Jr., *The Evening Star*, Sept. 9, 1961, DC Public Library, Washingtoniana section, Sept. 1-15, 1961, Reel 1477.

[283] "Zoo's Youngest Star Is a Sleepyhead," *The Washington Post*, Sept. 10, 1961, DC Public Library, Washingtoniana section, Sept. 1-15, 1961, Reel 1092.

[284] "Gorilla Birth at the National Zoological Park," Theodore Reed and Bernard Gallagher, *Der Zoologische Garten*, Oct. 21, 1961, page 283, Smithsonian Institution Archives, RU 326, Box 81.

[285] Board of Regents Annual Report, Smithsonian Institution, 1962, page 132, Smithsonian Institution Archives, 08-061.

[286] Encyclopedia of Journalism, Christopher H. Sterling, 2012, page 910, https://books.google.com/books?id=pLV1AwAAQBAJ&pg=PA910&lpg=PA910&dq=WAVA+all+news+radio+arundel&source=bl&ots=j66zd458Vf&sig=g7KnacJuJNpHPY94CQ1BJWhV-qM&hl=en&sa=X&ved=0CCoQ6AEwATgKahUKEwi_oczd_MTIAhXBGj4KHc5ZChM#v=onepage&q=WAVA%20all%20news%20radio%20arundel&f=false; Also "All-News Radio," Wikipedia, https://en.wikipedia.org/wiki/All-news_radio. Also, Life Chronology of Arthur W. (Nick) Arundel, Dec. 2, 2003.

[287] "Zoo's New Gorilla Is Yclept Tomoka," *The Washington Post, Times Herald*, Oct. 11, 1961, DC Public Library, Washingtoniana section, Oct. 1-15, 1961, Reel 1094; also, list of gorilla names, Nick Arundel personal files; also letter to Charlene Riggs from Nick Arundel, Oct. 12, 1961, Smithsonian Institution Archives, RU 326, Box 81.

[288] "To Zoo's Apes, 'Mother' Means Louise Gallagher," Mary M. Krug, The Smithsonian Torch, June 1969, page 2, Smithsonian Institution Archives, RU 371, Box 1.

[289] "The First Gorilla Ever Born in Captivity," Life Magazine, Jan. 14, 1957, pp. 57-58, online at https://books.google.com/books?id=P1QEAAAAMBAJ&q=gorilla#v=snippet&q=gorilla&f=false, accessed Oct. 27, 2016.

[290] "The First Gorilla Ever Born in Captivity," Life Magazine, Jan. 14, 1957, pp. 57-58, online at https://books.google.com/books?id=P1QEAAAAMBAJ&q=gorilla#v=snippet&q=gorilla&f=false, accessed Oct. 27, 2016; also "Colo's Life," Columbus Zoo Media, video uploaded May 28, 2009, https://www.youtube.com/watch?v=H_L4l7FLd6I, accessed Jan. 18, 2017.

[291] Colo's Birthday, Columbus Zoo and Aquarium, https://www.columbuszoo.org/colo/, accessed Jan. 18, 2017; also "Columbus Zoo Announces the Death of Colo, World's Oldest Zoo Gorilla," Columbus Zoo Media Alert, Jan. 17, 2017, https://www.columbuszoo.org/home/about/press-releases/press-release-articles/2017/01/17/columbus-zoo-announces-the-death-of-colo, accessed Jan. 18, 2017.

[292] "Fact: How Long Do Gorillas Live?" Berggorilla & Reginald Direkthilfee e.v., Website, http://www.berggorilla.org/en/gorillas/general/facts/how-long-do-gorillas-live/, accessed Dec. 1, 2016.

[293] *Stephi was also known as Christopher.* International Gorilla Studbook, Dec. 31, 2010, pages 88-89.

[294] Gorillas Land, Zoo Basel, Family Tree, Zoo website http://gorillasland.yolasite.com/basle-zoo.php, assessed Dec. 1, 2016.

[295] "Obituary: Ernst M. Lang," International Zoo News, Vol. 61, No. 6, 2014, pp. 419-421.

[296] "Famous Basel Zoo Gorilla Turns 55," Basel Zoo website, http://www.zoobasel.ch/en/aktuell/detail.php?NEWSID=791, Accessed July 12, 2016.

[297] International Gorilla Studbook, Dec. 31, 2010, pages 91, 92 and 108.

[298] Durrell Wildlife Conservation Website, http://www.durrell.org/; also, website of Brian Le Lion, photographer of the Jambo incident in 1986, http://lelion.co.uk/index.html, accessed Jan. 28, 2017.

[299] "Gorilla Birth at the National Zoological Park," Theodore Reed and Bernard Gallagher, *Der Zoologische Garten*, Oct. 21, 1961, page 279, Smithsonian Institution Archives, RU 326, Box 81.

[300] "The Washington National Zoological Park Gorilla Infant, Tomoka," Leonard Carmichael, Moselle Bigelow Kraus and Theodore Reed, reprint from *International Zoo Yearbook*, Vol. 3, 1961, Smithsonian Institution Archives, RU326, Box. 30.

[301] "To Zoo's Apes, 'Mother' Means Louise Gallagher," Mary M. Krug, *The Smithsonian Torch*, June 1969, page 2, Smithsonian Institution Archives, RU 371, Box 1.

[302] International Gorilla Studbook, Dec. 31, 2010, pages 89-102.

[303] Board of Regents Annual Report, 1962, page 132, Smithsonian Institution Archives, 08-061; also, video - https://www.youtube.com/watch?v=gVheSfblZrc.

[304] "Baby Gorilla Quits Life With People For Picture-Window Zoo Quarters," Albon B. Hailey, *The Washington Post*, April 25, 1962, DC Public Library, Washingtoniana section, April 16-30, 1962, Reel 1107.

[305] National Zoo Animal Acquisition Records, "Tomoka," Smithsonian Institution Archives, RU 386, Box 3.

[306] Letter to Dr. Fred L. Whipple from Theodore Reed, June 2, 1970, Smithsonian Institution Archives, RU326, Box 81.

[307] A Narrative Guide to the Park, National Zoological Park, September 1963, pp. 3-4, Smithsonian Institution Archives, 12-086, Box 2.

[308] A Narrative Guide to the Park, National Zoological Park, September 1963, pp. 3-4, Smithsonian Institution Archives, 12-086, Box 2.

[309] "A Brief History of Animals In Space," National Aeronautics and Space Administration, http://history.nasa.gov/animals.html, accessed Jan. 16, 2017.

[310] Memorandum to Theodore Reed from Lear Grimmer, "Acquisition of gorillas," July 16, 1964, Smithsonian Institution Archives, RU 365, Box 23.

[311] "To Zoo's Apes, 'Mother' Means Louise Gallagher," Mary M. Krug, Smithsonian Torch, June 1969, page 2, Smithsonian Institution Archives, RU 371, Box 1.

[312] *Spots and Stripes*, Jocelyn Arundel, Friends of the National Zoo newsletter, September 1964, Nick Arundel personal files.

[313] "Where Have All the White Tigers Gone?" Jada Jones, Aug. 13, 2015, Smithsonian Institution Archives online, http://siarchives.si.edu/blog/where-have-all-white-tigers-gone.

[314] Board of Regents Annual Report, 1964, page 111, Smithsonian Institution Archives, 08-061.

[315] Friends of the National Zoo memo, Mrs. Tom Kelly, undated, Smithsonian Institution Archives, RU365, Box 12; also, FONZ membership envelope, date unknown, Nick Arundel personal files; also National Zoo brochure, date unknown, RU 365, Box 16.

[316] Board of Regents Annual Report, 1964, page 112, Smithsonian Institution Archives, 08-061.

[317] Theodore Reed Oral History, interview by Pamela Henson, Sept. 25, 1990, page 11, Smithsonian Institution Archives, RU 9568.

[318] Theodore Reed Oral History, interview by Pamela Henson, Sept. 25, 1990, page 11, Smithsonian Institution Archives, RU 9568.

[319] Association of Zoos and Aquariums, "Welfare and Conservation Implications of Intentional Breeding for the Expression of Rare Recessive Alleles," June 2011, https://www.aza.org/uploadedFiles/About_Us/AZA%20White%20Paper%20Inbreeding%20for%20Rare%20Alleles%2018%20Jan%202012.pdf; Also, http://www.allaboutwhitetigers.com/whitetigerreport.pdf

[320] Memorandum to Theodore Reed from Lear Grimmer, April 30, 1964, Smithsonian Institution Archives, RU 365, Box 23.

[321] Letter to Nick Arundel from Lear Grimmer, Aug. 27, 1964, Smithsonian Institution Archives, RU 365, Box 23; also, letter to Walter Van den bergh from Lear Grimmer, July 9, 1964, Smithsonian Institution Archives, RU 365, Box 23.

[322] "WAVA Public Service Item," Gorilla Expedition. Summer 1963, Nick Arundel personal files.

[323] Letter to WAVA Gorilla Expedition from Nolan C. Hill, Jr. of Alitalia Airlines, Aug. 5, 1963, Nick Arundel personal files.

[324] Memorandum to Theodore Reed from Lear Grimmer, "Acquisition of gorillas," July 16, 1964, Smithsonian Institution Archives, RU 365, Box 23.

[325] National Zoological Park Animal Acquisition Record, "Femelle" #30,096, Jan. 21, 1965, Smithsonian Institution Archives, RU 386, Box 3; also International Gorilla Studbook, Dec. 31, 2010, page 97; also, National Zoo response to Frankfurt Zoological Gardens questionnaire, Feb. 27, 1969, Smithsonian Institution Archives, RU 365, Box 23; also, announcement of Moka's death, National Zoo press release, Sept. 3, 1968, Smithsonian Institution Archives, RU 365, Box 23; also Treasury Department Bureau of Customs, Entry No. 609918, Jan. 25, 1965, Smithsonian Institution Archives, 96-139, Box 3.

[326] "Female Gorilla On Way To National Zoo," WAVA newscast, January 1965, Nick Arundel personal files.

[327] Board of Regents Annual Report, 1967, page 158, Smithsonian Institution Archives, 08-061.

[328] "Profile: Nikumba," By Melanie Bond, *Gorilla Gazette*, April 1990, page 11.

[329] *In 1977, the doctors were asked by President Jimmy Carter's administration to help with an urgent request from the Iraq government to assess the cause of back pain in what the U.S. called Iraq's "number two strongman," Saddam Hussein.* "Obituary: Hugo V. Rizzoli, MD, FACS," Neurosurgery, May 2015, Volume 76, Issue 5, pages E641-E64, http://journals.lww.com/neurosurgery/Fulltext/2015/05000/Obituary,_Hugo_V__Rizzoli,_MD,_FACS.18.aspx, accessed Oct. 6, 2016; also, "Henry Feffer, Surgeon Who Treated Saddam Hussein and Gorilla, Dies at 93," *The Washington Post*, May 13, 2011, https://www.washingtonpost.com/local/obituaries/henry-feffer-back-surgeon-who-treated-dc-notables-and-gorilla-dies-at-93/2011/05/11/AF7ytNtG_story.html, accessed Oct. 6, 2016.

[330] "Paraplegia In a Male Lowland Gorilla At the National Zoological Park," C. W. Gray, *International Zoo Yearbook*, 1965, pages, 186-189, Smithsonian Institution Archives, RU 326, Box 30.

[331] "Profile: Nikumba," Melanie Bond, *Gorilla Gazette*, April 1990, pages, 11-13.

[332] "Paraplegia In a Male Lowland Gorilla At the National Zoological Park," C. W. Gray, *International Zoo Yearbook*, 1965, pages, 186-189, Smithsonian Institution Archives, RU 326, Box 30.

[333] Board of Regents Annual Report, Smithsonian Institution, 1963, page 135, Smithsonian Institution Archives, 08-061.

[334] Annual Report Board of Regents, Smithsonian Institution, 1969, pages 287-288, Smithsonian Institution Archives, 08-061.

[335] Scammell, Henry, "The New Arthritis Breakthrough: The Only Medical Therapy Clinically Proven to Produce Long-term Improvement and Remission of RA, Lupus, Juvenile RA…and Other Forms of Arthritis," M. Evans and Company, 1998, page 199; also, "Natural Occurrence of Rheumatoid Arthritis in Great Apes - A New Model," Thomas McPherson Brown, Harold Clark and Jack S. Bailey, The Arthritis Institute of the National Orthopaedic and Rehabilitation Hospital, paper presented at the Centennial Symposium on Science and Research, Zoological Society of Philadelphia, Nov. 13, 1974, Smithsonian Institution Archives, RU 326, Box 30.

[336] "Rheumatoid-type Illness in Gorilla with Immunologic Association of Isolated Mycoplasma and Clinical Remission Following Intravenous Tetracycline Therapy," Thomas McPherson Brown and zoo veterinarian, 1970, paper presented at the Infectious Diseases Section of the Ninth Interscience Conference on Antimicrobial Agents and Chemotherapy, portion of paper is included in Board of Regents Annual Report, Smithsonian Institution Archives, 1970, page 45-52, Smithsonian Institution Archives, 08-061.

[337] "Natural Occurrence of Rheumatoid Arthritis in Great Apes - A New Model," Thomas McPherson Brown, Harold Clark and Jack S. Bailey, The Arthritis Institute of the National Orthopaedic and Rehabilitation Hospital, paper presented at the Centennial Symposium on Science and Research, Zoological Society of Philadelphia, Nov. 13, 1974, Smithsonian Institution Archives, RU 326, Box 30.

[338] National Zoo Animal Records, Primates, 1973-1975, Smithsonian Institution Archives, RU 389, Box 4.

[339] "Natural Occurrence of Rheumatoid Arthritis in Great Apes - A New Model," Thomas McPherson Brown, Harold Clark and Jack S. Bailey, The Arthritis Institute of the National Orthopaedic and Rehabilitation Hospital, paper presented at the Centennial Symposium on Science and Research, Zoological Society of Philadelphia, Nov. 13, 1974, Smithsonian Institution Archives, RU 326, Box 30.

[340] Annual Report of the National Zoological Park, 1971, page 31-33, Smithsonian Institution Archives, 08-061.

[341] "Lead Poisoning in Captive Wild Animals," B.C. Zoo, R.M. Bauer, F.M. Garner, *Journal of Wildlife Diseases*, Vol. 8, July 1972, page 264-272, http://www.jwildlifedis.org/doi/pdf/10.7589/0090-3558-8.3.264, Accessed June 13, 2016; also Annual Report of the National Zoological Park, 1971, pp. 31-33, Smithsonian Institution Archives, 08-061.

[342] "Lead Poisoning in Captive Wild Animals," B.C. Zoo, R.M. Bauer, F.M. Garner, *Journal of Wildlife Diseases*, Vol. 8, July 1972, pp. 264-272.

[343] Annual Report of the National Zoological Park, 1971, page 31-33, Smithsonian Institution Archives, 08-061.

[344] 18-month Report of the National Zoological Park, July 1971-Dec. 31, 1972, page 22, Smithsonian Institution Archives, 08-061; also Kara Arundel interview with Bill Xanten, June 10, 2016.

[345] Annual Report of the National Zoological Park, 1971, page 31-33, Smithsonian Institution Archives, 08-061.

[346] "Rafters Ring at Zoo Clinic As Apes Take Physicals," Herman Schaden, *Washington Star*, 1969, Smithsonian Institution Archives, RU389, Box 4, Apes 1948-1978.

[347] "Rafters Ring at Zoo Clinic As Apes Take Physicals," Herman Schaden, *Washington Star*, 1969, Smithsonian Institution Archives, RU389, Box 4, Apes 1948-1978.

[348] "A Zoo For All Seasons," The Smithsonian Animal World, Smithsonian Exposition Books, 1979, pages 86-87, Smithsonian Institution Archives, RU 365, Box 36.

[349] Letter to Ted Reed from Anne Tierney, Oct. 27, 1963, Smithsonian Institution Archives, RU 326, Box 80.

[350] Letter to Anne Tierney from Ted Reed, Oct. 30, 1963, Smithsonian Institution Archives, RU 326, Box 80.

[351] Kara Arundel interview with Melanie Bond, May 15, 2014.

[352] Kara Arundel interview with Melanie Bond, May 15, 2014; also, "Urbane Gorillas, Cagey Critics," Judith Martin, *The Washington Post*, Jan. 15, 1976, DC Public Library, Washingtoniana section, Jan. 11-20, 1976, Reel 1656; also, "Gorillas Don't Go Ape Over Television Set," Phil Casey, *The Washington Post*, Nov. 26, 1965, DC Public Library, Washingtoniana section, Nov. 21-30, 1965, Reel 1225.

[353] Letter to Russell Arundel from Theodore Reed, Oct. 4, 1968, Nick Arundel personal files.

[354] Dewar Wildlife Trust, "Moka," http://www.dewarwildlife.org/jrdavis-gorilla-studbook/0043.htm, accessed Sept. 18, 2016; also letter to Russell Arundel from Theodore Reed, Oct. 4, 1968, Nick Arundel personal files.

[355] Theodore Reed Oral History, interview by Pamela Henson, Aug. 3, 1989, pp. 107, Smithsonian Institution Archives, RU 9568

[356] Theodore Reed Oral History, interview by Pamela Henson, Aug. 3, 1989, pp. 107-108, Smithsonian Institution Archives, RU 9568; also, "The Kingdom of Theodore Reed," Henry Mitchell, *The Washington Post*, March 11, 1983, DC Library Washingtoniana section, March 8-15, 1983, Reel 1933; also, Theodore Reed Oral History, interview by Pamela Henson, Oct. 13, 1989, pages 73-74, Smithsonian Institution Archives, RU 9568.

[357] "The Kingdom of Theodore Reed," Henry Mitchell, *The Washington Post*, March 11,

1983, DC Library Washingtoniana section, March 8-15, 1983, Reel 1933

[358] Board of Regents Annual Report, Smithsonian Institution, 1968, page 413, Smithsonian Institution Archives, 08-061.

[359] National Zoological Zoo Annual Report, 1970, page 1, Smithsonian Institution Archives, 08-061.

[360] Kara Arundel interview with Bill Xanten, Dec. 11, 2015.

[361] Theodore Reed Oral History, interview by Pamela Henson, Aug. 17, 1989, page 39-40, Smithsonian Institution Archives, RU 9568.

[362] Letter from Zoologischer Garten, Frankfurt Zoological Gardens, Dec. 30, 1968, Smithsonian Institution Archives, RU 365, Box 23.

[363] "The Kingdom of Theodore Reed," Henry Mitchell, *The Washington Post*, March 11, 1983, DC Library Washingtoniana section, March 8-15, 1983, Reel 1933.

[364] Annual Report, Board of Regents, Smithsonian Institution, 1958, page 169, Smithsonian Institution Archives, 08-061; also Kara Arundel interview with Bill Xanten Dec. 11, 2015.

[365] Theodore Reed Video History transcript, interviewed by Pamela Henson, Sept. 25, 1990, page 32, RU 9568.

[366] Kara Arundel interview with Bill Xanten, Dec. 11, 2015.

[367] Kara Arundel interview with Miles Roberts, April 14, 2016.

[368] "Research at the National Zoo," John Perry, *BioScience*, Vol. 16, No. 9, 1966, pp. 591-592, Smithsonian Institution Archives, RU 365, Box 15.

[369] Kara Arundel interview with Melanie Bond, May 15, 2014

[370] "A Zoo For All Seasons: The Smithsonian Animal World," Smithsonian Exposition Books, 1979, pages 64-65, Smithsonian Institution Archives, RU 365, Box 36; also Thompson, Peggy, "Keepers and Creatures at the National Zoo," Thomas Y. Crowell, 1988, pp. 84-85; also Kara Arundel interview with Melanie Bond, May 15, 2014.

[371] Annual Report, Board of Regents, Smithsonian Institution, 1965, page 205, Smithsonian Institution Archives, 08-061.

[372] Ted Reed said of John Eisenberg as told by Chris Wemmer, Zoo Symposium, May 21, 2014.

[373] "Research at the National Zoo," John Perry, *BioScience*, Vol. 16, No. 9, 1966, pp. 591-592, Smithsonian Institution Archives, RU 365, Box 15.

[374] "The Biography of Russell Moore Arundel," Marjorie Sale Arundel, Arthur Windsor Arundel, and Jocelyn Ann Alexander, 1978; also, Kara Arundel interview with Lee Talbot, Jan. 13, 2014.

[375] Talbot, Lee, "A Personal Perspective on the Endangered Species Act of 1973 (ESA) and the Convention on International Trade in Endangered Species of Wild Fauna and Flora (CITES)," July 9, 2013, Talbot's personal notes.

[376] Kara Arundel interview with Lee Talbot, Jan. 13, 2014.

[377] Talbot, Lee, "A Personal Perspective on the Endangered Species Act of 1973 (ESA) and the Convention on International Trade in Endangered Species of Wild Fauna and Flora (CITES)," July 9, 2013, Talbot's personal notes.

[378] Talbot, Lee, "A Personal Perspective on the Endangered Species Act of 1973 (ESA) and the Convention on International Trade in Endangered Species of Wild Fauna and Flora (CITES)," July 9, 2013, Talbot's personal notes.

[379] Kara Arundel interview with Lee Talbot, Jan. 13, 2014.

[380] Agreement between Nick Arundel and National Educational Television and Radio Center, June 22, 1965; also pamphlet from Audubon Lectures, 1960-61, Nick Arundel personal files. Multimedia

[381] Neumann, Roderick P., *Imposing Wilderness: Struggles Over Livelihood and Nature Preservation in Africa*, University of California Press, 1998, Chapter 4.

[382] "Wildlife Threat In Africa Studied," *New York Times*, Nov. 11, 1956, Smithsonian Institution Archives, RU326, Box 80; Kara Arundel interview with Lee Talbot, Jan. 13, 2014 and July 11, 2016; also Kara Arundel interview with Jocelyn (Arundel) Sladen, Dec. 11. 2013.

[383] Kara Arundel interview with Lee Talbot, Jan. 13, 2014 and July 11, 2016; also Kara Arundel interview with Jocelyn (Arundel) Sladen, Dec. 11, 2013.

[384] Neumann, Roderick P., "*Imposing Wilderness: Struggles Over Livelihood and Nature Preservation in Africa*," University of California Press, 1998, Chapter 4; also "Wildlife Threat In Africa Studied," *New York Times*, Nov. 11, 1956, Smithsonian Institution Archives, RU326, Box 80; also Kara Arundel interview with Lee Talbot, Jan. 13, 2014 and July 11, 2016; also Kara Arundel interview with Jocelyn Arundel, Dec. 11, 2013.

[385] Neumann, Roderick P., "Political Ecology: An Integrative Approach to Geography and Environment," Guilford Press, Chapter 12, 2012.

[386] Kara Arundel interview with Lee Talbot, Jan. 13, 2014.

[387] Kara Arundel interview with Lee Talbot, July 11, 2016.

[388] Convention on International Trade in Endangered Species (CITES), https://www.cites.org/eng/disc/what.php, accessed Oct. 6, 2016.

[389] Talbot, Lee, "A Personal Perspective on the Endangered Species Act of 1973 (ESA) and the Convention on International Trade in Endangered Species of Wild Fauna and Flora (CITES)," July 9, 2013, Lee Talbot's personal notes; also, Kara Arundel interview with Lee Talbot, Jan. 13, 2014 and July 11, 2016.

[390] National Zoological Zoo Annual Report, 1970, page 3, Smithsonian Institution Archives, 08-061.

[391] U.S. Fish and Wildlife Services, Federal Register, 35 FR 8491-8498, June 2, 1970, http://ecos.fws.gov/docs/federal_register/fr21.pdf, accessed Oct. 6, 2016.

[392] Kara Arundel interview with Lee Talbot, July 11, 2016.

[393] Kara Arundel interview with Pete McCloskey, Dec. 8, 2015 and Jan. 18, 2016.

[394] Report from Committee on Merchant Marines and Fisheries, Endangered and Threatened Species Conservation Act of 1973, submitted by Rep. Leonor Sullivan, Congressional Record, July 27, 1973, page 143, http://www.eswr.com/docs/lh/140-179.pdf, accessed Oct. 6, 2016.

[395] Kara Arundel interview with Jim Bugg, Sept. 9, 2014; also Roosevelt, Theodore, "African Game Trails," 1910, Reprint Editor Peter Capstick, St. Martin's Press, 1988.

[396] "Smithsonian-Roosevelt African Expedition," Museum of Natural History, Celebrating 100 Years, http://www.mnh.si.edu/onehundredyears/expeditions/SI-Roosevelt_Expedition.

html, accessed Oct. 6, 2016; also Board of Regents Annual Report, Smithsonian Institution, 1910, page 69.

[397] "The Roma Restaurant," Sen. Christopher Dodd, The Congressional Record, Vol. 143, page S8622, July 31, 1997, https://www.gpo.gov/fdsys/pkg/CREC-1997-07-31/pdf/ CREC-1997-07-31-pt2-PgS8622.pdf, accessed Oct. 6, 2016.

[398] Kara Arundel interview with Jim Bugg, Sept. 18, 2014; Kara Arundel interview with Carol Bugg, Jan. 7, 2016.

[399] Train, Russell, "Politics, Pollution and Pandas," Island Press, 2003, page 34.

[400] "Conserving Wildlife in Africa: AWF's 40-Year History," African Wildlife Foundation, Fall 2001, page 2, online at https://www.awf.org/old_files/documents/FALL01.pdf, document since removed.

[401] Kara Arundel interview with Lee Talbot, July 11, 2016.

[402] "Conserving Wildlife in Africa: AWF's 40-Year History," African Wildlife Foundation, Fall 2001, page 2, online at https://www.awf.org/old_files/documents/FALL01.pdf, document since removed.; also, "Our History," African Wildlife Foundation, http://www. awf.org/about/history, accessed Oct. 6, 2016.

[403] "Conserving Wildlife in Africa: AWF's 40-Year History," African Wildlife Foundation, Fall 2001, page 3 and 6 https://www.awf.org/old_files/documents/FALL01.pdf, document since removed; also, "Our History," African Wildlife Foundation, http://www.awf.org/ about/history, accessed Oct. 6, 2016.

[404] "Conserving Wildlife in Africa: AWF's 40-Year History," African Wildlife Foundation, Fall 2001, page 6, online at https://www.awf.org/old_files/documents/FALL01.pdf, document since removed.; also, "Our History," African Wildlife Foundation, http://www. awf.org/about/history, accessed Oct. 6, 2016.

[405] "Arundel Elected President of African Wildlife Unit," AWLF press release, May 12, 1977, Nick Arundel personal files.

[406] "Conserving Wildlife in Africa: AWF's 40-Year History," African Wildlife Foundation, Fall 2001, page 3, online at https://www.awf.org/old_files/documents/FALL01.pdf, document since removed.

[407] Kara Arundel interview with Jim Bugg, Sept. 9, 2014.

[408] "Conserving Wildlife in Africa: AWF's 40-Year History," African Wildlife Foundation, Fall 2001, pp. 1-16, online at https://www.awf.org/old_files/documents/FALL01.pdf, document since removed.

[409] National Zoological Park Three-Year Report, Theodore Reed, Jan. 1-1973-Dec. 31, 1975, page 7, Smithsonian Institution Archives, 08-061.

[410] Board of Regents Annual Report, Smithsonian Institution, 1949, page 97, Smithsonian Institution Archives, 08-061; also, Board of Regents Annual Report, Smithsonian Institution, 1969, page 246, Smithsonian Institution Archives, 08-061.

[411] National Zoological Park, Status of the Collection, December 31, 1978, Smithsonian Institution Archives, RU 326, Box 13.

[412] Board of Regents Annual Report, Smithsonian Institution, 1960, page 134, Smithsonian Institution Archives, 08-061.

[413] "National Zoo Will Establish Breeding Farm in Front Royal," Smithsonian Institution

press release, Jan. 21, 1974, Nick Arundel personal files.

414 National Zoological Park, 18-Month Report, John Perry, July 1, 1971 to Dec. 31, 1972, page 5, Smithsonian Institution Archives, 08-061.

415 National Zoological Park memo, "Why Does the National Zoo Need A Rural Annex?," Aug. 16, 1973, Nick Arundel personal files.

416 National Zoological Park, Report of the Director Theodore Reed, 1971, page 1, Smithsonian Institution Archives, 08-061.

417 National Zoological Park Three-Year Report, "Conservation and Research Center," Christen Wemmer, Jan. 1, 1973 - Dec. 31, 1975, page 99, Smithsonian Institution Archives, 08-061.

418 Theodore Reed Oral History, interview by Pamela Henson, Oct. 13, 1989, page 11, Smithsonian Institution Archives, RU 9568.

419 National Zoological Park, Three-Year Report, "Conservation and Research Center," Christen Wemmer, Smithsonian Institution, Jan. 1, 1973-Dec. 31, 1975, page 101, Smithsonian Institution Archives, 08-061.

420 National Zoological Park, Three-Year Report, "Conservation and Research Center," Christen Wemmer, Smithsonian Institution, Jan. 1, 1973-Dec. 31, 1975, pages 99-101, Smithsonian Institution Archives, 08-061.

421 Theodore Reed Oral History, interviewed by Pamela Henson, Smithsonian Institution, Oct. 13, 1989, page 18, Smithsonian Institution Archives, RU 9668.

422 Theodore Reed Oral History, interviewed by Pamela Henson, Smithsonian Institution, Sept. 27, 1990, page 2, Smithsonian Institution Archives, 08-061.

423 "A Zoo For All Seasons," Smithsonian Exposition Books, 1979, pages 128-131, Smithsonian Institution Archives, RU 365, Box 36; also, letter to Nick Arundel from Ted Reed, Nov. 13, 1973, Nick Arundel personal files.

424 Letter to John Hanes from Nick Arundel, Oct. 12, 1973, Nick Arundel personal files.

425 "A Zoo For All Seasons," Smithsonian Exposition Books, 1979, pages 128-131, Smithsonian Institution Archives, RU 365, Box 36.

426 Kara Arundel interview with Christen Wemmer, Feb. 18, 2016.

427 Kara Arundel interview with Christen Wemmer, Feb. 18, 2016; also "History and Status of Science Programs at the Smithsonian National Zoological Park's Conservation and Research Center," Christen Wemmer, et. al, 2001, page 13, Christen Wemmer personal files.

428 "Can Wildlife Be Saved In Zoos?" Chris Wemmer, New Scientist, Sept. 8, 1977, page 585, Smithsonian Institution Archives, RU 326, Box 9.

429 Theodore Reed Oral History, interviewed by Pamela Henson, Aug. 24, 1989, page 52, Smithsonian Institution Archives, RU 9568

430 Theodore Reed Oral History, interview by Pamela Henson, Oct. 13, 1989, page 19, Smithsonian Institution Archives, RU 9568.

431 Kara Arundel notes from Christen Wemmer presentation at National Zoo on SCBI history, May 21, 2014.

432 National Zoological Park, Three-Year Report, "Conservation and Research Center," Christen Wemmer, Smithsonian Institution, Jan. 1, 1973-Dec. 31, 1975, page 104,

Smithsonian Institution Archives, 08-061; also Kara Arundel notes from Christen Wemmer presentation at National Zoo on SCBI history, May 21, 2014.

433 "History and Status of Science Programs at the Smithsonian National Zoological Park's Conservation and Research Center," Christen Wemmer, et. al, 2001, page 13, Christen Wemmer personal files; also Friends of the National Zoo Annual Report, 1976-77, pages 16-17, Nick Arundel personal files.

434 *Today, zoo populations of scimitar-horned oryx are plentiful, but they did officially become extinct in the wild - the largest mammal to become extinct in the wild in the last 20 years, according to the Conservation Centers for Species Survival. But because of coordinated efforts across the globe, there are now 6,000 living in captivity and attempts have been made to release several back into the wild.* Conservation Center for Species Survival, http://conservationcenters.org/species-conservation-priorities/scimitar-horned-oryx/, accessed Aug. 28, 2016; Also, National Zoo, https://nationalzoo.si.edu/Animals/AfricanSavanna/Facts/fact-oryx.cfm, accessed Aug. 28, 2016; also "Rewinding the African Scimitar-Horned Oryx," Jackson Landers, Smithsonian. com, April 15, 2016, http://www.smithsonianmag.com/smithsonian-institution/rewilding-african-scimitar-horned-oryx-180958796/?no-ist, accessed June 14, 2016.

435 "Can Wildlife Be Saved In Zoos?" Chris Wemmer, *New Scientist*, Sept. 8, 1977, page 586 Smithsonian Institution Archives, RU 326, Box 9.

436 National Zoological Park, Annual Report, Smithsonian Institution, 1979, pages 39-43, Smithsonian Institution Archives, 08-061.

437 Theodore Reed Oral History, interviewed by Pamela Henson, Oct. 13, 1989, page 55, Smithsonian Institution Archives, RU 9568; also, International Studbook, Golden Lion Tamarin, 2nd edition, 1976; also 2008 International Golden Lion Tamarin Studbook, page 9, online at http://alouattasen.weebly.com/uploads/8/9/5/6/8956452/tamaringoldenlionin ternationalstudbook2008-cdbe6003.pdf, accessed April 11, 2016.

438 "History of the Golden Lion Tamarin Captive Breeding Program," Smithsonian Institution Press, J.D. Ballou, D.G. Kleiman, J.J.C. Mallinson, et al, online at https:// nationalzoo.si.edu/SCBI/EndangeredSpecies/GLTProgram/ZooLife/History.cfm, accessed Aug. 28, 2016.

439 "History of the Golden Lion Tamarin Captive Breeding Program." Smithsonian Institution Press, J.D. Ballou, D.G. Kleiman, J.J.C. Mallinson, et al, online at https:// nationalzoo.si.edu/SCBI/EndangeredSpecies/GLTProgram/ZooLife/History.cfm, accessed Aug. 28, 2016.

440 Kara Arundel interview with Benjamin Beck, March 4, 2016; also, "100th Golden Lion Marmoset Born at National Zoo," Smithsonian institution press release, March 31, 1978, Smithsonian Institution Archives, RU 326, Box 26.

441 "100th Golden Lion Marmoset Born at National Zoo," Smithsonian institution press release, March 31, 1978, Smithsonian Institution Archives, RU 326, Box 26.

442 "100th Golden Lion Marmoset Born at National Zoo," Smithsonian institution press release, March 31, 1978, Smithsonian Institution Archives, RU 326, Box 26.

443 "History of the Golden Lion Tamarin Captive Breeding Program," Smithsonian Institution Press, J.D. Ballou, D.G. Kleiman, J.J.C. Mallinson, et al, online at https:// nationalzoo.si.edu/SCBI/EndangeredSpecies/GLTProgram/ZooLife/History.cfm, accessed Aug. 28, 2016; also "Golden Lion Tamarin Conservation Program," National Zoo, online at https://nationalzoo.si.edu/scbi/endangeredspecies/GLTProgram/, accessed Aug. 28, 2016; also "History and Status of Science Programs at the Smithsonian National Zoological Park's

Conservation and Research Center," Christen Wemmer, et. al, 2001, page 30, Christen Wemmer personal files.

[444] "Zoos Involved in Retroductions," Save the Golden Lion Tamarin Website, http://savetheliontamarin.org/reintroduction/, accessed Nov. 22, 2016.

[445] International Union for the Conservation of Nature, Red List of Threatened Species, Leontopithecus rosaria, 2008, online at http://www.iucnredlist.org/details/11506/0, accessed Aug. 28, 2016.

[446] Kara Arundel interview with Miles Roberts, April 14, 2016.

[447] "Inbreeding Depression in a Herd of Captive Dorcas Gazelle, gazelle dorcas," Katherine Ralls, Kristin Brugger and Adam Glick, March 1979, Smithsonian Institution Archives, 01-044, Box 13.

[448] "Inbreeding and Juvenile Mortality in Small Populations of Ungulates," Katherine Ralls, Kristin Brugger and Jonathan Ballou, Science, Vol. 206, Nov. 30, 1979, page 1101-1103; also Kara Arundel interview with Benjamin Beck, March 4, 2016; also National Zoo's Annual Report, 1979, page 3, Smithsonian Institution Archives, 08-061; also "History and Status of Science Programs at the Smithsonian National Zoological Park's Conservation and Research Center," Christen Wemmer, et. al, 2001, page 14, Christen Wemmer personal files.

[449] Letter to Tom Lovejoy of the Wildlife Preservation Trust International, Inc., from Theodore Reed, March 28, 1979, Smithsonian Institution Archives, 07-168, Box 2.

[450] Theodore Reed Oral History, interview by Pamela Henson, Sept. 25, 1990, page 11, Smithsonian Institution Archives, RU 9568.

[451] Kara Arundel interview with Katherine Ralls, April 28, 2016.

[452] National Zoo's Annual Report, 1979, page 3, Smithsonian Institution Archives, 08-061.

[453] Hearings Before A Subcommittee of the Committee on Appropriations, House of Representatives, Chairman Sidney Yates, Nov. 4, 1982, pp. 5-6, Smithsonian Libraries.

[454] Hearings Before A Subcommittee of the Committee on Appropriations, House of Representatives, Chairman Sidney Yates, Nov. 4, 1982, pp. 3-14, Smithsonian Libraries.

[455] Hearings Before A· Subcommittee of the Committee on Appropriations, House of Representatives, Chairman Sidney Yates, Nov. 4, 1982, pp. 3-14, Smithsonian Libraries; also Kara Arundel interview with Chris Wemmer, Feb. 12 and Dec. 1, 2016.

[456] Hearings Before A Subcommittee of the Committee on Appropriations, House of Representatives, Chairman Sidney Yates, Nov. 4, 1982, pp. 3-14, Smithsonian Libraries; Also Kara Arundel interview with Christen Wemmer, Feb. 12 and Feb. 19, 2016.

[457] Kara Arundel interview with Christen Wemmer, Feb. 12 and Feb. 19, 2016.

[458] Hearings Before A Subcommittee of the Committee on Appropriations, House of Representatives, Chairman Sidney Yates, Nov. 4, 1982, pp. 3-14, Smithsonian Libraries.

[459] Hearings Before A Subcommittee of the Committee on Appropriations, House of Representatives, Chairman Sidney Yates, Nov. 4, 1982, p 66, Smithsonian Libraries,

[460] Email to Kara Arundel from Chris Wemmer, Nov. 30, 2016.

[461] Kara Arundel interview with Christen Wemmer, Feb. 19, 2016.

[462] Theodore Reed Oral History, interviewed by Pamela Henson, July 12, 1994, page 102, Smithsonian Institution Archives, RU 9568.

[463] Theodore Reed Video History, interviewed by Pamela Henson, Sept. 27, 1990, page 6, transcript, Smithsonian Institution Archives, RU 9568.

[464] Memo to FONZ Panda Watchers from Devra Kleiman, March 31, 1975, Smithsonian Institution Archives, 01-227, Box 1.

[465] Memorandum to Jaren Horsely from Mitch Bush, June 16, 1975, Smithsonian Institution Archives, RU 326, Box 13; "Feeding Survey" memo to David Challinor from Ted Reed, April 9, 1976, Smithsonian Institution Archives, RU 326, Box 13.

[466] "Draft Memo to All Employees" from Ted Reed, July 1976, Smithsonian Institution Archives, RU 326, Box 13; "Feeding Survey" memo to David Challinor from Ted Reed, April 9, 1976, Smithsonian Institution Archives, RU 326, Box 13.

[467] Theodore Reed Video History, interviewed by Pamela Henson, Sept. 25, 1990, page. 13, transcript, Smithsonian Institution, RU 9568.

[468] National Zoo Animal Records, 1971-72, Smithsonian Institution Archives, RU 389, Box 5.

[469] Pregnancy Watch Log, Femelle, May 21, 1972, Smithsonian Institution Archives 11-221, Box 1.

[470] Pregnancy Watch Log, Femelle, March 8, 1972, Smithsonian Institution Archives, 11-221, Box 1.

[471] "Description of Femelle's First Birth," By N. Muckenhirn, May 29, 1972, Smithsonian Institution Archives RU 326, Box 20.

[472] Kara Arundel interview with Mitchell Bush, Feb. 22, and Dec. 8, 2016.

[473] "Description of Femelle's First Birth," By N. Muckenhirn, May 29, 1972, Smithsonian Institution Archives RU 326, Box 20.

[474] Annual Report of the Smithsonian Institution, 1972, Smithsonian Institution Archives, 08-061; also National Zoo Animal Records, Daily Reports Small Mammals and Primates, May 20, 1972, RU 389, Box 1.

[475] Friends of the National Zoo, The *Zoogoer*, Vol. 1, Number 5, Dec. 1972-Jan. 1973, Smithsonian Institution Archives, 07-023, Box 3.

[476] National Zoo Animal Records, Daily Reports Small Mammals and Primates, Dec. 9-15, 31, 1972, Smithsonian Institution Archives, RU 389, Box 1.

[477] "Observations on gorillas: Nicki and Femelle," Oct. 25, 1973 and Nov. 5, 1973, Smithsonian Institution Archives, 11-221, Box 1.

[478] Kara Arundel interview with Miles Roberts, April 14, 2016; also "Access to Gorilla Room Behind Barricades," from William Xanten to various National Zoo staff, Nov. 7, 1973, Smithsonian Institution Archives, RU 326, Box. 20.

[479] Gorilla Birth memorandum from Devra Kleiman to E. Kohn, Oct. 30, 1973, Smithsonian Institution Archives, RU 326, Box 20

[480] Gorilla Birth memorandum from Devra Kleiman to E. Kohn, Oct. 30, 1973, page 5, Smithsonian Institution Archives, RU 326, Box 20.

[481] Board of Regents Annual Report, 1968, Smithsonian Institution Archives, 08-061, Page 408.

[482] *There are no documents in the Smithsonian Archives regarding this incident that could be found. It is*

unclear on what date this took place and whether Gallagher resigned or was fired. This information is based on Kara Arundel interviews with Michael Davenport, April 29, 2016; with Bill Xanten, Dec. 11, 2015 and March 31, 2016; with Judith Block, March 16, 2016 and March 31, 2016; with Miles Roberts, April 14, 2016; and with Mark Reed, June 8, 2016.

[483] "To Zoo's Apes, 'Mother' Means Louise Gallagher," The Smithsonian Torch, June 1969, page 2, Smithsonian Institution Archives, RU 371, Box 1.

[484] Smithsonian Institution National Zoological Park: A Historic Resource Analysis, Gavin Farrell and Dr. Cynthia Field, Sept. 10, 2004, Zoo Development 1971-1980, Smithsonian Institution Archives, 12-086, Box 2; also Kara Arundel interview with Bill Xanten, Dec. 11, 2015.

[485] Smithsonian Institution National Zoological Park: A Historic Resource Analysis, Gavin Farrell and Dr. Cynthia Field, Sept. 10, 2004, Zoo Development 1971-1980, Smithsonian Institution Archives, 12-086, Box 2.

[486] Theodore Reed Video History, interviewed by Pamela Henson, Sept. 25, 1990, page 8, transcript, Smithsonian Institution Archives, RU 9568.

[487] "New Lion and Tiger Exhibit to be dedicated at the National Zoo," National Zoo press release, May 1976, Smithsonian Institution Archives, RU365, Box 14.

[488] Kara Arundel interview with Judith Block, March 31, 2016.

[489] Letter to Nick Arundel from Lear Grimmer, April 1, 1959, Smithsonian Institution Archives, RU 326, Box 80.

[490] Letter to Katherine Scrivener from Miles Roberts, Sept. 13, 1978, Smithsonian Institution Archives, RU 326, Box 20.

[491] Kara Arundel interview with Bill Xanten, March 31, 2016.

[492] Daily Animal Department report, Small Mammal and Primate Division, June 16 and 17, 1972, Smithsonian Institution Archives, RU 389, Box 1; also Kara Arundel interview with Bill Xanten, March 31, 2016.

[493] Email to Kara Arundel from Melanie Bond, May 31, 2016.

[494] Animal Records, 1943-1988, Smithsonian Institution Archives, RU389, Box 4 and 5; also Kara Arundel interview with Bill Xanten, Sept. 29, 2016.

[495] "Gorilla observations," June 27- Sept. 21, 1977, Smithsonian Institution Archives, 11-221, Box 1; also letter to Theodore Reed from Jaren Horsley, Jan. 14, 1977, Smithsonian Institution Archives, 11-221, Box 1.

[496] Letter to Dr. Mitchell Bush from Dr. John Tyson, Oct. 31, 1977, Smithsonian Institution Archives, 11-221, Box 1.

[497] Kara Arundel interview with Lisa Stevens, March 30, 2016.

[498] Memo to Jaren Horsley from Nan Muckenhirn, "Ape Breeding Program," Jan. 10, 1973, Smithsonian Institution Archives, RU 385, Box 2; "Acquisition of Gorillas," memo to Theodore Reed from Lear Grimmer, July 16, 1964, Smithsonian Institution Archives, RU 365, Box 23.

[499] International Studbook for Gorilla, Gorilla, Gorilla, M'Wasi, Dec. 31, 2010.

[500] National Zoological Park Annual Report, 1979, page 122, Smithsonian Institution Archives, 08-061; also National Zoological Park Annual Report, 1980, page 123, Smithsonian Institution Archives, 02-239, Box 1.

[501] Smithsonian Institution National Zoological Park: A Historic Resource Analysis, September 10, 2004, page 5, Smithsonian Institution Archives, 12-086, Box 2.

[502] Kara Arundel interview with Bill Xanten, April 29, 2014.

[503] Kara Arundel interview with Miles Robert, April 14, 2016.

[504] "Nikumba Has Stopped Grinding His Teeth," John Sherwood, *The Washingtonian*, April 1981, page 149, DC Public Library, Washingtoniana section, , April 1981-Sept. 1981; also, "Going Ape: National Zoo's Gorillas and Orangs Get Rooms With a View," By Mike Morgan, *The Torch*, Smithsonian Institutional Archives May 1981, Smithsonian Institution Archives, RU 371, Box 3; also, FONZ booklet, "The National Zoo: Great Ape House," 1982, page 31, Smithsonian Institution Archives, RU 380, Box 3.

[505] Theodore Reed Video History, interviewed by Pamela Henson, June 23, 1994, page 61, transcript, Smithsonian Institution Archives, RU 9568.

[506] National Zoo, Daily Animal Records, 1971-72, Apes, Smithsonian Institution Archives, RU 389, Box 5; also "Nikumba Has Stopped Grinding His Teeth," John Sherwood, *The Washingtonian*, April 1981, page 149, DC Public Library, Washingtoniana section, , April 1981-Sept. 1981.

[507] "Gorillas Take An Inside-Out Look at Yard," Leah Y. Latimer, *The Washington Post*, July 9, 1981, Washington Post archives, accessed Feb. 22, 2016.

[508] Daily Report Animal Programs, July 8, 1981, Smithsonian Institution Archives, 08-099, Box 2.

[509] "Declaration for Free Entry Or Articles For Colleges, Religious Institutions, Etc., U.S. Treasury Department Bureau of Customs, Entry No. 609918, Jan. 25, 1965, Smithsonian Institution Archives, 96-139, Box 3; also Letter to the National Zoo from Lansen-Naeve Corp, New York City, June 10, 1965, Smithsonian Institution Archives, 96-139, Box 3; also National Zoo Animal Acquisition Record, Jan. 21, 1965, Smithsonian Institution Archives, RU 386, Box 3.

[510] "Keeper Has Big Love for Big Animals," John Rivera, *The Baltimore Sun*, July 14, 1996, accessed April 24, 2016, http://articles.baltimoresun.com/1996-07-14/news/1996196117_1_animal-keeper-mary-wilson-baltimore-zoo, accessed April 24, 2016

[511] "Gorillas at the National Zoological Park," 1984-85, Appendix 2, date unknown, Smithsonian Institution Archives, 02-235, Box 1.

[512] "Gorillas at the National Zoological Park," 1984-85, Appendix 2, date unknown, Smithsonian Institution Archives, 02-235, Box 1.

[513] "Gorillas at the National Zoological Park," 1984-85, Appendix 2, date unknown, Smithsonian Institution Archives, 02-235, Box 1; also, Kara Arundel interview with William Xanten, March 31, 2016.

[514] "Double Jeopardy: The Gorilla Dilemma," By Benjamin Beck, *Zoogoer* magazine, Jan./Feb. 1985, pp. 9-16, Benjamin Beck's personal files; also Kara Arundel interview with Benjamin Beck, March 4, 2016; also "Gorilla Research Project" memo, Appendix 1, date unknown, Smithsonian Institution Archives, 01-044, Box 9.

[515] Kara Arundel interview with Benjamin Beck, March 4, 2016.

[516] Untitled memo, National Zoological Park, Smithsonian Institution Archives, Smithsonian Institution Archives, 02-235, Box 1.

[517] "Gorillas at NZP," memo to Michael Robinson from Ben Beck, Oct. 18, 1984,

Smithsonian Institution Archives, RU01-044, Box 9.

518 Kara Arundel interview with Lisa Stevens, April 16, 2014.

519 "History and Status of the Science Programs at the Smithsonian National Zoo," Christen Wemmer et. al, 2001, page 9, Christen Wemmer's personal files; also Kara Arundel interview with Mitchell Bush, Feb. 22, and Dec. 8, 2016.

520 "History and Status of the Science Programs at the Smithsonian National Zoo," Christen Wemmer et. al, 2001, page 37, Christen Wemmer's personal files.

521 AZA Reproductive Management Center, "The Importance of Reproductive Management," St. Louis Zoo, http://www.stlzoo.org/animals/scienceresearch/reproductivemanagementcenter/, accessed May 20, 2016.

522 "Meeting the Challenge of Preserving Global Biodiversity Through Reproductive Science," Smithsonian Conservation Biology Institute, Smithsonian Institution Archives online https://nationalzoo.si.edu/SCBI/ReproductiveScience/, accessed May 20, 2016.

523 "Population Analysis and Breeding and Transfer Plan," Western Lowland Gorilla (Gorilla, Gorilla, Gorilla), AZA Species Survival Plan, Population Management Center, Kristen Lukas, Roby Elsner and Sarah Long, published by Population Management Center, Lincoln Park Zoo and Association of Zoos and Aquariums, Dec. 22, 2015, page 11.

524 *From various correspondence from the Conservation and Research Center. Memos considered room for 20 "delicate arboreal animals" (gorillas and orangutans) at cost of $1 million for facility.* "Cost Analysis of Potential Animal Programs at CRC," Smithsonian Institution Archives, RU 326 Boxes 7, 8, 9; also "Gorillas at the National Zoological Park," 1984-85, Appendix 2, date unknown, Smithsonian Institution Archives, 01-044, Box 1

525 "Gorillas at the National Zoological Park, 1984-85, Appendix 2, date unknown, Smithsonian Institution Archives, 02-235, Box. 1.

526 "Saving Giant Pandas: Conservation at the National Zoo," Kira M. Sobers, Smithsonian Institution Archives blogpost, http://siarchives.si.edu/blog/saving-giant-pandas-conservation-national-zoo, accessed Aug. 23, 2016.

527 "The Kingdom of Theodore Reed," Henry Mitchell, *The Washington Post*, March 11, 1983, DC Library Washingtoniana section, March 8-15, 1983, Reel 1933.

528 Kara Arundel interview with Lisa Stevens, March 30, 2016.

529 "Gorillas at the National Zoological Park, 1984-85, Appendix 2, date unknown, Smithsonian Institution Archives, 02-235, Box. 1.

530 Regional Action Plan for the Conservation of Western Lowland Gorillas and Central Chimpanzees 2015-2025, International Union for Conservation of Nature, IUCN SSC Primate Specialist Group, 2014.

531 "Western Lowland Gorilla," World Wildlife Fund Website, http://wwf.panda.org/what_we_do/endangered_species/great_apes/gorillas/western_lowland_gorilla/, accessed Sept. 3, 2016.

532 International Union for Conservation of Nature's Red List of Threatened Species, Gorilla Gorilla, 2008 Assessment, http://www.iucnredlist.org/details/9404/0, accessed July 24, 2016; also "Action Plan for African Primate Conservation: 1986-1990, J.F. Oates, Hunter College and the Graduate Center City University of New York and Regional Coordinator for Africa, IUCN/SSC Primate Specialist Group, 1985, pp. 16-18, http://static1.1.sqspcdn.com/static/f/1200343/24851543/1399638765277/Oates1986.pdf?token=X3d%2FvUAxIi8EuQWIzO

UOrjxxfeM%3D, accessed Oct. 12, 2016.

533 Management of Gorillas In Captivity; Husbandry Manual, Gorilla Species Survival Plan, Jacqueline Ogden and Dan Wharton, 1997.

534 "The Kingdom of Theodore Reed," Henry Mitchell, *The Washington Post*, March 11, 1983, DC Library Washingtoniana section, March 8-15, 1983, Reel 1933.

535 "Profile: Nikumba," Melanie Bond, *Gorilla Gazette*, Vol 4, No.1, April 1990, page 1; also Dewar Wildlife Trust online says Leonard died of poisoning, http://www.dewarwildlife.org/jrdavis-gorilla-studbook/0173.htm, accessed Aug. 28, 2016.

536 Board of Regents Annual Report, Smithsonian Institution, 1956, page 117, Smithsonian Institution Archives, 08-061; also Theodore Reed Oral History, interview by Pamela Henson, July 12, 1994, page 64, Smithsonian Institution Archives, RU 9568.

537 Theodore Reed Oral History, interview by Pamela Henson, July 12, 1994, page 64, Smithsonian Institution Archives, RU 9568.

538 Kara Arundel interviews with Bill Xanten March 31, 2016 and Mark Reed June 8, 2016.

539 Kara Arundel interview with Mark Reed, June 8, 2016.

540 Kara Arundel interview with Bill Xanten, April 29, 2014; Miles Roberts, April 14, 2016, Mike Davenport, May 5, 2016.

541 Smithsonian Archives Oral History interview with Theodore Reed, interviewer Pamela Henson, Sept. 25, 1990, page 26.

542 "Michael Robinson, 79: Director Widened Scope of National Zoo," Joe Holley, *The Washington Post*, March 24, 2008. http://www.washingtonpost.com/wp-dyn/content/article/2008/03/23/AR2008032301778.html, accessed May 16, 2016.

543 "History and Status of Science Programs at the Smithsonian National Zoological Park's Conservation and Research Center," Christen Wemmer, et. al, 2001, pages 35 and 43, Christen Wemmer's personal files.

544 "Michael Robinson, 79; Director Widened Scope of National Zoo, Joe Holly, *The Washington Post*, March 24, 2008, http://www.washingtonpost.com/wp-dyn/content/article/2008/03/23/AR2008032301778.html, accessed Oct. 11, 2016.

545 "International Studbook for the Western Lowland Gorilla," Gorilla g. Gorilla, Savage & Wyman, 1847, Frankfurt Zoo, 2011, page 136.

546 "Gorilla a Good Mom," Brenda Fowler, *The Milwaukee Journal*, Dec. 9, 1986, https://news.google.com/newspapers?nid=1499&dat=19861209&id=EAIkAAAAIBAJ&sjid=xH4EAAAAIBAJ&pg=3952,261636&hl=en, accessed April 16, 2016.

547 "International Studbook for the Western Lowland Gorilla," Gorilla g. Gorilla, Savage & Wyman, 1847, Frankfurt Zoo, 2011, page 146.

548 "Gorilla a Good Mom," Brenda Fowler, *The Milwaukee Journal*, Dec. 9, 1986, https://news.google.com/newspapers?nid=1499&dat=19861209&id=EAIkAAAAIBAJ&sjid=xH4EAAAAIBAJ&pg=3952,261636&hl=en, accessed April 16, 2016, also "Senior Gorilla Femelle Dies at Milwaukee County Zoo," Erin Richards and Meg Jones, Milwaukee Journal Sentinel, Dec. 15, 2016, http://www.jsonline.com/story/news/local/2016/12/15/senior-gorilla-femelle-dies-milwaukee-county-zoo/95471254/, accessed Jan. 4, 2017)

549 "International Studbook for the Western Lowland Gorilla," Gorilla g. Gorilla, Savage & Wyman, 1847, Frankfurt Zoo, 2011, pp. 98 and 146.

550 "Keeper Has Big Love For Big Animals," By John Rivera, *The Baltimore Sun*, July 14, 1996.http://articles.baltimoresun.com/1996-07-14/news/1996196117_1_animal-keeper-mary-wilson-baltimore-zoo, accessed April 18, 2016.

551 Kara Arundel interview with Robert Shumaker, Aug. 12, 2016.

552 "International Studbook for the Western Lowland Gorilla," Gorilla g. Gorilla, Savage & Wyman, 1847, Frankfurt Zoo, 2011, pp. 130, 132.

553 "Gorillas Just Want To Have Fun," By Kim Eisler, *Washingtonian Magazine*, May 1, 1995, DC Public Library, Washingtoniana section, Jan.-June 1995; also "How Four Strangers Became A Family And Mothers Swapped Babies," Robert Shumaker, *Gorilla Gazette*, Vol. 8, No. 1, May 1994, pages 6 and 7; also Kara Arundel interview with Robert Shumaker, July 21, 2016.

554 "How Four Strangers Became a Family and Mothers Swapped Babies," Robert Shumaker, The *Gorilla Gazette*, Vol. 8, No. 1, May 1994, page 6-7.

555 Kara Arundel interview with Lisa Stevens, March 30, 2016.

556 "Profile: Nikumba," Melanie Bond, *Gorilla Gazette*, April 1990, page 11-13.

557 "Hercules Unchained," Ann Zimmerman, *The Dallas Observer*, April 1, 1999. http://www.dallasobserver.com/news/hercules-unchained-6419828, accessed May 16, 2016.

558 "Hercules, gorilla that once attacked handler, dies," Associated Press, appearing in USA Today, Aug. 15, 2008, http://usatoday30.usatoday.com/news/nation/2008-08-15-gorilla-dies_N.htm, accessed Oct. 11, 2016; also Western Lowland Gorilla 2013 North American Regional Studbook, By Roby Elsner, Knoxville Zoo

559 Western Lowland Gorilla 2013 North American Regional Studbook, By Roby Elsner, Knoxville Zoo.

560 Dewar Wildlife, http://www.dewarwildlife.org/jrdavis-gorilla-studbook/0393.htm, accessed Nov. 24, 2016; also interview with Benjamin Beck, Nov. 22, 2016.

561 Kara Arundel interview with Lisa Stevens, March 30, 2016.

562 Kara Arundel interview with Robert Shumaker, July 21, 2016.

563 "Nick, the 37-year-old gorilla, dies at National Zoo," Associated Press, July 25, 1990, Associate Press News Archives, http://www.apnewsarchive.com/1990/Nick-The-37-year-old-Gorilla-Dies-at-National-Zoo/id-2302697346beea74fca8e852bab84548, accessed Oct. 11, 2016.

564 *A variety of spellings for Nick and Nicky appear in documents from Nikumba's life.* Kara Arundel interview with Melanie Bond, May 15, 2014; also Kara Arundel interview with Lisa Stevens and Bill Xanten, April 29, 2014; also Kara Arundel interview with Robert Shumaker, Aug. 12, 2016.

565 Letter to Lisa Stevens from Nick Arundel, June 24, 1991, Nick Arundel personal files.

566 Kara Arundel interview with Lisa Stevens, March 30, 2016.

567 "Mopie Gets The Call," Russell Smith, San Antonio Zoo newsletter, 1990, Smithsonian Institution Archives, 07-023, Box 3.

568 Kara Arundel interview with Robert Shumaker, July 21, 2016.

569 Kara Arundel interview with Lisa Stevens, March 30, 2016; also Kara Arundel interview with Robert Shumaker Aug. 12, 2016.

[570] "How Four Strangers Became a Family And Mothers Swapped Babies," Robert Shumaker, *Gorilla Gazette*, Vol. 8, No. 1, May 1994, page 6 and 7.

[571] Western Lowland Gorilla (Gorilla gorilla gorilla) 2013 North American Regional Studbook, By Roby Elsner, Knoxville Zoo, 2013.

[572] Kara Arundel interview with Lisa Stevens, March 30, 2016; also Kara Arundel interview with Robert Shumaker July 21, 2016.

[573] "How Four Strangers Became a Family And Mothers Swapped Babies," Robert Shumaker, *Gorilla Gazette*, Vol. 8, No. 1, May 1994, page 6 and 7.

[574] "Correlates of Sexual and Maternal Competence in Captive Gorillas," Benjamin Beck and Michael Power, *Zoo Biology*, Vol. 7, pages 339-350, 1988; also Kara Arundel interview with Benjamin Beck, March 4, 2016 and Nov. 22, 2016.

[575] "Management of Captive Gorillas," Gorilla Species Survival Plan and Atlanta/Fulton County Zoo, 1997, page 51, 72 and 116, http://www.gorillassp.org/MembersSection/MembersOnlyForms/Gorilla%20Husbandry%20Manual.pdf, accessed May 24, 2016.

[576] "Correlates of Sexual and Maternal Competence in Captive Gorillas," Benjamin Beck and Michael Power, *Zoo Biology*, Vol. 7, pages 339-350, 1988; also Kara Arundel interview with Benjamin Beck, March 4, 2016 and Nov. 22, 2016; also "Management of Captive Gorillas," Gorilla Species Survival Plan and Atlanta/Fulton County Zoo, 1997, page 51 and 72, http://www.gorillassp.org/MembersSection/MembersOnlyForms/Gorilla%20Husbandry%20Manual.pdf, accessed May 24, 2016.

[577] Kara Arundel interview with Robert Shumaker, July 21, 2016.

[578] "How Four Strangers Became a Family And Mothers Swapped Babies," By Robert Shumaker, *Gorilla Gazette*, Vol. 8, No. 1, May 1994, page 6 and 7.

[579] "Tomoka," By Lisa Stevens, *Gorilla Gazette*, Vol. 6, No. 1, March 1992, page 9.

[580] "Tomoka," By Lisa Stevens, *Gorilla Gazette*, Vol. 6, No. 1, March 1992, page 9; also Kara Arundel interview with Robert Shumaker, Aug. 12, 2016.

[581] Kara Arundel interview with Robert Shumaker, July 21, 2016.

[582] Melanie Bond email to Kara Arundel, May 31, 2016; also Kara Arundel interview with Lisa Stevens, March 30, 2016.

[583] "Gorillas Just Want To Have Fun," Kim Eisler, *The Washingtonian Magazine*, May 1, 1995, DC Public Library, Washingtoniana section, Jan.-June 1995.

[584] "How Four Strangers Became a Family And Mothers Swapped Babies," Robert Shumaker, *Gorilla Gazette*, Vol. 8, No. 1, May 1994, page 6 and 7; also "Gorillas Just Want To Have Fun," Kim Eisler, *The Washingtonian Magazine*, May 1, 1995. DC Public Library, Washingtoniana section, Jan.-June 1995; also Melanie Bond email to Kara Arundel, May 31, 2016.

[585] "How Four Strangers Became a Family And Mothers Swapped Babies," Robert Shumaker, *Gorilla Gazette*, Vol. 8, No. 1, May 1994, page 6 and 7.

[586] Western Lowland Gorilla 2013 North American Regional Studbook, By Roby Elsner, Knoxville Zoo.

[587] Western Lowland Gorilla 2013 North American Regional Studbook, By Roby Elsner, Knoxville Zoo; also Kara Arundel interview with Lisa Stevens, March 30, 2016.

[588] "Profile: Nikumba," Melanie Bond, *Gorilla Gazette*, Vol 4, No.1, April 1990, page 1;

also Dewar Wildlife Trust online says Leonard died of poisoning, http://www.dewarwildlife.org/jrdavis-gorilla-studbook/0173.htm, accessed Aug. 28, 2016.

589 "Inaki", Dewar Wildlife Trust online, http://www.dewarwildlife.org/jrdavis-gorilla-studbook/0289.htm, accessed Oct. 16, 2016; also Gorilla Passion Project, https://www.facebook.com/625918240776106/photos/a.630190760348854.1073741836.625918240776106/743418109026118/?type=1&theater, accessed May 16, 2016.

590 "Gorillas Just Want To Have Fun," Kim Eisler, *The Washingtonian Magazine,* May 1, 1995, DC Public Library, Washingtoniana section, Jan.-June 1995.

591 Western Lowland Gorilla 2013 North American Regional Studbook, By Roby Elsner, Knoxville Zoo.

592 Kara Arundel interviews with Lisa Stevens, March 30, 2016; Miles Roberts, April, 14, 2016; Robert Shumaker, Aug. 12, 2016.

593 *Accredited zoos in North America estimate they can maintain a 90 percent genetic diversity rate for captive western lowland gorillas for the next 400 years.* Western Lowland Gorilla (Gorilla gorilla gorilla) AZA Species Survival Plan Green Program, 2015, page 1.

594 Email to Kara Arundel from Benjamin Beck, Nov. 24, 2016.

595 Kara Arundel interviews with Lisa Stevens, March 30, 2016; Miles Roberts, April, 14, 2016; Robert Shumaker, Aug. 12, 2016.

596 Kara Arundel interview with Melanie Bond, May 15, 2014.

597 "History and Status of Science Programs at the Smithsonian National Zoological Park's Conservation and Research Center," Christen Wemmer, et. al, 2001, pages 23, 35 and 36, Christen Wemmer's personal files; also Kara Arundel interview with Chris Wemmer, Dec. 1, 2016.

598 Kara Arundel interview with Christen Wemmer, Feb. 18, 2016.

599 Smithsonian Institution FY 2002 Budget Justification to the Office of Management and Budget, January 2001, page 49-51, https://archive.org/stream/smithsonianinst2002smit#page/n0/mode/2up, accessed June 1, 2016; also "History and Status of Science Programs at the Smithsonian National Zoological Park's Conservation and Research Center," Christen Wemmer, et. al, 2001, pages 4 and 35, Christen Wemmer's personal files.

600 Kara Arundel interview with Christen Wemmer, Feb. 18, 2016 and Nov. 29, 2016.

601 Kara Arundel interview with Christen Wemmer, Feb. 18, 2016.

602 "History and Status of Science Programs at the Smithsonian National Zoological Park's Conservation and Research Center," Christen Wemmer, et. al, 2001, page 4, Christen Wemmer's personal files.

603 Smithsonian Conservation Biology Institute, National Zoo website, https://nationalzoo.si.edu/SCBI/, accessed June 2016.

604 "National Zoo Gorillas Are the First to Participate in Heart Disease Study," Smithsonian's National Zoo and Conservation Biology Institute, March 29, 2012, National Zoo website, https://nationalzoo.si.edu/animals/news/national-zoo-gorillas-are-first-participate-heart-disease-study, accessed Dec. 1, 2016.

605 A few include: World Wildlife Fund, http://www.worldwildlife.org/species/gorilla; Wildlife Conservation Society, https://www.wcs.org/our-work/wildlife/apes; International

Union for Conservation of Nature (Primate Specialists Group, Species Programme and Species Survival Commission), http://www.primate-sg.org/action_plans/, all accessed Oct. 12, 2016.

606 Walsh, P.D., Tutin, C.E.G., Oates, J.F., Baillie, J.E.M., Maisels, F., Stokes, E.J., Gatti, S., Bergl, R.A., Sunderland-Groves, J. & Dunn. A. 2008. *Gorilla gorilla.* The IUCN Red List of Threatened Species 2008: e.T9404A12983787. http://dx.doi.org/10.2305/IUCN.UK.2008. RLTS.T9404A12983787.en, accessed Aug. 9, 2016.

607 Based on author familiarity of the home.

608 "Celebrating 125 years at the Smithsonian 's National Zoo: How Ted Reed Envisioned the Modern Zoo," Dennis Kelly speech, Academic Symposium at National Zoo, May 21, 2014.

609 Kara Arundel interview with Melanie Bond, May 15, 2014.

610 "Population Analysis and Breeding and Transfer Plan," Western Lowland Gorilla (Gorilla, Gorilla, Gorilla), AZA Species Survival Plan, Population Management Center, Kristen Lukas, Roby Elsner and Sarah Long, published by Population Management Center, Lincoln Park Zoo and Association of Zoos and Aquariums, Dec. 22, 2015, page 7 and 8.

611 Conservation Breeding Programmes, World Association of Zoos and Aquariums, Website, http://www.waza.org/en/site/conservation/conservation-breeding-programmes, accessed Dec. 12, 2016.

612 "Population Analysis and Breeding and Transfer Plan," Western Lowland Gorilla (Gorilla, Gorilla, Gorilla), AZA Species Survival Plan, Population Management Center, Kristen Lukas, Roby Elsner and Sarah Long, published by Population Management Center, Lincoln Park Zoo and Association of Zoos and Aquariums, Dec. 22, 2015, pp. 1 and 9.

613 "Population Analysis and Breeding and Transfer Plan," Western Lowland Gorilla (Gorilla, Gorilla, Gorilla), AZA Species Survival Plan, Population Management Center, Kristen Lukas, Roby Elsner and Sarah Long, published by Population Management Center, Lincoln Park Zoo and Association of Zoos and Aquariums, Dec. 22, 2015, page 1.

614 Maisels, F., Bergl, R.A. & Williamson, E.A. 2016. *Gorilla gorilla.* The IUCN Red List of Threatened Species 2016: e.T9404A17963949, http://www.iucnredlist.org/details/9404/0, accessed Oct. 12, 2016.

615 *The population of wild western lowland gorillas is estimated to be between 150,000-250,000.* Maisels, F., Bergl, R.A. & Williamson, E.A. 2016. *Gorilla gorilla.* The IUCN Red List of Threatened Species 2016: e.T9404A17963949, http://www.iucnredlist.org/details/9404/0, accessed Oct. 12, 2016.

616 Maisels, F., Bergl, R.A. & Williamson, E.A. 2016. *Gorilla gorilla.* The IUCN Red List of Threatened Species 2016: e.T9404A17963949, http://www.iucnredlist.org/details/9404/0, accessed Oct. 12, 2016.

617 Plumptre, A., Robbins, M. & Williamson, E.A. 2016. *Gorilla beringei.* (errata version published in 2016) The IUCN Red List of Threatened Species 2016: e.T39994A102325702, http://www.iucnredlist.org/details/39994/0, accessed Dec. 16, 2016.

618 Steven Monfort speech, SCBI 40th anniversary dinner, Nov. 14, 2015; also Kara Arundel interview with Steve Monfort, Feb. 13, 2016 and Dec. 13, 2016.

619 Zoo and Aquarium Statistics, Association of Zoos and Aquariums, https://www.aza.org/zoo-and-aquarium-statistics, accessed Jan. 29, 2017.

[620] "All Things Wild: An Essential Animal Resource Guide for Today's Zoo and Aquarium Director," Association of Zoos and Aquariums, January 2015, page 20, https://www.aza.org/assets/2332/allthingswildlife.pdf, accessed Jan. 29, 2017; also Dennis Kelly speech, AZA Annual Conference, Sept. 10, 2016.

[621] Born Free Foundation website, http://www.bornfree.org.uk/campaigns/zoo-check/zoos/, accessed May 30, 2016; also People for the Ethical Treatment of Animals Website, http://www.peta.org/issues/animals-in-entertainment/zoos/, accessed May 30, 2016; also Last Chance for Animals, http://www.lcanimal.org/index.php/campaigns/animals-in-entertainment/zoos, accessed Dec. 1, 2016.

[622] Seaworld website, https://seaworldcares.com/future?from=SWParksPortal, accessed May 31, 2016.

[623] Ringing Bros. and Barnum & Bailey Center for Elephant Conservation website, https://www.ringlingelephantcenter.com, accessed May 31, 2016.

[624] Smithsonian Annual Report 2015, https://www.si.edu/Content/Pdf/About/2015-Smithsonian-Annual-Report.pdf, page 14, accessed Dec. 15, 2016.

[625] Smithsonian National Zoological Park, Facilities Master Plan and Environmental Assessment, Office of Planning and Project Management, May 2008, https://www.yumpu.com/en/document/view/18018710/national-zoo-master-plan-nearing-completion; also comments by Dennis Kelly, National Zoo Symposium, May 21, 2014